THE RECORD SOCIETY OF LANCASHIRE AND CHESHIRE

FOUNDED TO TRANSCRIBE AND PUBLISH
ORIGINAL DOCUMENTS RELATING TO THE TWO COUNTIES

VOLUME CXXX

The Society wishes to acknowledge with gratitude the assistance given
towards the cost of publication by
Cheshire County Council
Lancashire County Council

ISBN 0 902593 21 8

Produced by Alan Sutton Publishing Limited, Stroud, Gloucestershire
Printed in Great Britain

THE FAMILY RECORDS OF BENJAMIN SHAW MECHANIC OF DENT, DOLPHINHOLME AND PRESTON, 1772–1841

Edited by
Alan G. Crosby

PRINTED FOR THE SOCIETY
1991

CONTENTS

In memory of the author, Benjamin Shaw of Preston (1772–1841)

PREFACE AND ACKNOWLEDGMENTS

In May 1826 Benjamin Shaw (1772–1841), a mechanic and turner living in Dale Street, Preston, began to write his *Family Records*, a detailed account of the lives of his forebears and relations, combined with his own autobiography. The work, written in small neat script in a home-made notebook, was completed in August, and then updated at intervals during 1827 and 1828. The results evidently pleased Benjamin: in 1829 he began a second volume, written up annually until old age and failing powers put an end to his serious writing at the beginning of 1837.

The two volumes of Benjamin's *Family Records* are fascinating in their own right, since he had a long and interesting life and his powers as a writer were considerable. They are also of very great historical significance. Benjamin was unable to write until he was twenty, when he taught himself, and he was one of only a handful of working-class men who, before the days of universal education, were willing and able to record their stories. The background to his life was the Industrial Revolution, as a consequence of which he and his family experienced the traumatic upheaval of migration from the country to the town, and from domestic labour to the factory system. It was an experience which was shared by millions of their contemporaries in England at the same time, and is a familiar tale, but it is rare indeed for it to be recounted by one who was a participant.

Benjamin's papers, including these two volumes and a wide range of his other writings, were preserved by his descendants – as he had intended – and in 1984 were deposited in the Lancashire Record Office, where they have the reference DDX/1554. This present edition comprises a complete transcript of both volumes of the *Family Records*, together with detailed notes on the text, and an introduction giving the background to the work and pointing to some of the valuable historical material which it contains. In writing the introductory sections I have not attempted to give an in-depth analysis of the subjects covered, but rather to indicate some of the issues raised and the strengths and weaknesses of Benjamin's account. Neither have I felt it appropriate to include comparative analysis of other works of this type, since this volume is intended as a primary source in its own right.

I am grateful to the Record Society of Lancashire and Cheshire for making this publication possible. Its General Editor, Dr Peter McNiven, has made many helpful suggestions and has checked the text with scrupulous accuracy. The staff of the Lancashire Record Office, the Cumbria Record Office at Kendal and the Harris Library, Preston, have given invaluable assistance in many ways, and I would like to express my special thanks to them. Ken Hall, the County Archivist of Lancashire, not only allowed me to use the material in his custody, but also gave his strong personal support to the idea of publication. Acknowledgment is also due to the Cheshire Record Office, Leeds District Archives, and other branches of the West Yorkshire Archive Service. The interest of Dr Shani d'Cruze, a fellow Benjamin-enthusiast, has made the work on this edition even more enjoyable. Discussion with her has stimulated consideration of the material from different perspectives, and I am indebted to her for several key references and for allowing me access to her unpublished work.

My wife Jacquie has wielded the censor's pen over grammatical, stylistic and typographical infelicities, and has valiantly undertaken the laborious task of checking the original transcript and typescript. Above all, though, I am grateful to Mr. Henry Shaw, a direct descendant of Benjamin Shaw and the present owner of his papers. He has most generously allowed me complete freedom to publish the present edition in whatever style I wished, and to make use of other documents in his ownership. He has been full of encouragement and enthusiasm for the project, and I hope very much that his ancestor, Benjamin Shaw, would have approved of the results.

INTRODUCTION

The writings of Benjamin Shaw

The text in this book comprises the two separate volumes of Benjamin Shaw's autobiographical and biographical writings. The first, ninety pages in length, is entitled *Benjamin Shaw^s Family Records a Short account of Benjamin Shaw and his Family*[1] and the second, only fourteen pages long, is *A Short Account of Benjamin Shaw and his Family continued.*[2] Both books were handmade by the author himself, of cheap soft paper sewn with thread and bound in brown paper. A note at the end of the original text of the first volume states 'wrote and bound by the author Benjⁿ Shaw 1826 august 20th 1826 Preston in lancashire'. There is a reliable belief within the Shaw family that not only were the books made by Benjamin, but that he also made his own steel-nibbed pen – something he would have been more than capable of doing. Unsplit steel nibs were first manufactured in 1803, and Benjamin would thus have had a model to work from. The more efficient split-nibbed pens were commercially produced from 1826, after the writing of the first volume, but it may well have been that Benjamin made his own version of that refinement using the ideas already in circulation. The writing, which is fine and extremely regular, has no evidence of blotting or drying-up of the ink supply, and was certainly done with a steel nib.[3]

These two volumes are only part of Benjamin's surviving writings. The collection of his papers which has been deposited in the Lancashire Record Office (DDX/1554) includes several compendia of epigrams, phrases, proverbs and mottoes; notes on herbal remedies and indexes to published flora; rough notes of dates and events; arithmetical and geometrical notes, including specifications for the sizes and calibration of tools; and couplets and verse written partly by Benjamin and partly derived from other sources. In addition, there are several letters to Benjamin from other members of his family.

Benjamin's other writings reveal the catholicity of his tastes and the variety of his interests, and hint at his remarkable talents and originality of thought. He had received only the minimum of formal schooling in his youth, and could not write until he was twenty – when he taught himself – but it is clear that he had a 'fine mind'. The account of his family and his own life which he wrote in the summer of 1826 was his most ambitious, original and important work. He planned the project well in advance, preparing notes and gathering information, and it is likely that for many years he had been intending to write such an

---

1   LRO: DDX/1554/1.
2   LRO: DDX/1554/2.
3   Personal communication from Mr Henry Shaw, 24 August 1989.

account. The results seem to have pleased him, for he continued his story, in a necessarily less ambitious form, after 1828. Of his surviving writings these two volumes are by far the most important. They have a special value for historians as a detailed and accurate tale of the progress of an ordinary family, in its many branches, over almost 150 years, combined with a careful and frank account of the life of the author himself.

The *Family Records* were written for posterity. In his preface to the first volume Benjamin specifically explains that he undertook the work partly for his own use, but partly for his children after his time. This means that the account is more reflective, ordered and rounded than a daily or yearly review would have been – it is certainly not a diary or journal, in format, aim or content. The second volume, which was intended to bring the original account up to date, was written as an annual review. Its form is therefore markedly different, with less coherence and less of an overview than the first volume.

Primarily because it was intended for posterity – and therefore was written in an explanatory and descriptive style – and also because it was produced as a planned project, the first volume shows a high degree of organization. It was clearly designed in advance with a particular arrangement, and was not shaped as writing progressed. The first section comprises short biographical sketches of the members of previous generations, on both the paternal and maternal sides, including not only the direct but also the collateral forebears. The most important characters, Benjamin's parents, Joseph and Isabella Shaw, are described in greater detail. The core of the book is a long chronological account of Benjamin's own life up to 1826, combining a large quantity of precise and pertinent factual material with some anecdotal and descriptive passages.

There is also a certain amount of what might be termed 'emotional writing'. Although Benjamin generally eschews a polemical or intensely personal approach, he does employ such a style in describing, for example, his often troubled relationship with his wife, the religious conversion which he experienced in 1800, the death of his daughter Hannah in 1824, and the resentment and bitterness of his quarrel with his sister Hannah in the previous year. In these passages he gives vent to feelings and personal opinion. The original text concluded with accounts of his wife and her family, and separate biographies of each of their children, which to some extent duplicate material found in the autobiographical section. The arrangement of the writing is complemented by a series of brief passages which serve as extended introductory headings, and the text was made usable as a practical document of reference by a detailed index, arranged by first name, which listed all the characters appearing in the work and noted their relationship to the author. The index is not reproduced in this edition.

The first volume was started, as the title page indicates, on 31 May 1826 and, in its initial form, was completed on 20 August. However, between the last page of the original text and the index which was written at the back of the book were several blank pages. These were filled, after August 1826, by a further section which brought the book up to date. It gave a detailed account of the illness and death of Benjamin's wife Betty – she had fallen ill with consumption in July 1826, while the book was being written – and noted current events and recent happenings in the family. The first volume concludes with a series of verses about Betty Shaw, and with a note that writing was finished on 20 April 1828 (two months after her death).

On 15 February 1829 he began work on 'Volume the 2nd', which of necessity was written with a more immediate perspective. It was an annually updated journal: each January or February, Benjamin wrote a review of the main happenings of the previous year, in the same fashion as the additional (post-August 1826) material in the first volume. This inevitably resulted in a more disjointed style. The second volume was maintained until the end of 1836, a year in which Benjamin experienced much ill health and personal distress. While it is not possible to be certain, these experiences seem to have caused him to lose interest in the journal, so that although there are a few fragmentary notes among his papers relating to events after the autumn of 1836, the account itself stops abruptly at that point. He died in June 1841, and does not seem to have undertaken any serious narrative writing during the last five years of his life.

Benjamin was deeply interested in politics and current affairs. The autobiographical section, its updating of 1826–8, and the whole of the second volume, contain extensive notes relating to what was happening in Preston and the wider world. This material was probably included for two main reasons. First, he found the political material of intrinsic interest, and felt that those who read the book would also value it. Second, the inclusion of details of wars, battles, political upheavals, the births and deaths of royalty and famous people, and of trends in society – taxation, civil unrest, good and bad harvests, unemployment and inflation – set the personal narrative firmly in perspective.

Benjamin had a sophisticated appreciation of comparative chronology, and seems to have felt a need to set the events in their proper historical context. At its most mundane level this feeling might be expressed as 'I have lived in interesting times – this is what happened while I was around', but there is good reason to believe that he saw a relationship between his own life and experience and what was going on beyond that horizon. That he was well aware of the influences – beneficial or detrimental – of wars, economic cycles and political changes is clear. He points to direct relationships between price changes and the availability of food on the one hand, and the effects of the Napoleonic Wars, the taxation policies of successive governments, and the fluctuations in the harvest on the other. These events were recorded not just for academic interest, but for the impact which they had upon his own life.

Undoubtedly, much of the information must have been included because it also provided a yardstick by which to measure the progress of his life – births of children happened in the same year as famous battles, changes in his circumstances at the same time as upheavals in Europe. These dates and events were pegs on which to hang his own story. Right at the beginning of his autobiographical account he notes how his birth and infancy were 'about the middle of the Americam [*sic*] war'.[4] Characteristically he goes on to mention the Boston Tea Party, which happened 'because the English government had laid a duty of 3^d per lb on tea – which now pays here 10^s & excise duty beside'. Benjamin's personal financial caution was combined with a strong dislike of taxation and government revenue-raising.

The inclusion of so much political history, spanning the whole period from the 1770s until the end of his writing in 1836 – by which time it had become more important than the family record – poses the question of the source both of this information, and of the family history which is recounted. At the beginning of the first volume there are some indications of sources. The preface states that he had no records available from previous generations, and that 'if any records had been handed down to me, I should have considered it as a Vallueable treasure' – indeed, in writing these volumes he intended to provide just such a record for subsequent generations.[5] The lack of written material from his own family meant that what Benjamin learned about the past had to be derived from questioning older relatives, and from his own recollections: he knew nothing of his family except 'what I remember to have heard, by word of mouth, or seen'.

It is certain that the chief source for such family detail was his father. Joseph Shaw did not have any personal memories of his own grandfather, but his father, Benjamin Shaw senior, born in 1708, lived until 1794, so that Joseph would have had a rich fund of stories about the family going back to the early eighteenth century. Joseph moved to Preston in 1795, and lived the rest of his life within yards of Benjamin. The two were 'constant companions', discussing religious and political matters as well as the family, and when Benjamin began to write extensively, after the amputation of his leg in 1810, Joseph must have told many tales of the past. He – and to a lesser extent his wife Isabella, who died in 1798 – provided Benjamin with much of the material for the potted biographies of relatives. Benjamin was able to add his own, perhaps more impressionistic, recollections of the more long-lived members of previous generations. He had known his Shaw grandparents, and his grandmother Noddle, very well. When he was a boy many of his aunts and uncles had lived near his family, in Dentdale or Garsdale, and were known personally to him.

Benjamin and his father, combining their memories, produced an account which is remarkably accurate. Since Benjamin could not have had any means of corroborating most of the information from manuscript sources, all the information about names, dates and places which he gives was necessarily derived from careful calculation and memory. There is no suggestion of a list of dates in a family bible, although it is just possible that there was such a record of his own

4   *Benjamin Shaw's Family Records* (the present volume: noted hereafter as *Family Records*), p. 21.
5   *Family Records*, p. 1.

brothers and sisters. The accuracy of his information is impressive: rarely is the year or the location of an event significantly wrong, and only occasionally, if due allowance is made for the vagaries of spelling, is a name given incorrectly. When inaccuracies have crept in, they tend to relate to distant events or remoter relatives. Research in parish records and other sources now readily available almost always confirms Benjamin's statements.

From 1811 or thereabouts, Benjamin began to keep a rough notebook in which he jotted down significant events – the births, deaths and marriages of his children, the changes in his wages and employment, news of acquaintances and employers – and it was from these rough notes that the later part of the first volume was written. One of these notebooks, containing a miscellany of memoranda and dates between 1813 and 1840, has survived. Most of the notes have been worked into the text, but a few – mainly those which relate to people who were not members of the family – were omitted from the final version.[6] These jottings may well also have been intended as an *aide memoire*, for Benjamin must have had an exceptionally clear and quick memory, and may have needed to consult only an outline record for events, feelings and scenes to be brought vividly to mind. Given the accuracy of the factual material, it is reasonable to suppose that the discursive passages are similarly reliable, and that his memory did not play serious tricks.

The source of the political notes and information about current events is less clear. My own view is that he is likely to have had access to some form of almanac or textbook of dates and events at least for the period up to 1811. Until that year the political notes are almost invariably laconic and factual – in the manner of an almanac – while some of the dates are of events so obscure that it is difficult to believe Benjamin would have noted them at the time or remembered them later. It was not until 1793 that he learned to write, and he had no opportunity for extended writing until 1810, so these details were probably added from a printed source available in 1826. After 1811, as with the family details, he may have kept some rough notes of current events – especially those which were taking place in Preston and neighbourhood, for the amount of specific detail and the quantity of subjective opinion increase markedly after this time. These were events which Benjamin experienced as a mature adult, and he must have had a very clear personal recollection of them and their impact.

Benjamin's recollections, the use of an almanac, and perhaps some rough notes, were augmented by the reading of newspapers. There is only one specific reference to this: he notes in July 1826 that 'the last weeks paper stated, that 200.000 were out of work within 20 miles of manchester'.[7] Nevertheless, the style and content of the local and political notes made in the second half of the first volume make it plain that he used such a source regularly. The newspaper

6 LRO: DDX/1554/3.
7 *Family Records*, p. 70.

would have been the *Preston Chronicle*, which was founded in 1812 and was the only newspaper in the town until 1844. It is probably no coincidence that there is an increased volume of local news in Benjamin's political and current events record at the same time as a regular newspaper became available, although it is unclear whether he bought the paper or had sight of someone else's copy: there was no public free library in Preston until 1879.

The grammar and punctuation of Benjamin's writing are erratic. There are some colloquialisms and dialect words, though perhaps fewer than might have been expected, and the vocabulary is extensive, formal and mature. The punctuation is distinctive, with ubiquitous use of '&c &c –' to end a sentence or phrase, and with minimal use of full stops and paragraphs. Spelling is also highly variable. There are many words which are misspelled where it is certain Benjamin must have known the correct form – 'toly' instead of 'told' or 'ut' rather than 'up' are examples. These are errors of oversight rather than ignorance. Elsewhere, some consistent spellings suggest phonetic interpretation of his own pronunciation – 'contlude' (conclude), 'difequilty' and 'prostect' (prospect) are examples. In these he trusted his own judgment, but for many longer and more complex words – 'rhumatism', 'predicament', 'subscriptions' the spellings are more or less correct, implying that he made use of a dictionary or other printed source.

Benjamin had a natural gift for writing. For this reason, and perhaps also because he was self-taught from published books, his vocabulary, sentence construction and ability to convey complex abstract ideas are remarkably sophisticated. There are some passages which suggest, by their style and arrangement, that he copied or adapted extracts from published sources – the newspapers or an almanac – but much of the writing conveys the clear impression of original thought. The turn of phrase is often vivid and striking, his powers of terse descriptive writing are considerable, and his understated style is in some places intensely moving. Among Benjamin's surviving writings there is no other material which involves lengthy narrative composition, but his epigrams, couplets and verses indicate clearly that he had great gifts of inventive literary ability. The lack of formal education is always apparent, but the power of his mind and its intellectual potential equally so.

The autobiography and biographical sketches are not as full and extensive in their descriptive scope as, for example, the autobiographies of Samuel Bamford or William Stout. This is primarily because Benjamin's writing reflects the motive which lay behind his project – to portray the history of a man and of his family within the context of the wider events of the times – and therefore he had no wish to include extensive ancillary detail. Nevertheless, their importance as historical evidence is tremendous. Benjamin Shaw is one of the few genuinely working-class autobiographers before the age of universal elementary education. His schooling was rudimentary and his learning acquired by his own efforts. He was, for much of his life, really poor and living in the most difficult conditions.

From the historical viewpoint this rarity is made all the more valuable by the wider circumstances of his life, which coincided with a crucial period in the development of modern England. In his progress from a childhood in a beautiful Pennine valley, via apprenticeship at one of the earliest large mechanized textile mills, to long years lived in the shadow of John Horrocks's cotton factories in booming, dirty Preston, he mirrors the experience of the English Industrial Revolution.

Benjamin Shaw

Benjamin Shaw was born at Dent, in the West Riding of Yorkshire, in December 1772. His father, Joseph, was a weaver who was already experimenting with the clock-mending and small-scale mechanical repair work which were soon to become his major employment. The Shaw family came originally from Garsdale, the valley north of Dentdale across the long high whaleback of Rise Hill. Joseph had moved to Dent only two years earlier, on his marriage to Isabella Noddle. There were many members of his family in Garsdale, where their ancestors had lived since the early seventeenth century and probably for generations before then. The Noddle family also came from Garsdale: Benjamin's grandparents, George and Peggy Noddle, had come to live in Dent soon after their marriage in 1739. Links between the two valleys were strong, and both had close ties with the nearby market town of Sedbergh, but there were also economic and social connections from Dentdale southwards, to Ingleton and into the Craven district.

In 1791 Miles Burton, a Dent man who had gone to work at the new worsted mill on the River Wyre at Dolphinholme near Lancaster, went back to his home valley with the task of recruiting labour for that factory. He told of the good wages which were on offer, and of the excellent employment prospects for families, and his propaganda was effective. The Shaws, and many of their neighbours, were persuaded by his account and moved to Dolphinholme in the summer of 1791. No member of Benjamin's immediate family ever returned, though his mother was, for the remaining few years of her life, constantly homesick and lamented the leaving of her native 'Countery'.[8] Dolphinholme proved to be a place of misery and distress for the Shaw family. Employment, far from being secure, was uncertain and unpredictable there; the masters found Joseph Shaw too independent of spirit and dismissed him, only reinstating him in a different and more lowly job; one of Benjamin's brothers, a boy of ten, was severely injured working in the mill; and fevers raged, so that three of the children died within twelve months. The family began to disintegrate and, to make bad much worse, in 1793–4 the mill gradually ceased operations.

Benjamin, who was nineteen when he went to Dolphinholme, signed on as an

8 ibid., p. 26.

apprentice turner and filer in the mechanics' shop. Soon after he arrived he began to court Betty Leeming, a Lancaster girl who had moved to Dolphin-holme with her family. They had a quarrel in 1792, and although they were reconciled she decided to go to Preston to find work in the mills there. Betty, who could apparently write, sent letters to Benjamin, and he – not wanting to send verbal messages with the carrier – taught himself to write so he could send her love letters. Early in 1793, after hearing disquieting reports and gossip about her infidelity, Benjamin went to Preston to see Betty. He spent one night with her, and a few weeks later she wrote to tell him of her pregnancy. Aged twenty, still an apprentice and with scarcely any means of supporting a family, he married her in September 1793 and their child was born in November. He confessed that he thought of abandoning her and running to another place, and during her labour he wished that she and the baby might die, but it was not to be. The shape of the whole of the rest of his life was determined on the night of 11 February 1793, when he stayed with Betty in Preston. From all this trouble there was one tangible benefit: he could now write. He gives his own wry verdict: 'It is an ill thing that is good for nothing'.[9]

Their first winter was a time of intense hardship, of bitter cold in a house with no fuel except what sticks they could gather on the riverbank. They had the barest minimum of possessions, and too little food: 'we were wed now indeed'.[10] In 1795 the mill finally closed completely and, thrown out of work, Benjamin took his family to Preston, where he obtained employment at Horrocks's cotton mill on the east side of the town. In March 1795 they moved into the two rooms in Dale Street where he was to live for over forty-six years, until immediately before his death. Children came regularly, the family grew, and Benjamin changed jobs from time to time as he was laid off at one works and taken on at another. Most of his work was in the machine shops, making tools and equipment for the cotton mills and carrying out repairs – his special skill was on the lathe, and he seems to have been highly regarded by employers as a reliable and talented workman.

In 1793, at Dolphinholme, a thoughtless lad had thrown a stick at him, and had injured his leg. The damage was exacerbated by his having to stand for hours at a time in the icy waters of the river, repairing the dam, and later by the frostbite which his feet suffered when he walked to Preston. Ointments and patent remedies failed to heal the wound, which became ulcerous. By the end of the 1790s he was suffering acutely and constantly from pain and open sores, and realized that he was growing gradually lame. During 1807–9 he had ever-longer periods off work, and began to think that he would not have long to live. Fortunately the Preston Dispensary, a charitable medical institution, opened at the beginning of 1810, and in April the doctors at the Dispensary amputated

9   ibid., p. 28.
10 ibid., p. 32.

Benjamin's right leg. They saved his life. The wound quickly healed, his health was restored and, although it was seven years before he was able to resume full-time work, he was once more mobile with the help of a crutch.

During the period in which he was growing lame, Benjamin found comfort in religion. In 1800 he was converted to active Christianity, initially by a Baptist preacher who was a spinning master at the Lord Street factory where Benjamin worked. This helped to relieve the gloom of his existence. Another comfort was education and self-improvement. He used the long days after the amputation and when, later, he was at part-time work, to further his studies, teaching himself mathematics, reading textbooks, and making copious notes on remedies, mechanics, epigrams and verse. This was his solace, for in addition to his troubled health he had an unhappy domestic life. Benjamin and Betty differed fundamentally and irreconcilably over household management, he being of an exceptionally thrifty and cautious disposition, while she – so he considered – was careless, casual and generous to excess.

They had eight children, only one of whom, his favourite child the 'first Mary', died in infancy. The children meant more expense and more crowding – in the summer of 1813 there were nine people living in the two rooms[11] – but gradually they began to earn their own keep, going to the factory at the age of nine or ten. From 1815 onwards, as they grew to adulthood, the children caused Benjamin and Betty an endless succession of problems. The last twenty-seven years of Benjamin's life were perpetually clouded by anxiety and practical difficulties as a result. William, when aged nineteen, fathered two children on different women within a year. Bella had an illegitimate child and did not marry the father for over three years, during which time she and her son lived at home. Hannah, aged eighteen, had a child – which died in infancy – and never properly recovered, becoming consumptive and dying a lingering and harrowing death in 1824.

Shortly before her death Joseph Shaw, Benjamin's father, died. Benjamin and his sister Hannah, whom he had already grown to dislike, quarrelled bitterly over their father's paltry estate. And in 1826 Betty, the wife with whom he had such a stormy relationship, but who had been his constant companion through hard and unhappy times for thirty-four years, fell fatally ill with consumption. In the same year the last unmarried son, Thomas, lost his job: Benjamin had taken great pains to secure work for him, using his influence with employers and trying hard to get him a good place, but his efforts were not crowned with success. In October 1826 Thomas married secretly and his wife had their child shortly afterwards. Penniless, homeless and with a tiny baby, they moved in with Ben and Betty. It was in these somewhat inauspicious circumstances that, during

---

11 It has been suggested to me that the family may have rented additional rooms, other than the two taken in 1795. This view is based on an ambiguous phrase in the text, and I think the case for it is at best non proven.

May 1826, Benjamin began work on the first volume of his autobiography and family record.

Betty died in February 1828, leaving Benjamin, then fifty-five, with their two teenage daughters, Agnes and Mary. Both were – in their father's view – wilful and headstrong, and Benjamin was ill-suited to deal with them. They stole money from him, he criticized their extravagance and frivolity, and mournfully noted his loneliness and how much he missed his wife – troublesome and infuriating she might have been, but she had been a friend and a support. Mary became pregnant in 1829, when she was seventeen, and announced that the baby's father was in prison for assault. After his release (and after the child was born) they married – only to separate four months later. In another context, Benjamin had said how the burdens of parents were not finished when their children were grown. In his case the burdens grew ever heavier.

The last child, Agnes, was described by Benjamin as a pert and saucy girl. She left home when she was young, went to Manchester, and in 1834 had a child which died in infancy. A year later she was back in Preston, working at Horrocks's mill, but was soon dismissed when it was discovered that she was pregnant again. Her child was born in February 1836, but she did not recover her health, and died in August. Benjamin, a lonely, tired and failing widower of sixty-four, was left in charge of Betty, his baby granddaughter.

Since 1828 he had been writing, probably once a year, an account of the events of the previous twelve months in his family and in the wider world. The last such review was written up in late 1836 or at the start of 1837, and thereafter Benjamin is silent. In January 1840 his daughter and son-in-law, Bella and William Roberts, wrote to him from Manchester – the main subject of the letter, characteristically, is the whereabouts of some pawn tickets – and they asked after their niece Betty, Agnes's daughter. The child was taken elsewhere not long afterwards – probably to live with her uncle Joseph – and in April 1841, when the census was taken, Benjamin was living alone in his rooms in Dale Street. He died aged sixty-eight on 7 June 1841, at Joseph's house in Park Lane, Preston. His death certificate gives the cause of death as 'natural decay'.[12] It was forty-six years since he had come to live in the shadow of Horrocks's factory, and over fifty since he and his family had left the green fields of Dent to work in the mill at Dolphinholme.

The character of the author

There is much that we shall never know about Benjamin Shaw, for despite the detail, accuracy and frankness of his autobiography he is reticent about himself

---

12 The death certificate does not state the place of death (other than 'Preston'), but when Benjamin was buried at St Paul's church, Preston on 9 June 1841 his place of residence was given as Park Lane (LRO: St Paul's Burial Register Transcript).

as an individual. Although he gives a careful description of the physical appearance of many of the people he writes about, there is no indication at all of what he himself looked like. His character is, however, plainly identifiable.

He was a cautious, methodical, organized man. His writing is neat and regular, his page layouts – in the family records but especially in the lists which he compiled of epigrams and aphorisms – are orderly and tidy. He had a passion for indexes: his surviving writings include several examples prepared by him for existing published works, while his quotations and mottoes are carefully arranged in alphabetical order. The love of order and regularity is immediately apparent in the arrangement of the two volumes of his family record – these are no spontaneous scribblings, but an organized and carefully-planned project executed over several months.

These characteristics, so clear in his written work, are evident in every aspect of his daily life. His greatest battles were fought as planned campaigns, and it was infuriating and exasperating when others failed to play the appropriate part. The tone in which he recounts the story of his early, hasty marriage, brought about by Betty's pregnancy, shows the great contempt which he felt for himself because he had, momentarily but disastrously, been carried away by passion. Instead of the rational, cautious, sensible approach which he admired, he had acted carelessly and impetuously, and the consequences had moulded, for the worse, all his later life. Thirty-five years later his anger with himself was still strong:

> How seldom wisdom guides the Stubern choice
> In love affairs, tis cappreece whim or chance[13]

The regrets began immediately. He and Betty had had a tempestuous courtship, with quarrels and differences, reconciliations and partings. They were physically attracted, and he was in love with her, but temperamentally they proved to be well-nigh incompatible, and in retrospect he saw not just marriage, but also his choice of partner, as a mistake. With brutal frankness he tells of his thoughts of escape, either by running away or by the fervent wish that she and the baby might die and he might then be free. He must often have wished that he had been guided by the philosophy of caution which he later summarized in a couplet:

> Quick Promises oft causes sorrow,
> I'lle consider on't, call tomorrow[14]

Yet the same sense of order and caution had another aspect – throughout his adult life he seems to have had a firm moral code, involving a sense of honour

13 LRO: DDX/1554/13.
14 LRO: DDX/1554/12.

and obligation. His ideas of running away were dismissed: 'I sometimes thought I would not have her, but then this came to my mind, how must She do'.[15] That sense of duty is recalled in his attitude to his employers in later years. Those who were unjust to him were censured, and on one occasion taken to court, but those who were fair to him were repaid by his best efforts to do good work and to serve them well. His strong feelings of family duty, perhaps inevitable in a man so conscious of the family as an institution, are apparent in the support and protection he gave to his children through the years of their adulthood, long after he had ceased to have direct responsibility for their actions or needs.

His marriage would have been less regretted had his wife been of a like mind, but their characters were radically different. Benjamin's caution in his financial affairs matched his rational, ordered approach to life in general. The endless arguments with Betty over the management of their household accounts perfectly exemplify his character. He wanted to be obliged to nobody, to be independent and in control. Solvency, savings and sensible purchasing were essential. Debts, credit trading, unwise lending, hasty borrowing and living from day to day were all anathema to Benjamin. Unfortunately, Betty was unwilling or unable to conform to his ideas. He was generous in his contributions to the household budget; he earned – for substantial periods – a decent wage; and he claims to have been modest in his own requirements, but she remained insolvent. The prudence and restraint which marked his character were not shared by the rest of his family.

Benjamin cannot have been an easy man to live with – sometimes stern, frequently censorious, for long periods in great pain and then an invalid, often moralizing and possessed of a firm belief in the correctness of his own views. Betty comes across as a sympathetic character, who must have been long-suffering and who, eventually and too late, was found by Benjamin to have been a greater support and comfort than he had realized. These aspects of his character may also perhaps explain why Benjamin apparently had few friends. He scarcely mentions people outside the family except in so far as they appear in the story as employers. There are no references at all to the term 'friend', and in the whole of the work only Frank Sleddon, the masters Park and Hope, and the Baptist spinning master, Frank Lambert, are described in other than impersonal terms.

In the rough notes started about 1813 there is a series of entries recording the deaths of, and sometimes the births of children to, people who were definitely not members of the Shaw and Leeming families – for example, '1829 March 15 tom wignal died'.[16] These brief notes must refer to acquaintances or neighbours, yet none is mentioned in the main work and there is only one definite reference to a fellow-worker – James Kay, who in 1799 moved with Benjamin to work at

---

15 *Family Records*, p. 30.
16 LRO: DDX/1554/3.

the Lord's Factory in Dale Street. In a history of the family it might have been inappropriate to describe friends, acquaintances and neighbours, but this is unlikely to have been the sole reason for the absence of references.

Benjamin enjoyed a normal and – as far as we can tell – happy childhood, and had a good relationship with his parents then and in his adult life. He recalled how, when sixteen or seventeen, he sought the company of his comrades and wanted to be with 'the lasses' who were always in his thoughts. But the troubles of his early and hasty marriage and increasing lameness, together with the family's poverty, seem to have turned him in on himself, and as these problems loomed larger his introversion grew. For much of his adult life Benjamin was a solitary person, spending his leisure time in reading, writing and doing arithmetical exercises, making notes and indexing textbooks. He tells how in 1811–12, when he was unable to work because his leg had been amputated, their desperate poverty meant that he and Betty stayed indoors day in and day out, winding twist and baking oatcakes while their neighbours were enjoying a night out after the labours of the week. Any friendships he might have had at work probably faded away during his prolonged absence. His wife, father and children were his only companions.

He appears to have disliked or despised most of his neighbours, seeing them as poor and undeserving, scrounging from Betty and taking advantage of her generosity, or gossiping and passing on tittle-tattle. There was early experience of this: the people who, in 1792, had interfered between him and Betty, telling him of her unfaithfulness and casting doubt on her character, had indirectly been responsible for his early marriage and for his lingering doubts about Joseph's paternity. Such tale-telling was alien to his character and repugnant to him. Later, in Dale Street, he thought that the poor neighbours took advantage of Betty's generosity and casual ways with money. A verse which he composed makes his views of gossiping neighbours quite clear. Referring to the reliability and accuracy of the tale told by an echo, he says:

> O, would women be so faithfull,
> In their report,
> Neigbours would not seem so hatefull
> Naught of the sort[17]

The lack of references to friends is not only because he did not think them worthy of mention, but also because there was comparatively little friendship in his adult life. A man who saw his neighbours as 'hatefull', who despised them for their financial inadequacies, and detested the gossip and chatter which was one of the few consolations to women leading a hard and downtrodden existence, was unlikely to have a wide circle of friends.

17 LRO: DDX/1554/12.

He was a cynical man, with a jaundiced view of authority. His references to governments often make a sharp political statement about their self-interest and incompetence. He notes sourly the vagaries of the Poor Law system and the ways of employers. Much of the early part of the book, describing his various relations, gives an impression of an aloof, amused, though not necessarily unsympathetic, outsider observing the waywardness and weakness of human kind. His sense of humour, which certainly existed, was dry and sardonic – there is a neat and wry play on words in his reference to the anxious months before his marriage: '& the lass quite big, (alass for Poor Ben)'.[18]

In all the work which survives there is a powerful feeling for truth. There are inevitably points at which there must be suspicion about the completeness or reliability of an account – the most significant is Betty's deathbed speech – but in general a very high degree of factual accuracy seems to be matched by the truthfulness of the story. Some aspects of his life – for example, the houses he lived in and their conditions, and the details of his work – are given very little coverage, but that is not the result of deception or a wish to conceal, but simply because Benjamin did not consider them worthy of detailed reporting. As in all autobiographies it is necessary to bear in mind that we have only one perspective upon the story. This is one man's account of people and events, and one man's assessment of their character and importance. Inevitably, it is an account seen from his perspective.

Despite these reservations, the honesty and straightforwardness which he required – though often did not receive – in matters as diverse as the behaviour of his employers and the accounting system of his wife, shine through the narrative. The preface to the first volume gives a superb and forthright explanation of the need for truth and objectivity in historical writing, and Benjamin amply fulfils his own conditions in this respect.

Education and learning

It was remarkable that a man who only learned to write at the age of twenty was able to compose such a philosophical and elegantly-phrased preface, and that Benjamin did so is a tribute to the effectiveness of his self-education. Widening his intellectual horizons was a central theme in Benjamin's adult life. He placed the highest value on learning, and derived immense satisfaction from his own achievement in that field. He was also acutely conscious of this skill – or its absence – in others. Many of the biographical sketches refer to the education, or lack of education, of their subjects. In the longer and more detailed accounts of the more immediate members of the family the ability to read and write is frequently mentioned, directly or indirectly. Benjamin not only prized education for the advantages it offered and for its practical value, but also considered

18 *Family Records*, p. 30.

learning as a worthy object in its own right and a key to wisdom. In his adult years, especially after the amputation of his leg and in the period of troubled and unhappy relations with his wife, he found reading, arithmetical exercises and technical drawing a comfort and a solace in his depression.

Richard Shaw, Benjamin's great-grandfather, was probably illiterate. When he signed his will, written in 1737, seven years before he died, he made a cross.[19] But he clearly saw the worth of giving his sons a sound education for, as Benjamin records, his 'easy circumstances' (he was a small farmer) gave him the chance to do this, and it was a wise investment. One son, Joseph, was the chapel clerk at Garsdale for many years, and his neat regular signature appears many times in the parish register and other documents of the mid-eighteenth century. His son Edward was sufficiently well-educated to enter the Church as a clergyman. Joseph also educated his daughters: Margaret (1729–93) signed as a marriage witness.[20] Another signatory was Benjamin Shaw the elder, grandfather of the autobiographer, whose 'Hobby was Books [he] was a great reeder & writer'.[21] Benjamin senior was a small farmer and weaver, and it is significant that studying could be described as a 'hobby': perhaps the younger Benjamin, in very different circumstances, recognized a like mind.

The level of education among the next two generations seems to have been less adequate, and it is possible to detect a steady general decline which can be related to the changing fortunes of the family. William Shaw, Benjamin's uncle, was 'a good reeder & writer', but Benjamin's father, Joseph, 'Read & wrote Slowly'.[22] More serious was the very poor education given to Joseph's children, including Benjamin himself. The village schoolmistress in Dent, Peggy Winn, was claimed to be very good at her work, but although Benjamin went to her school for about six years he learned only to read. His younger brother George also went to the village school, and could also read, but it is clear that this was at best only a part-time schooling. The main purpose of the school was to teach knitting. Benjamin himself 'continued to go to School, & learned to knit stockings as was the fashon of the place, & day', while George 'went to school, & learnt to Read & knit'.[23]

This evidence supports the view that in the eighteenth century learning to read and to write were considered to be separate and sequential processes. Reading was held to be of much greater importance. It was only in later life, and as a result of his own efforts, that Benjamin reached the second stage. The education of the other children of Joseph and Isabella Shaw is not directly recorded, but the eldest daughter, Benjamin's sister Hannah, was barely literate. On the death of their father Benjamin was bitter that she had been left 'his large Bible &

19 LRO: WRW(L) 1744 Richard Shaw of Garsdale.
20 CROK: WPR/60/2.
21 *Family Records*, p. 4.
22 ibid., pp. 15, 9.
23 ibid., pp. 23, 80.

Birketts Notes on the new testament also though my sister could not read either of them for she scarce knew her letters'.[24] The younger son William, the only other child who grew to adulthood, could write – although his letters are badly formed, his spelling extremely erratic, and his whole style gives the impression that writing was a great labour. He emigrated to America, and Benjamin received several letters from him, some of which survive.[25]

The education of Benjamin's mother, Isabella Noddle, and her family was similarly restricted. Margaret (Peggy) Noddle, widowed young with a large family, was only able to send 'the younger [children] to Scool, untill they were able to go to Service'.[26] The elder children apparently had no education, and none of the family was apprenticed to a trade. Isabella, the eldest living daughter, was fully occupied from a very early age with bringing up her younger brothers and sisters, and with knitting and winding in her spare moments. Her son records that 'She was no Scholler', and the entry in the Dent parish register for her marriage to Joseph Shaw shows his signature and her mark.[27] There is no reference in the biographies of any of Isabella's siblings to education, schooling or ability to read or write – a negative which must be taken as a clear sign that they could not, for elsewhere Benjamin is careful to record such information.

Benjamin himself learned to write and to do written arithmetic when he was twenty. Betty Leeming, his sweetheart at Dolphinholme, was better educated than he. As a small girl she had attended the Bluecoat Charity School in Lancaster for several years, and had received a competent basic education, being able to read with some fluency, and apparently to write. Her ability to read was 'retained in a good degree', and as she lay dying in 1827 she 'had many a Comfortable hour when She could not Sleep in reading her testament & hymn book'.[28] Her few personal possessions included the testament, two 'smallbooks' and the hymn book. During their courtship Betty went to live in Preston and wrote letters to Benjamin, sent by the carrier to Dolphinholme: 'this was the begining of my writing, for I never went to any school to write in my life – and wanting to send to her I was ashamed to let anybody know my secrets, I set about writing love letters'.[29]

Benjamin had an obvious aptitude for learning. The circumstances in which he lived militated against productive use being made of his talent, but nevertheless learning became basic to his very existence. He quickly began to extend his self-taught education. Buying a book and slate, and with the help of someone in the mill at Dolphinholme, he taught himself the methods of arithmetical calculation and accounting procedures. After he went to live in Preston, lame

---

24   ibid., p. 63.
25   LRO: DDX/1554/22–4.
26   *Family Records*, p. 11.
27   ibid., p. 12 and CROK: WPR/70/3.
28   ibid., pp. 74, 99.
29   ibid., p. 28.

and exhausted by work, he spent his limited spare time in reading, practising drawing and beginning to write. Although the domestic budget was limited, he saved up to buy himself books. When he was converted to Methodism in 1802 he could 'read the Scriptures with great delight'.[30]

He gives little specific information about the education of his children. His financial position after 1806 was so precarious, because of the long periods he had off work as a result of his lameness, that there was an urgent need to have the children earning an income as soon as possible. Opportunities for their education were thus severely restricted, but it is likely – indeed almost certain – that all could at least read. During the lingering and heartbreaking illness before her death in 1823, Hannah 'delighted in . . . reading the Scriptures, Particularly the 14 Chapter of John'.[31] Thomas and Agnes both went to school, when very young, but both were soon sent to work in the factory – Thomas at the age of nine – and their education must have been very limited. Agnes could apparently write, as in 1836 Benjamin records that he had received two letters from her 'informing us she was in the family way' (someone else might perhaps have written them on her behalf).[32] Joseph, the eldest child, could certainly sign his name, but his signature on the administration bond for his father's estate granted in June 1841 is awkward and ill-formed, as though writing did not come easily,[33] and when he registered Benjamin's death on 7 June 1841 he made his mark.

Benjamin's enthusiastic and enlightened attitude towards education was undoubtedly exceptional. It was formed, in part, from his background: his father, Joseph, had an inquiring mind and a great curiosity about how things worked, and could read and write, albeit slowly. He seems to have shared Benjamin's thirst for knowledge and enlightenment. After 1800, when Joseph was living alone and Benjamin was converted to religion, the two spent much time together in discussion, and this intellectual companionship continued almost until Joseph's death in 1823. This undoubtedly had a strong influence upon Benjamin, but much of his particular passion for learning must have been spontaneous. Nobody in the family, apart from his father, appears to have shared or encouraged it, and there is indeed evidence that his daughters found it, if not tiresome, at least unnecessary. In the early 1830s Agnes and Mary stole his books and pawned them to raise money for their own purposes.

Benjamin was fascinated by information, and voraciously devoured facts and figures. The 'current events' sections of the autobiography are one result, but another, far more significant, is the extraordinarily accurate and clear descriptions of the members of his family and himself. The arrangement of the work, its clarity and its sophisticated nature bear witness to the level of Benjamin's self-taught learning. This is no rambling, incoherent jotting, but a carefully

30   ibid., p. 40.
31   ibid., p. 92.
32   ibid., p. 112.
33   LRO: WRW(A) 1841 Benjamin Shaw of Preston.

planned, even polished, piece of writing. He was also deeply interested in more abstract concepts. His love of the sound and feel of language is perhaps less apparent in the autobiography and related writings than it is in the several books of poems, couplets and one-line epigrams. He particularly appreciated the succinct and pithy qualities of the epigrams, and filled page after page with many hundreds. Some were copied from published works, some were commonplace sayings of the time (and of our time), but others were his own original thoughts. These reveal his thinking on a very wide range of matters, often in a more intimate and personal way than the factual accounts given in the autobiography: 'An apt saying, pertainently apply'd, gives life to Conversation, & teaches more than we are aware of'. Two such epigrams sum up his attitude perfectly:

> Education clears the views & enlarges the mind
> Learning is wisdom to the studious and riches to the carefull[34]

Once he had learned to write fluently he collected such fragments, and in the last years of his life he painstakingly copied them into a series of notebooks: *Benjamin Shaws Scrap Book of Moral & Religious Tendancy Sometimes Humourous &c* (August 1833) and *Proverbs, Morrals, Addeges, Sayings, Remarks &c gather'd from various authors & aranged Alphabettically Many of them are purely Originals also.*[35] He appears to have read extensively and widely, though whether from original authors or from anthologies and extracts is unclear, and he collected examples from these sources – particularly those with an apposite moral message, or which made a pungent comment upon an aspect of daily life. Identifiable quotations in his writings come from such diverse poets as Pope, Cowper, Milton and Burns, while he not only read Cobbett's political and social tracts but also criticized their style:

> The too frequent use's of I and me
> Was a fault in Cobbett that all could see,
> This aragonce ne'er fail's to give offence,
> And pregudice the mind at his expence.[36]

The comfort of learning was crucial to Benjamin's well-being. He passed the long lonely days after Betty's death in reading and gathering information, and in improving his knowledge by arithmetical problems and puzzles. He collected medicinal cures and remedies and he filled notebooks with technical drawings. He clearly found a physical release in writing, a pleasure and an outlet for his energies in compiling page after page of notes which, he must have realized,

---

34   LRO: DDX/1554/14.
35   LRO: DDX/1554/13, 14.
36   LRO: DDX/1554/13.

perhaps only he would ever read. Learning was central to his philosophy of life, and it can only have been a matter of regret to Benjamin that his children could not be educated adequately – but even more bitter must have been the realization that only he among his immediate family had any inclination towards learning. Writing of his mother, he says that she was no scholar, which was 'a great loss in her family'. Later he recommended the reading of the scriptures to his wife and father, and he seems to have wanted to share his knowledge with those around him, but they were, in general, unresponsive. The title page of *Family Scetches* (1826) says that the work is 'partly for his children after his time', but there is a clear note of disillusionment in the statement on the first page of *Proverbs, Morrals etc.* (1836), that the contents are 'for the use of those into whose hands it may fall, for it is not worth publishing'.[37]

One of the sadnesses of his life was that in his studies he ploughed a lonely furrow. Another is that his circumstances did not allow him the peace and happiness embodied in another epigram which, when he wrote it out, must have brought back memories of Dentdale half a century before: 'Rural quiet, friends & books, Alternate ease & labour, a competence for me'.[38]

Migration

Benjamin Shaw and his family were country people, raised in the remote Pennine dales on the borders of the West Riding and Westmorland. They moved to new employment in the textile mills, first of rural Dolphinholme and eventually of urban Preston, and never returned to their birthplace. His brother William, who became a blacksmith, eventually emigrated to the United States. Other members of the family also moved to Preston, or left Dentdale and Garsdale for the North East of England. Migration from the country to the town, with its attendant social and economic upheaval, is thus an underlying theme of the story which Benjamin tells. His own experiences were shared by many thousands of his contemporaries, but he was one of the handful who left a personal testimony of a process which played a major part in transforming the nation.

The detail which Benjamin includes in his biographical accounts of different members of the Shaw family, and the fact that his story spans several generations, gives his work a particular importance as historical evidence. Reconstruction of the shape and experiences of this large and complex family by any conventional means would be almost impossible: the name is common, the distances travelled were great, and the directions and chronological staging of travel confused and diverse. Genealogical methodology would not allow such a reconstruction without a herculean effort and an enormous amount of searching

37 *Family Records*, p. 12 and LRO: DDX/1554/14.
38 LRO: DDX/1554/14.

of parish registers, even supposing that the data were available and in a suitable form. Such an exercise would produce a body of information which would, in many instances, suffer from a lack of proven connection, while the great quantity of ancillary circumstantial and supporting material given by Benjamin would inevitably be absent. Benjamin's account also includes extensive coverage of two other families, the Noddles and the Leemings, allowing the possibility of comparative analysis and revealing the effects of different circumstances upon patterns of movement.

The common myth that 'in the old days' people were immobile, and that families stayed in the same villages for generations, has long been disproved by research, but is still a potent image. Benjamin's story provides a further confutation of the belief, for long before the Industrial Revolution members of his family were travelling widely. Although there had been Shaws in Garsdale for several generations the Noddles, his mother's family, came from elsewhere – the place is not yet identified – only seventy years before Benjamin was born, and his grandmother Noddle was from Swaledale. And while some of the Shaw family did indeed stay in their home valley, others moved away. His aunt, Peggy Shaw, married and went to live in County Durham; his uncle, John Shaw, after two childless marriages in Garsdale, went to Kirkby Stephen; his other uncles, Richard and Benjamin, went to live and work in Kendal. Of the nine children who lived to adulthood in his father's generation, only four died in their home valley, and two of these had spent large parts of their lives far afield.

Analysing the motives for migration has long exercised the minds of researchers, but all too often there is little detailed contemporary evidence. Using present-day analogies, as well as historical material, a basic division has often been recognized between 'push' motives – in which people were driven to another location because of particular or general problems at home – and 'pull' motives, in which the attractions of another location were the inducement to mobility. This has been alternatively considered as a division between the aim for improvement and the need for subsistence – moving in order to better the circumstances of the individual or family, or moving simply to survive. It is, perhaps, inevitable that the distinctions are far from clear, and that in individual instances the two motives were frequently, and perhaps even usually, combined. At the most basic level a move, even for continued subsistence, represents a move for improvement when the alternative is destitution or starvation.

Joseph Shaw moved with his family from Dent to Dolphinholme in 1791. Dentdale, like neighbouring Garsdale, was an agricultural valley with a variety of industrial and semi-industrial employment. The coal mines and stone quarries of the upper slopes were significant, but the economic mainstays of the dales were agriculture and the domestic knitting and weaving industry, very often in combination within the same farming and knitting family. Benjamin records how many members of his family were employed in knitting stockings and other small items of clothing: because it was a cottage industry it was particularly suitable for all members of the family. Children were brought up to knit and spin and women could work in the trade as well as doing their domestic duties and looking after children. Benjamin's mother 'employed herself with winding, sewing, & knitting, & Spining, when she was able & learned & kept her Children to the same work'. It was also the near-universal part-time occupation of men, who would knit at the times when farm work was slack. Benjamin's uncle, Edward Shaw, was 'employed in the land, as they had a little farm, & in the wooling at times in winter & when there was no work without'. If the children were sent to school it was customary for them to be taught to knit and sew, with some reading and other learning. Benjamin himself 'continued to go to School, & learned to knit Stockings as was the fashon of the place, & day'.[39]

The apparently thriving nature of this domestic industry, in a superb and beautiful natural setting, led some outsider observers – and some insiders – to view Dent as a rural paradise. The great geologist Adam Sedgwick, a native of Dent and the son of its vicar, was one such. In his classic works about the valley, written in Cambridge in his old age, he gives a deeply nostalgic and optimistic view of the knitting industry and the industrious cottagers in what he calls 'a land of rural opulence and glee'. David Boulton, a recent historian of the valley, is far more realistic: 'one doubts whether there was ever much opulence or glee in the densely-packed galleried tenements of the little slum which was Dent's town, or the weavers' and knitters' cottages and day labourers' hovels in the dale'.[40] Neither were all nineteenth-century observers as sanguine as Sedgwick. In 1834 the poet Robert Southey wrote *The Doctor*, a novel partly set in Dent: its celebrated phrase 'the terrible knitters e'Dent' has passed into local lore. It is based on the true story of two little girls who, in the mid-eighteenth century, ran away from a knitting school at Kirthwaite, in the upper valley. In a powerful statement they are told that they 'had duun re'et to com away, for Dent was t'poorest plaace in t'warld'.

It was from this valley that Joseph took his family. Life was hard and uncertain, and when Miles Burton came to Dent in 1791 and in glowing terms extolled the virtues of the new worsted mill at Dolphinholme, he met with a receptive and hopeful audience. The apparent advantages of the mill were clear. Already the small cotton mill at Millthrop near Sedbergh had offered better wages for domestic outwork, and these had been eagerly seized upon. Dolphinholme, which was a larger and more ambitious undertaking, might reasonably be supposed to give even better prospects. Furthermore, there would be regular waged employment for all members of the family including the children, who were particularly wanted by the mill management. The opportunities were enticing and Joseph, like his neighbours, had no hesitation in leaving the 'rural opulence and glee' of Dent. In retrospect it is clear that this was a very mixed blessing but, if the wisdom given by hindsight is ignored, his decision becomes

---

39 *Family Records*, pp. 12, 16, 23.
40 Sedgwick, p. xiii.

quite comprehensible. Life stood to be greatly improved by a move to the factory. There was no overt compulsion to leave Dent, but there was a good deal of potential for improvement by moving to Dolphinholme.

This change, a voluntary move from a rural domestic industry to a rural factory industry, may be contrasted with Joseph's next relocation. Shortly after his arrival at Dolphinholme he fell into disagreement with the mill managers about wages, and he lost his job. Dolphinholme had no other employment – it was a large industrial enterprise in a rural setting, with scarcely even a village nearby – and so Joseph was compelled to move elsewhere. He went to Ackenthwaite Green near Milnthorpe and found work there, weaving sacking. This move was quite clearly motivated by dire necessity, not by any idea of improvement. Joseph eventually returned to Dolphinholme and then, in 1795, followed Benjamin to Preston.

The closure of Dolphinholme Mill at the end of 1794 had thrown Benjamin out of work. If he had ever thought of moving to improve his lot in the years between 1791 and 1794, he had been unable to do anything about it – as an apprentice, he was tied to the mill. Even as the mill wound down, and even after he had completed his apprenticeship and was no longer bound to Dolphinholme, he stayed. His move at the start of 1795 was, unquestionably, the result of the utmost necessity. He had no job, a little child, and a pregnant wife. In this instance we can see in detail the decision-making process which lay behind the eventual migration. Benjamin wanted to stay in the same area, which he knew well and where members of his and his wife's families were living. He walked first to Lancaster and then to the mills at Caton, unsuccessfully seeking work. The failure of these quests made Preston the only alternative, and eventually he found work in the mills there.

Preston, which was undergoing a boom, offered plenty of work, but Benjamin did not initially head in that direction. His necessity was dire, but the attraction of the town was not sufficiently powerful in its own right. It is striking that although he already knew Preston slightly, and Betty had worked in the textile mills of Preston for a year before pregnancy had forced her to leave, only after local possibilities were shown to be hopeless did he consider moving further afield. The desire to stay settled was strong, but ultimately futile. Once Benjamin was established in Preston he acted as a magnet for other members of his family: they were less compelled by necessity and more drawn by the attractions of family ties and the job opportunities which they heard about. Within a few years his parents, sister, parents-in-law and their children, and several more distant members of the family had all come to live near Benjamin in the town.

It is easier to establish the motives for migration than to ascertain how the move was regarded by those affected. Nowhere does Benjamin explicitly state his own feelings on going from the beauty and poverty of Dentdale to Dolphinholme and then to the noise, dirt and industrial hubbub of Preston. Writing in 1826, when he was in his late fifties, he recalls his childhood and the rural lifestyle with affection, remembering the haymaking in Garsdale and the houses with gardens, berry trees and beehives at Dent. This slightly wistful nostalgia might be construed as the inevitable product of advancing years, but it seems likely that, dispassionate observer as he usually was, he saw that there were many advantages to such a place. The fresh air, open space and clean water of Ellel, where he and the family lived in 1808–9, were noted with approval, and there is little doubt that he recognized the merits of the country environment even if the circumstances of rural life were less than idyllic.

Benjamin's most direct statement on this subject is in connection with his mother, whose feelings must have been shared by countless thousands who made the move from country to town: 'this leaving our own Country was a great cross to my mother, for she was greatly atached to her Native town, & had she known what would follow, I am sure that she never would have left her relations & countery on any account'.[41] Dent might have been poor, and the life of its knitters and weavers harsh, but a settled, familiar and friendly existence in the dale of her birth was, Isabella thought, infinitely preferable to the unbroken misery and uncertainty of life centred on the mill, or passed in the hard environment of an industrial town. By implication, Benjamin was by no means unsympathetic to this view. In some circumstances the close proximity of his family might have offered some compensation, but in his case that too, in many respects, brought troubles.

The family and its relationships

The nature and significance of family relationships in the past has been the subject of extensive research. Definitions of what constitutes 'the family', its role in the lives of its members, and their attitudes towards each other, have all been investigated. These issues have tremendous significance in their own right and are also important because of their fundamental influence upon wider social and economic questions. Rarely, however, is there sufficient contemporary evidence, particularly in respect of the poorer and less literate households, and only rarely does the available evidence extend widely over time and space. Benjamin's account charts in detail the progress of three families over a period of more than sixty years. It gives a substantial amount of information about the interaction between the members of those families, and about the state of their relationships with each other. From this one can obtain a far more rounded and comprehensive picture than is usually possible, and the factual detail is complemented by a wealth of evidence as to attitudes and feelings.

This evidence suggests very strongly that the family was – with comparatively few exceptions – of crucial importance not only before but even more so *after* the migration to the factories and towns. There is in this work a great deal to support

41 *Family Records*, p. 26.

Anderson's contention that the Industrial Revolution and the migration which accompanied it, far from weakening 'traditional' family ties and bonds, actually reinforced them.[42] It is immediately apparent that the move from the familiar environment of the Sedbergh area, first to Dolphinholme and Milnthorpe, and later to Preston, did not result in the spontaneous disintegration of the Shaw family. Certainly there were losses – four of the seven children died in childhood before they reached Preston, and another son was apprenticed to a Westmorland man and subsequently lived at Kirkby Lonsdale – but this could well have happened even if the family had stayed in Dent. Deaths in childhood were frequent in town and country alike, during epidemics and in the 'normal' course of events, while William might well have moved away from Dent as an apprentice, just as his father had done thirty years before.

Against these losses to the completeness of the family must be set the remarkable degree of continuing attachment which is apparent from the account. Benjamin moved to Preston in 1795 and his parents followed only a few weeks later. His wife's father and stepmother then moved to the town, accompanied by their children, several of whom settled there permanently. Other members of Benjamin's family also turned up in Preston at different times – his sister, Hannah Walker (later Jackson); his uncle, William Shaw, with his second wife and children; his cousin Molly Greaves and her husband Anthony; his aunt, Mary Davis (who later returned to Garsdale) and her brother Edward Shaw. The result was that in 1826, when he wrote the first volume of his story, many members of the Shaw and Leeming families were living in Preston – a large proportion of them in streets within yards of Benjamin's own home in Dale Street.

The migration and relocation of the 1790s had not destroyed either the intangible sense of family and feeling of identity with it, or the practical and emotional ties between its members. This is further indicated by the immense amount of detail which Benjamin is able to give about the lives and careers of his contemporaries. It is quite clear that many members of the family kept in touch. The comparative difficulties involved in such communication – problems of physical distance, extensive illiteracy and the cost and inefficiency of postal services – made the circulation of information far from straightforward. News and gossip were perhaps distributed verbally and by notes sent by carrier, but members of the family might have paid occasional visits to each other. Whatever the source of family news, there is no doubt that it circulated.

The extent of Benjamin's family contacts is also clear from the quantity of recent information which he was able to give in 1826. It is apparent that communications with more distant relatives had, predictably, faded. A large

---

42   This is one of the main conclusions of Anderson's very detailed analysis of the migration and kinship patterns evidenced by the 1851 census of Preston. Although Benjamin's experience pre-dated the study period the evidence suggests that the processes in his period were not significantly different in character.

proportion of the information about earlier generations, including his half-uncles and aunts, had been derived from non-contemporary sources, and he says in several instances that he knew nothing of their fate after they had left the Sedbergh district. There was thus a point after which fresh information was no longer available: much of the information is detailed and accurate up to the end of the eighteenth century, but the biographies of many of the more peripheral characters are not continued after that time.

However, the members of the family who remained in Dent and district are recorded, albeit rather sketchily, well into the 1820s. This suggests that those relatives who went further afield in the 1780s and 1790s were eventually cut off from the family, whereas communication with Dent itself continued long after Joseph and Benjamin had moved to Preston. For example, the life of Benjamin's aunt Marian Noddle is given in some detail up to her marriage in 1787, but nothing is told after that point. While she remained in the Dent area she had contact with the family, but when she moved to Pendleton, near Whalley, communication was lost. In contrast, the stories of his aunt Isabella Watson and her family, and of his uncle James Noddle, are continued into the 1820s. Of Isabella's daughter, Benjamin's cousin Agnes Holme, he specifically states that 'she drives the carts with coals to Sedburgh &c now (1826)'.[43]

It was even possible to maintain desultory contact with Benjamin's brother William, who emigrated to the United States in 1812. Among the family papers are a few letters written by members of the family from America: as late as 1842 William's son was writing to his uncle Benjamin in England, not knowing that his uncle had died the previous year. Three thousand miles of ocean precluded any possibility of antagonism between the two brothers, but there was a desire to maintain family contacts, despite there being little hope of them ever meeting again, and even though writing was clearly a painfully laborious business for William.

Among those members of the family who came at different times to Preston there was a variable degree of contact. This is to be expected, since members of any family do not necessarily get on with each other or need each other. The Leeming family, Benjamin's brothers-in-law, do not seem to have had much contact with the Shaws – which, given his low opinion of most of them, is not surprising. There is a lack of detailed information about some of the Leemings, and Benjamin appears to be uncertain of their more recent history. But Betty Shaw's brother, John Leeming, was present at her bedside with Benjamin, joining him in prayers as she died. Benjamin's view of that family, far from unique, was that his in-laws were an unreliable and feckless lot.

Relationships within the immediate family were of differing significance. Benjamin shows eloquently how close he was to his father's parents, and with what warmth his grandparents regarded him. The account of his annual

---

43 *Family Records*, p. 15.

'holidays' in Garsdale, over half a century earlier, is moving and affectionate, while the sense of disillusionment which crept in as his young cousin supplanted him is also sharp and vivid. Just as clearly expressed is his adolescent change of feeling, when the 'lasses' and the companionship of his comrades mattered more to him than his family ties. He looks back on his early interest in the lasses knowing that it was, before long, to lead him to great misfortune.

Also apparent, by its frequent repetition as well as by the clarity with which he expresses the feeling, is his closeness to his parents. He notes of Isabella Shaw that she was a 'loving mother' and a 'careful wife', and sympathizes with the burdens of her life – the leaving of her native countryside and the misery and pain of her rheumatism. Like many in similar circumstances, he failed to appreciate her qualities at the time, and only fully realized and understood how he needed his mother after she was gone. Writing of the time when his family had moved to Milnthorpe, leaving him alone at Dolphinholme, he says that 'I now began to feel the want of my mother, who had been very kind to me, though I did not Prize that kindness as I ought'.[44] The same personal conviction is apparent when, writing of his wife's brothers who had lost their mother young, he records how they were the worse for their loss.

The Shaws were far from united – witness the great quarrel between Benjamin and his sister Hannah over their father's estate – yet their geographical proximity meant a good deal of social contact and mutual assistance. The relationship between brother and sister seems to have been satisfactory until about 1820: Benjamin makes no reference to hostility or tension until the account of the last year of his father's life. In 1808, when the Shaws were removed to Ellel by the overseers and spent thirty weeks in lodgings, the two elder boys, Joseph and William, were looked after by their aunt Hannah. That certainly implies a friendliness and a willingness to help her brother in a time of great need.

Not until their father, Joseph senior, was elderly did this harmony disintegrate. Benjamin thought that his sister took excessive advantage of the old man, and that he, in turn, showed her favouritism. This growing antagonism was heightened by the question of Joseph's savings, which seemed to be dwindling as a result of Hannah's depredations, and was brought to a head by Benjamin's outrage over Hannah's behaviour after the death of Joseph. In this increasingly troubled relationship Hannah's husband, Henry Jackson, remains a shadowy but crucial figure. He was educated and – as clerk to Holy Trinity church – socially superior to Benjamin. It is possible to speculate that Benjamin may have felt envy and jealousy towards his brother-in-law, and that Henry may in turn have been patronizing. It is clear that Benjamin cordially disliked Henry, and perhaps Hannah suffered partly by association.

Benjamin was especially close to his father, whom he resembled in several important respects. Both had a remarkable aptitude for things mechanical, and

44   ibid., p. 29.

for the execution of detailed, intricate and skilled projects, and they had long worked together at the lathe and in mending. Joseph Shaw, like his son, was a rather solitary, serious man and, although it is not expressly stated, it seems likely that they shared a similar outlook on life. Benjamin's assessment of his father's character – 'sober, frugal, & temperate' – could equally well apply to his own, though another of Joseph's qualities, that he was 'rather Pationate', seems less applicable. After their religious conversion in 1800 his father was Benjamin's 'constant companion' and they regularly discussed 'devine Subjects'.[45] This closeness was diminished in later years when Joseph seemed to show much greater favour to Hannah. Benjamin is nowhere directly reproachful of his father for this, but his depth of feeling is striking – he devotes almost four pages to an exceptionally detailed and angry denunciation of Hannah and her behaviour, and accuses his father indirectly: '[he] was very Partial to my sister hannah she could not do wrong for him . . . in everything his Partialaty was seen'.[46]

He quarrelled bitterly with the Jacksons, and there is no evidence that they were ever close again. Although his affection for Joseph remained strong, and he visited his father each evening while the older man was dying, these unhappy times must have been especially painful to Benjamin. He was himself in need of comfort, for his relationships with his wife and children were troubled and distressing, and he was deeply anxious about his own daughter Hannah, who was seriously ill. The companionship of his father, which might have been a solace, was diminished by Benjamin's jealousy of Hannah and her family, and by his father's own deteriorating health. Nevertheless, his final verdict on his father, as expressed in the writings of three years later, is favourable – in marked contrast to his opinion of Hannah. His dislike of her is abundantly clear not only from the account of Joseph's death and the division of his goods, but also from the terse comment: 'Hannah is a managing woman, but very Covetious & earnest to get money, She is rather inclined to be fat, of a middle Size, &c'.[47]

The role of the family as a supportive institution is perhaps best seen in the workings of Benjamin's own household, and in particular the way in which he and Betty helped their generally troublesome brood. Of the seven children who grew to adulthood only one, Joseph, seems to have caused his parents no grief or anxiety. Joseph, the eldest child, married at twenty and had at least nine children but, tragically, no fewer than seven of these died before the age of five. Benjamin appears to have had a somewhat ambiguous attitude to Joseph, giving no hint anywhere as to his character, appearance or qualities. This coolness may have been the consequence of lingering doubts as to Joseph's paternity – a matter considered in more detail in notes to the text.[48]

---

45   ibid., pp. 9, 40.
46   ibid., pp. 62–63.
47   ibid., p. 80.
48   ibid., p. 31, n. 188.

Each one of the others caused some difficulty, emotionally and in practical terms, for their parents. When writing of his children Benjamin frequently uses the word 'trouble' and, except in relation to his daughter Mary, who died as a baby, he never expresses any overt pleasure in them. It is clear that he loved Hannah dearly, and her early death caused him great distress, but even in her case he is extremely restrained in his approbation. Hannah was perhaps a substitute for the 'first Mary', and he retained a very clear picture of her appearance and character when he wrote his first volume, almost three years after her death. Her pregnancy must have come as a considerable shock to him – he admits that it caused him great grief – and she is the only one of his surviving children about whom his writing becomes sentimental.

He was not a violent or aggressive man, and must in many ways have been an excellent father, but his caution and critical nature would have presented his children with many difficulties. His gentleness is well-illustrated by the sensitive descriptions of the temperaments of the children he describes. It is also shown by his very clear disapproval, and acute observation, of the physical abuse of a child: his brother-in-law, John Leeming, 'Seemed as though he had been ill used in his infantcy, he was a Sour looking child, Scarce ever laughed, & was not fond of Play, but Soletery, & Stayed, & Seemed as though he had bad health &c'.[49] The overall impression, though, is that, while he was supportive of his children and did a great deal for them, he did not find them congenial company, and regarded their behaviour as a considerable burden. It is not hard to see why that should be so, but we cannot know the reasons for the waywardness of Benjamin's offspring – the influences of their respective parents can only be conjectured.

In 1815 William, aged nineteen, fathered two illegitimate children on different women. Benjamin is very casual in his recollection of the affair – '1815 this year, I dont remember anything remarkable that took place in our family' – but, in something of an understatement, notes that 'we had a good deal of trouble on that account'.[50] William was imprisoned for not keeping up his maintenance payments for the children, but eventually married the mother of the second child. As a man he could – with luck or skill – take care of himself, and Benjamin was apparently not too concerned. But it was a quite different matter when, four years later, Bella became pregnant: 'this year we had trouble from a new quarter, & of a new description, our oldest daughter Bella was with child, which gave us now Smale concern for her, as we feared, & it proved so, that she did not get married soon'.[51]

Bella and her child lived at home with her parents, and Benjamin and Betty had the additional responsibility of looking after the child, although their

49 ibid., p. 83.
50 ibid., p. 52.
51 ibid., p. 56.

daughter could presumably have married William at any time. Her income from factory work went towards general housekeeping and the couple did not marry until 1822, when Bella was pregnant again. In the summer of 1820 Benjamin's burden was greatly increased when the next daughter, Hannah, revealed that she was expecting the child of their neighbour, Samuel Whittle. Benjamin obviously found this particularly distressing, for Hannah was only seventeen, was considered delicate, and was his favourite daughter – he does not say so, but his lengthy descriptions of her make this quite clear. The news was therefore not only the cause of anxiety but was also 'a mater of greif'. The effect on her parents is vividly expressed: 'we had Bella Child to keep, & all the trouble atending it, & now likely to have another, Parents trouble is not done when they have reared their Children'.[52]

The child died when it was only a few weeks old – it 'was a very little one, & Seemed not likely for life . . . it was never well from its birth'.[53] This, in the cruellest way, solved one of their problems, but Benjamin considered that Hannah herself never really recovered from the birth. She grew weaker, although she returned to work for some months. By the end of 1823 it became clear that she was dying of consumption. Her long and distressing decline, characteristic of the disease, was a harrowing experience for her parents and utterly miserable for Hannah. Her family did all they could for her: 'we used every means in our Power to aleviate her condition, but what is it that we can do for the destrest with Pain, but to be kind & to encourage them to look to god . . . & to be ready & willing to asist in every way Posible, to Comfort & wait with Patience on them'.[54] The misery of this time is movingly portrayed, and the struggles of her parents and family to ease Hannah's last months were clearly overwhelming. For a year the life of the family centred on the dying girl.

During the autumn of 1826 Benjamin updated the first volume of his family record, which had been written that summer. The family living at home in Dale Street comprised Benjamin and Betty (who was then dying – also of consumption); the surviving younger daughters, Mary and Agnes; and the youngest son, Thomas. Bella had married in 1822, and Joseph as long ago as 1813. Benjamin records that in October Thomas, who was nineteen, married Ann Richardson, a servant girl living in Preston but originally from Newton near Kirkham. They were married at Kirkham, and Thomas did not tell Benjamin and Betty until two weeks later – his child was born in Preston on 12 January. The reason for Thomas's secrecy is not stated, but it was undoubtedly because he had been unemployed since late March 1826, and had no possible means of supporting a wife and baby: Benjamin notes that during that period 'we had to keep him'.[55]

The responsibility for looking after Thomas and his family fell on Benjamin,

52 ibid., p. 58.
53 ibid., pp. 58–59.
54 ibid., p. 66.
55 ibid., p. 97.

now deeply troubled by Betty's worsening illness. Having to cope with an out-of-work son, a new daughter-in-law, and a tiny baby, in addition to two teenage daughters and a dying wife, was a tremendous problem for a tired man in his mid-fifties. Thomas and Ann lived with them for three weeks at Christmas (they had presumably stayed with her parents for some of the time) and the baby was apparently born at Benjamin's home, for when it was baptized on 14 January the parents' address was stated to be Dale Street. At the end of February 1827 Thomas got work with Benjamin's old master and friend, Frank Sleddon, and at the beginning of March Ann and the baby, Jane, 'came to live at our house & we kept them until april 28 for 9 Shilling per week'. By that time the couple had bought or borrowed a few household goods, and Benjamin 'found them a few more', and they set up house near the *Three Tuns* in North Road, on the edge of the town.[56]

In times of economic depression, when work was scarce and wages low, it was almost impossible for young couples to set up home on their own. Thomas and Ann Shaw offer a good example of the way in which the family – and particularly the parents – assisted by providing accommodation (despite the very limited space available to them) and by finding household goods. The use of the parental home as a place of refuge is also revealed by the experiences of both Mary and Agnes. Early in 1829 Benjamin discovered that Mary, still only seventeen, was pregnant, and that Robert Smith, the child's father, was in prison at Lancaster Castle – he was nineteen, and had been found guilty of assault during a brawl. The circumstances were far from encouraging. Mary was clearly desperate, since apart from the developing pregnancy she had to cope with finding support for Bob's needs. As Benjamin notes, she 'began to use all kinds of fraud upon me', including stealing money set aside to pay bills, and using Benjamin's name to obtain goods on credit.[57]

Bob Smith was released on 14 June, the baby was born on 3 September, and the couple were married on 24 October. They were nineteen and eighteen, Bob had no job (he was previously an ordinary labourer) and had just come out of prison, and they had a tiny baby. By this time Benjamin was widowed; apart from Mary herself, the only other person living with him was Agnes. There was thus room for Bob and the baby, William, and the family therefore went to live with Benjamin, staying there between their marriage and late January, when they rented a room. Benjamin records that they quarrelled and parted soon afterwards and 'she came home'. The foundations of the marriage – their youth, the miserable circumstances and, it may be suspected, the characters of both Mary and Bob – were to say the least shaky, and a parting after three months cannot have been a surprise. After January 1830 Benjamin lived with Mary, her baby, and Agnes. With evident disillusionment and great honesty, he tells how

56   ibid., p. 97.
57   ibid., p. 104.

they 'did badly for me by runing into Debt and Pawning their Clothes & my Bed Cloths & Book or any thing that they Make Money off . . . this year I lost 7 or 8 Pound in Money by them & lost very many thing alltogether'. Subsequently, at the end of 1830, he notes again how Mary 'has been with me & her lad all the year, & has behaved Badly, putting me to much expences & trouble'.[58]

Family life was a very mixed blessing. The loneliness of widowhood was painful, and in late 1828, the year of Betty's death, Benjamin described his state plaintively and with an understandable hint of self-pity: 'this has been a troublesom year to me having no wife to care for the concerns of the House nor any Company or any to care for me'.[59] The behaviour of his daughters, who might have lessened his loneliness, merely gave it emphasis, and he found their continued presence a great weight to bear. They had little mutual understanding or sympathy, and Benjamin considered that the girls used him without gratitude or feeling – though we do not know their version of events. In April 1830 Agnes, then seventeen, went to Manchester for work, and returned on Whit Sunday having pawned most of her clothes in Preston to raise money, even though she was in work. Her father records sourly that while she was running the house he had paid the bills, and she had kept her own wages, but she still had no money – having spent it on '7 or 8 gowns in a little more than 2 years'.[60]

In 1832 Benjamin was sixty years old, and although his physical health was fair he could see that he was ageing and shrinking – 'I have gone smaller & weaker'. He was depressed by the death of his son William, who was only thirty-five and had seven small children, and wrote a moving and forlorn obituary upon him. His annual review is increasingly taken up with political events and current affairs, as though his family was no longer of interest to him. Some time in 1831 Bob Smith and Mary had patched up their quarrel and Bob, who had obtained work as a spinner, moved back to the rooms in Dale Street. On 1 April 1832 their second child, Elizabeth, was born. Bob and Mary stayed with Benjamin until 13 December 1834, by which time they had a third child, John. For a brief period after Christmas 1834 Benjamin was probably entirely alone, but the peace and quiet was short-lived. At some point in 1835 Agnes returned from Manchester and went to work at Horrocks's.

Benjamin was finding life difficult, for he felt 'the growing efects of age and infirmity' and as a consequence his wages were not increased. Agnes was discharged from work in the winter of 1835, and evidently did not tell Benjamin the reason. On his reduced wages he had to keep them both, and she then revealed that she was pregnant: she was twenty-three and had already had a child, which had died in infancy, in Manchester in 1834. She was ill and weak in

58 ibid., pp. 105–107.
59 ibid., pp. 103–104.
60 ibid., p. 107.

mid-February when the baby was born, and she thereafter 'never recoverd only so far as to Stirr about for a few weeks very feebly indeed'.[61]

Mary gave some help with nursing her sister, though her own son, John, was seriously ill and her crippled daughter, Betty, died in late April. Bella Roberts and her daughter then came from Manchester for six weeks to help, but Agnes died in mid-August, leaving Benjamin in sole charge of her baby daughter, Betty. He wrote of his plight: he had to work all day in spite of his age and infirmity, and to tend the child at night. She was ill and frail and needed medicine – 'at night [I] went about the town for some thing for her, till late oft, then got up 2 or 3 times at night'. The baby was wet-nursed and weaned very early; it had spells of violent convulsions, and then recovered but, Benjamin recorded at the end of 1836 'it . . . is a Small pittifull ill doing thing Still'.[62] He was sixty-four years old, widowed, tired and weary. He had buried his wife and four of his eight children, and had seen many of his numerous grandchildren die in infancy. His words of ten years earlier, ' Parents trouble is not done when they have reared their children', were still all too appropriate.

Benjamin's household thus fluctuated markedly in size. The maximum number of people living at one time in the two rooms in Dale Street was nine, attained on two occasions – between the birth of Agnes in July 1813, and the marriage and departure of Joseph in the December of that year, and again in February-May 1821 between the birth and death of Hannah's baby, Elizabeth. Thereafter there was a steady decline in the size of the household, broken only briefly in December 1826–April 1827 when Thomas's new wife and son were living with the family. By January 1830, when Mary and Bob Smith set up home on their own, only Benjamin and Agnes were left. Yet the to-ing and fro-ing of his daughters and their families meant that even in the 1830s Benjamin was on his own for a short time only, late in 1834. This was the sole occasion, apart from a few months in Dolphinholme in 1792, when he had ever been living alone.

The conventional view that households grow as the children are born, remain stable for some years, and then shrink as children marry and leave, is thus shown to be untenable in the case of the Shaws – and analogy and evidence from other families suggest that they were by no means unusual. Instead, the parental household seems to have been regarded by all members of the family as a fixed point, which could be used in times of crisis such as the breakdown of Mary's marriage and the pregnancies of Bella and Agnes. The parents therefore played a very important protective and sheltering role in the lives of their adult children, a role which might well have been unwillingly taken on – Benjamin was clearly not at all pleased with having his daughters at home – but one which, unless the parents were to be exceptionally firm and cold, was almost inevitable. Benjamin himself, because of his particular circumstances, had not used his

---

61 ibid., p. 115.
62 ibid., p. 116.

parents in this way, but during her first marriage and widowhood Hannah regularly spent long periods living with her father, seeing him as her 'place of refuge'.

Family life for Benjamin was a constant source of trouble and anxiety. There was no time, between the news of Betty's pregnancy in the spring of 1793 and his own death in June 1841, when he was free of the care and responsibility which his family brought him, and there is no doubt that he was acutely conscious of the weight which a dutiful parent carried. In 1826, writing the short biography of his aunt Isabella Watson (who had only one child), Benjamin had used a telling phrase: 'they enjoyed all the advantages of a married life without much of the care & labour common to rearing a family.[63]

He was an unusual man and it could be argued that, simply because he produced such a detailed family record, his views, experiences and attitudes towards the family cannot be accepted as typical. Undoubtedly his personal feeling for the family as an institution was intensely strong, and inevitably his views, in the most technical sense, cannot be taken as representative. Like the views and experiences of everyone else at all times, they were unique and personal, but that does not diminish their historical value. There is nothing to suggest that Benjamin's family, as a whole, was at all unrepresentative. His relatives did not share his passionate intellectual commitment to the abstract concept of the family. They maintained communications and contacts for more practical and unarticulated reasons, and there is little reason to suppose that in this they differed greatly in their experiences or attitudes from other people at the time. Their circumstances, and their economic and social characteristics, were by no means remarkable. What is exceptional about this family is that one of its members was deeply interested in its history, and was able to record its story.

Sex, marriage and women

Moralizing was evidently a habit of Benjamin's. The hundreds of worthy and sententious epigrams which he painstakingly copied into notebooks not only show his delight in and feeling for language but also reflect his sometimes priggish views. Nevertheless, moralizing on sexual matters is conspicuously lacking, and his severest censure is reserved for those who were unable to manage their daily lives with efficiency and order. In his family record, which in parts becomes almost a catalogue of illegitimacies and hasty marriages, Benjamin usually expresses no strong moral disapproval, but condemns the offenders only for their bad management, and for the financial and practical troubles which they brought upon themselves and others.

He was, of course, in no position to be over-censorious. His own marriage was

63 ibid., p. 15.

the result of Betty's pregnancy, when he was twenty and she was eighteen, and there is no doubt that he ever afterwards regretted his lack of care. He was not a man of impetuousness and passion, and the phrasing of the relevant passages suggests that the night of 11 February 1793 was an aberration, a lapse from his normally circumspect behaviour brought about by the relief he felt on finding Betty still 'faithful'. The consequences were dire, and in later life he traced many of his domestic problems from this moment of folly.

Of his seven children who survived to adulthood only one, Joseph, avoided the complications of illegitimate children or hasty marriage. Each of the four daughters had a child out of wedlock; Agnes had two, and she and Hannah died from the complications of childbirth. The second son, William, fathered two illegitimate children on different women in the same year, when he was only nineteen. Yet in Benjamin's accounts of these events there is no suggestion of condemnation on moral grounds. In the whole work there is only one instance when such disapproval is unambiguously expressed. His uncle William Shaw, widowed with several small children, took in his wife's niece as a housekeeper, and soon fathered a child on her. Benjamin said that this was 'a Shamefull affair' – it bordered on incest, and was clearly a breaking of family honour and of the trust involved in bringing Mally Winn into his house.[64] Illegitimacy and sexual freedom among the young and unmarried simply did not matter to Benjamin, and he seems to have accepted these as perfectly normal and unremarkable – though he was clearly unhappy at the prospect of Betty's being unfaithful to him before their marriage.

Greater condemnation was reserved for married women who were unfaithful to their husbands – though the casualness with which he includes such information suggests that he did not consider it a particularly unusual occurrence. It was whispered, he says, that his uncle William Noddle's second wife was 'unfaithful to the marrig contract', while his uncle Robert Noddle married a woman who had previously had a child by another man, and who was 'said to have been to much atached to him after her marrig with my uncle'. Benjamin's verdict on Robert's early death – he 'did not live long after, but left his wife to her dear dixon' – smacks not of condemnation but rather of cynical amusement.[65] He recognized, too, that a woman could be unhappy in marriage because of the behaviour of her husband though, significantly, when writing of his aunt Molly Noddle who married Frank Allen, a wild and drunken man 'of turbelent bad tempers', it is his extravagance and financial recklessness which Benjamin finds especially contemptible: 'nothing prospered with him . . . She was a managing woman, & very careful, but She could not be happy with such a man'.[66]

The Leeming family, Betty Shaw's father and brothers, were on the whole

---

64   ibid., p. 14.
65   ibid., pp. 18, 19.
66   ibid., pp. 20–21.

regarded by Benjamin as of doubtful character and reliability. Her father, Edward Leeming, was thrice married, something his son-in-law may have regarded not just as weakness but as being a glutton for punishment. Edward was 'an easy man (rather fond on woman as it was reported)' – something which could not be said of Benjamin himself. Robert Leeming, one of the younger sons, had married an Irishwoman, while serving in the Militia in about 1815, and was notorious within the family as being a battered husband: 'this woman . . . is a limb of the divil as we say, She frequently Beats him'. There is no suggestion of condemnation there: rather, Margaret Leeming almost seems to be regarded with credit for her behaviour. Benjamin hints, again without any overt criticism, that Robert was a bigamist as well: 'it is said . . . this Robert married a woman in Ireland, Before this wife & left her in that Countery'. He merely comments, with his dry sense of humour, 'this was lucky for her'. It is indicative of his concept of 'respectability', and his view that financial rectitude was of far greater *moral* importance than sexual restraint, that the youngest son, James Leeming could be described in the same sentence as the father of a bastard child and as 'the most respectable man of any of the younger Brothers'. James was respectable because he had a settled job: his having a bastard evokes no disapproval.[67]

Benjamin implies, in relation not only to others but also to his own wife, that happiness in marriage did not derive solely, or even especially, from sexual conduct but also from the woman's 'managing' qualities – a good wife should be clean and tidy, careful with money, sober and restrained in her behaviour. His grandfather, Benjamin Shaw, was said to be 'rather unhappy in his first marrige' to Jane Plummer because although she was a 'cleanly' woman she was not a good manager of money, so they were poor.[68] This is contrasted, probably deliberately, with the second wife (Benjamin's grandmother Hannah Handley) who was diligent, thrifty and hardworking, and so made the family prosper. The adjectives used in praise of Benjamin's own mother are an interesting reflection of his preferences in a woman – she was a loving mother, but a 'careful' wife.[69] Writing as he was after thirty-three years of marriage to a woman who, although a loving mother, was (he considered) profligate and hopeless with money, the word is an important one.

Underlying his opinions of the women in his life – his mother, his sister Hannah, his wife and his daughters – is Benjamin's unflattering view of women in general. While it would be going too far to suggest that he was a misogynist, it is clear that he did not regard the abilities of women in a favourable light. He was suspicious of their motives, critical of their behaviour, and condemnatory of what he saw as their manifold failings and weaknesses. This attitude is more apparent in his other writings than in the family record, perhaps because family

67   ibid., pp. 73, 86, 87.
68   ibid., p. 3.
69   ibid., p. 12.

feeling for female relations to some extent counterbalanced his suspicions of women as a group. Women, in his view, were foolish and frivolous gossips, fickle and unreliable, and he expresses these opinions forcefully in his epigrams and adages: 'Womans minds are like a sive – secrets they cannot hold'; 'Women carry two faces – when they are hot as mustard, they seem cold as ice'.[70] One of his longer poems, *on Women*, summarizes his views effectively:

> 'A woman's a Riddle, not easy to guess,
> Her life is all Pretence, not open and Plain,
> An actris, a mimick, a Humbug at Best,
> A dealer in double intender, for gain,
> Not only while acting the farce of untruth,
> When dress'd in her ruffles & Plumes in youth,
> But raise her a step, suppose her a wife,
> She's the same sly unknown, in all parts of life
> some say she no secrets can keep, but she can
> The drift of her life is to keep them from man,
> Her face, and her conduct, is hansom and fair
> If you stand at a distance and dont come too near'[71]

The verse called *The Echoe* is equally forthright in its condemnation of what Benjamin saw as the weaknesses and failings of women.

> I wish to see more simplicity,
> Become common,
> And not to Doubt the veracity,
> Of the women,
>
> But I'me afraid, they'll not redeem,
> Their character
> So prone to tattle, it would seem
> Their great charter[72]

As far as romantic love and physical attraction were concerned, Benjamin was cynical about both. Many of his collected epigrams and phrases are on the theme that such attractions last only for a brief period and then fade, but that their consequences are there for life – and a lifetime of regret: 'Boys before you marry, learn the golden Rule – Look before you leap or else you'll play the fool'; 'Early marriages [*sic*] & early old age, follow of corse, or are sisters'; 'Love takes the allarm at sight of human ties, Spreads her light wings and in a moment

---

70 LRO: DDX/1554/14.
71 LRO: DDX/1554/12.
72 LRO: DDX/1554/12.

flyes'.[73] He explicitly states that he loved Betty, and that their attraction was a romantic one, but in retrospect he viewed his experience of love as an ill-considered youthful folly. There is no doubt that for most of his married life he regretted that short period of infatuation, and he also considered that at twenty and eighteen he and Betty had been far too young to marry. Another verse expresses, from the heart, his view of marriage:

> Men ruin themselves, very oft for life,
> By promises made to a noughty wife[74]

Their characters, utterly different and often completely irreconcilable, produced no common interest, and their endless arguments about household management scarred almost the whole of their married life. He wrote various short verses on the subject:

> 'Alass! is domestic life,
> That soorest ill of human life,
> A plague so little to be feared,
> As to be wantonly incurred'

> 'What bicerings and angry strife
> Have we seen, between man and wife,
> These are united but in part,
> Quite disimular in mind & heart'[75]

When, in 1826, he wrote his first biographical volume he and Betty had been married for thirty-three years, but his condemnation of her ways and the detailed accounts of her bad management and dishonesty, which appear throughout the work, show that he still had a very considerable antagonism towards her. His sense of honesty compelled him to make frequent references to her good points, while his sense of guilt results in such phrases as 'I have my doubts whether I can gain credit for what I now say' when he is condemning her wholeheartedly.[76] Yet scarcely ever is a word of praise allowed to stand alone: there is almost always a qualification which takes the edge off his approval.

Summarizing her character in the summer of 1826 he filled several pages with criticisms of her reckless and feckless ways, her lack of pride, her habit of keeping company with 'the very Poorest of her Neighbours', her cheating and deceiving. Then, to redress the balance, he listed her virtues – she was sober, steady, temperate in her diet, loving to her children, sympathetic and of a

---

73 LRO: DDX/1554/19.
74 LRO: DDX/1554/13.
75 LRO: DDX/1554/12.
76 *Family Records*, p. 76.

'feeling temper', faithful in marriage, not a common liar or swearer. But the balance is not redressed, for the paragraphs are hedged with qualifications: she is loving to her children, 'to a Blame'; her sympathetic nature has led her to be imposed upon and deceived; her marital faithfulness is 'for any thing that I know'. This somewhat grudging list of good points then turns into a further catalogue of failings – a reiteration of what has been said several times before.[77]

Theirs cannot have been a happy marriage. It began badly, and grew worse, as poverty and ill-health worked their corrosive powers and as their mutual incomprehension became ever more apparent. For Betty, a warm-hearted, generous and careless woman, Benjamin must have been a remarkably difficult husband – strict, censorious, self-righteous and cold. His interests were solitary, his illness and lameness often made him unable to enjoy such leisure as he had, and his philosophy was the opposite of hers. Nonetheless, thirty-three years of living and quarrelling together meant that they became mutually dependent, and in the better times he must have had a good deal of affection for her. By the time of her death, after a long and distressing illness, Benjamin had had many months during which to reflect on Betty's character and his feelings. Even in 1826 he recognized that he too had his own faults and failings: 'every one has their way, and their faults, and it is not easy to say who hath the advantage, for every one thinks that if their wives, or Husbands, had any other fault, or way, they could do better, it would be more tolerable, or they could Bear it Better'.[78]

Despite the evidence of Benjamin's negative view of Betty, there are significant areas in which he does not criticize her. In particular, there is no reference anywhere to slovenliness or low standards of housekeeping. Indeed, there are hints that the opposite may have been true. For example, he notes that 'she did not like to be poor & seem so', which is a very clear statement of a high standard on her part.[79] Betty did not like to 'make do and mend' but wanted to have new clothes and possessions. She may not have practised the thrift and financial caution which he wanted, but she did aspire to better status and circumstances. This might seem surprising in view of her background (which included a long period in the workhouse as a child), but she had examples to emulate. The Charity School at Lancaster conveyed the message of improvement and domestic standards to its pupils, and in her youth Betty worked as a servant in the houses of James Skirrow, a prosperous publican and merchant, and Mrs Dove, a sea-captain's wife. This gave her an insight into the lifestyles and standards of the middle class, which must have been fundamental to her desire 'not to seem poor'. Although there is little specific evidence, it may be supposed that as far as she could she tried to achieve those aspirations: her few possessions included such 'middle class' objects as a tea canister, a tea tray, a

77   ibid., pp. 77–78.
78   ibid., p. 77.
79   ibid., p. 44.

clock and handkerchiefs. The irony of their marriage is that although Benjamin constantly pointed to alleged weaknesses in her character, they in fact shared a similar goal – improvement and escape from working-class poverty.

The account of Betty's death reflects the mixed feelings which her husband felt. He cannot resist the qualifying phrase – 'She told me of her debts at least some of them' – but he was clearly moved by what was happening. The speech which he reports her making, on her deathbed, is out of character: I suspect that he edited it heavily so that it conformed with his own view of life, for the edification of his descendants. It refers to the need for sobriety, industry, economy and carefulness, concepts which were not espoused by Betty and which contradict what he had written of her thoughts only eighteen months before. He wrote out – and perhaps composed – two poems on her death. One is in conventional form, expressing worthy sentiments of her lasting memory and his grief. The other – more obviously from the heart, even if not from his own pen – expresses perfectly his view of her in life and death:

> The time is past that I should her condemn,
> Child of caprice, and to her will the slave,
> She had her virtues let me think of them,
> Her faults be buried with her in the Grave.[80]

The domestic economy

Benjamin gives a substantial amount of factual information relating to the family economy, and expresses at considerable length his strongly-held views on economic management.[81] He gives a great deal of attention to wages and to changes in income and, especially, to expenditure and indebtedness. These matters lay at the heart of his personal philosophy, and were also the most important immediate cause of the troubles in his married life and his difficult relationship with Betty. The root of their constant disagreements was the fundamental difference in their attitudes to money. Betty was of a generous and somewhat feckless spirit, unconcerned with careful accounting or with where the money would come from, while – in total contrast – Benjamin was exceptionally careful, thrifty and economical. For him saving was not just a practical necessity but integral to his beliefs – caution and prudence in all matters was the basis of his view of life and its purpose. Such abstract and elevated concepts were entirely alien to Betty and to most, if not all, of their children.

Benjamin was not a miser, and he certainly prided himself on his generosity to

---

80 ibid., p. 100.
81 A comparative analysis of the evidence given in Benjamin's writings for the workings of the domestic economy is being undertaken by Dr. Shani d'Cruze. The work is as yet unpublished, but she has generously allowed me access to her working paper, *Care, Diligence and 'Usfull Pride'*.

Betty. At several points in his story he makes the important point that she had a greater amount of free money, not committed in advance and available for her to spend as she wished, than most women who managed households. He not only paid her a relatively large weekly allowance, but also spent from his own pocket significant sums on items which in other families would have been the responsibility of the woman. Clothes for the children, his own clothing and some of hers, significant quantities of food and other essential commodities, his own 'pocket money' and, latterly, the rent, were all provided by him, leaving Betty with far less direct responsibility than she might have expected. In addition, when he was in full-time employment Benjamin earned a good wage, so that the amount of money available was often surprisingly large. According to his account, none of this was sufficient to avoid indebtedness, solely because Betty so grossly mismanaged her part in the running of the household.

There is comparatively little information about Benjamin's own spending patterns. His personal tastes were, as far as can be ascertained, frugal. He does not seem to have spent substantially on drink or entertainment, although he did smoke – a letter written to him by Bella and William Roberts in 1840 refers to pawn tickets hidden under his tobacco, and a verse refers to a question which 'I desided while smooking last night'.[82] Instead of buying furnishings and equipment for the household he regularly made them himself: when describing his period of lameness before 1810 he notes how he spent much of his leisure time in making things. Items of regular expenditure were probably quite limited. He did spend on books, although there is no information about the size, content or value of his library. It is possible that he bought a weekly newspaper, although that is by no means certain. This comparative frugality meant that, with his often quite good wages, he could afford to save a little, to pay a sizeable proportion of the household expenses, and to give Betty money as well.

Benjamin thought that the early death of her mother was partly to blame for Betty's fecklessness with money, since it meant that she received no proper training in the running of a poor household. Her childhood and youth were, he thought, passed in families where she was not taught such lessons, or where suitable frugality was not practised – or, as he cynically noted, maybe it was that she had simply not learned from the good examples that she was given. Although her education at the Girls Charity School in Lancaster had included instruction in household management, this had no apparent benefit. It is, however, likely that these lessons were more practical than financial, being intended to prepare girls for going into ordinary domestic service. Whatever the cause of Betty's alleged inability to manage her affairs, her husband was in no doubt at all that she was very seriously at fault.

His great grievance was that, despite all his efforts to assist with managing the money, and his relieving her of many of the burdens of running a household, she

---

82 LRO: DDX/1554/22 and 12.

still managed to accumulate very large debts. Her careless generosity meant that she lent money without security to neighbours who – Benjamin thought – were undeserving and dishonest. She could not resist the blandishments of pedlars and credit traders, and bought from them at high interest so that she was forced to borrow to repay the debts due to them. That, in turn, produced further debt. She bought goods on credit, and paid off one shop by borrowing on the slate from the next. It was a classic tale of inability to escape from a vicious circle of mounting debt. Benjamin was especially aggrieved that she completely failed to learn any lessons which he tried to give her, and that when he had paid off her debts she went straight back to her old ways. He wrote in 1826 that in all their married life they had never been solvent.

His bitterness towards Betty was further increased when he learned that on several occasions she had 'borrowed' his personal items for pawning. Towards the end of her life, worn out by this endlessly repeated circumstance, he 'turned tyrant' (a phrase which Benjamin clearly found pleasing – he uses it on more than one occasion) and ordered her to reveal her debts. These were huge, in relation to the family income, and it was distressing for him to find that she had stolen from his box of savings. After her death it must have caused him a great deal of pain to realize that his daughters, Agnes and Mary, showed clear signs of being cast in their mother's mould. They stole their father's possessions, including some of his precious books, to be pawned to raise money for their own needs or wants (among them, supporting Mary's young man, Bob Smith, in jail at Lancaster Castle).

It is remarkable that, despite his problems and difficult circumstances, Benjamin was able to save substantial sums. By 1809, the year before the amputation of his leg, he had managed to accumulate no less than £26. In part this was the result of his financial caution, in part because the early years of the nineteenth century (especially 1802–5) were a period of real prosperity in trade. With factories flourishing and unemployment low, a mechanic was able to earn a very respectable income. In the spring of 1803 Benjamin was bringing home a regular wage of 25s (£1.25) per week, but when doing piecework on a specific project this was increased to the surprisingly high figure of £2 6s (£2.30) or even £2 8s (£2.40) per week. Such an income meant that Benjamin and his fellow-mechanics were earning more than most manual workers, and were indeed well-paid by the standards of most of their contemporaries. That Benjamin was, for several years, a pauper in receipt of poor relief was the consequence of his invalidity and lameness, for even in the bad times his wages were higher than those of most of his neighbours.

He carefully charts the fluctuations in wages, from his first employment, as an apprentice filer at Dolphinholme for 8s (40p) per week in August 1791, through relative prosperity, then growing poverty as lameness forced him to spend long periods off work, until in 1809 he was compelled to give up his trade. In December 1815, when he returned to more or less full-time employment after a break of over seven years, he earned markedly less than previously, and never again did his wages match even the basic earnings of 1803. In 1822, at 19s (90p) per week, they were 23% lower than they had been twenty years before.

The combination of wage levels and food prices was the basic determinant of the family fortunes. Benjamin gives values for both in some detail throughout the period 1800–30. Like all who lived in a world of actual or imminent pauperism and even starvation, he was acutely aware of the costs of staple foodstuffs – bread, oats and flour – and he makes frequent reference to their prices. It is clear that he, like social and economic historians of a later time, regarded these prices as a yardstick by which to measure the state of the world. In the spring of 1795 bread was 'now very dear, the quarter loaf 3½ pound was at 1s 3d' [6p]. By 1801, he records, the same size of loaf had increased to 1s 10½d [9p], and became more expensive until well after the end of the Napoleonic Wars. Throughout that period the cost of bread is used as a refrain against which the dark days and the desperate burdens of the poor are described.

In his account of the year 1815 Benjamin blamed the Government and its restrictive trade laws for this state of affairs – in which view he was far from alone – but for 1816 the effects of the disastrous harvest are held responsible. The year was extremely wet, and cold, so that 'every sort of Vegitation partly failed, So that from the time of Harvest, there was scarce any wheat Sound, & Scarce a pudding made all year among the poor'. It was not only the price of grain which was a problem. The grain spoiled in storage, giving a foul taste which was made worse by the adulteration of the bread because of the scarcity of flour: 'Bread very dear, & very Bad, the worst that I ever remember in all my life, oweing to the wet & cold weather last year, Scarce any wheat could be got that was grown that year & nothing had a proper taste'.[83]

He later observes how, suddenly, the price of bread fell sharply. In the winter of 1822–3 'Bread was cheaper than it had ever been in our life time before'. It was a short interlude, marred for Benjamin by the unhappy discovery that his wife could not take advantage of the cheapness of food because she was, yet again, heavily in debt. The drought of 1826 ruined the harvest just as the exceptional wetness of 1816 had done. Perhaps it was an even worse year than 1816, or perhaps Benjamin, tired and feeling old and depressed, was full of anxiety about the future, but his writing takes on a deeply pessimistic and doom-laden air: 'the long drought is expected to have materially ingured the Harvest . . . in all this Island, & we fear for the Corn, the poor are in a Pitiful State, and what will be the end we cannot tell may god Bless us & Save us'.[84]

83 *Family Records*, pp. 54–55.
84 ibid., p. 70.

Wage information

1791 August	8s per week (apprenticeship at Dolphinholme)
1793 August	9s per week (apprenticeship at Dolphinholme)
1795 January	14s per week (Horrocks's in Preston)
1797 summer	16s per week
1799 January	1 guinea per week (Riley & Paley)
	(but only 16s payable until frames made, and the master eventually paid only £1 per week)
1800 summer	1 guinea per week (Frank Sleddon)
1801	'wages a little better'
1803 February	25s per week
	(with piecework £2 6s–£2 8s per week)
1807	'wages pulled down' (trade depression)
	Benjamin often off work with lameness
1808	20s poor relief from Ellel township
1809–15	no regular wage because no regular work:
	income only from 'casual' wages, since unable to work because leg lame/amputated
1815 December	20s per week (first regular work since 1809)
	(at Hope & Park)
1816 late	wages dropped in trade depression
1818 September	wages raised 2s per week (to 25s)
1821 January	wages dropped 2s per week (to 23s)
1822 February	19s per week (Frank Sleddon)
1822 spring	20s per week
1823 March	raised by 3s per week to 23s
	(the last specific information he gives)
1824 early	4s per week for Thomas's apprenticeship
1824 June	Thomas raised to 8s per week
1825 May	Thomas earns 14s per week at Watts & Hodgson
1825 December	wages dropped
1826 April	wages dropped for the third time in a year
1827	wages 4s per week less than in 1825
1833	wages improved: raised 1s per week

Prices of bread and grain given in the text

1795 spring	Quarter loaf (3½lb) 1s 3d
1801	Quarter loaf 1s 10½d
1813	[Oat]meal £5 per load
1826 early	Wheat 31s per load
1826 September	Wheat 51s per load
1827 May	Superfine flour 44–48s per pack

	Oatmeal 41–42s per pack
1827 end	Superfine flour 40–42s per pack
	Oatmeal 27–28s per pack
1828 January	Wheat 50s per quarter
	Oats 26s per quarter
1828 October	Wheat 72s 10d per quarter
1829 January	Old wheat 92s per quarter
1831 January	Wheat 73s per quarter
	Oats 26s per quarter
1834 autumn	Wheat 36–44s per quarter
	Oatmeal 26–28s per load

The Poor Law system

The operation of the Poor Law had a direct impact upon the Shaw family. Benjamin and his brothers and sisters had their original settlement not at Dent, where they were born and where their parents lived, nor at Garsdale, the birthplace of their father and the home township of their ancestors, but at Preston Richard in Westmorland. It was there that Joseph Shaw had finished his apprenticeship as a weaver, and therefore it was to that township that he legally belonged. He left Preston Richard immediately on the completion of his apprenticeship and went back to his native valley and township of Garsdale. Nevertheless, although – as far as can be ascertained – he never again lived in or visited Preston Richard, that was deemed to be his place of settlement for Poor Law purposes.

Benjamin retained his father's settlement of Preston Richard until 1794 when, on completing an apprenticeship at the mill at Dolphinholme, he acquired his own settlement. There was a good deal of confusion about this, since initially the precise location of the settlement was unclear. The mill (on the south bank of the River Wyre) was in the township of Nether Wyresdale in the parish of Garstang, but Benjamin actually lived on the north bank, in the township of Ellel in the parish of Cockerham. At first the location of the family's settlement was of no immediate importance, but as he grew lame Benjamin began to realize that he was in danger of losing his income and might require parish relief to support his family.

Knowing the likelihood of increasing poverty and eventual destitution, and knowing too the uncertainty of his settlement, he took steps to seek legal or quasi-legal opinion on the case, and to ascertain his rights. He was comparatively literate, articulate and determined, and he met the challenge with vigour. He records how he applied to the Mayor for a decision, but received a doubtful answer, so he took advice from different 'law men' in the town. They, too, gave conflicting answers – all of which illustrates well the arcane and confused state of the law, and the frequently arbitrary and random nature of the decision-making. He therefore applied for relief from Preston deliberately to test the case. The townships of Ellel and Nether Wyresdale argued with each other and with Preston over responsibility. Finally, Ellel accepted that he had gained his settlement in that township by residing there when serving and completing his indentures.

The experiences of Benjamin and his family were by no means untypical. Many hundreds of families in Preston each year were subjected to the vagaries of the Poor Law, its eccentricities and ambiguities, the varying policies of individual overseers and the often labyrinthine processes by which assistance could be obtained. The Preston overseers, quite legitimately, consistently refused any assistance to the family apart from a trifling amount to tide them over their immediate predicament. When, later in 1808, the family were in urgent need of poor relief, they were removed by the Preston overseers and, having been passed back and forth, eventually stayed for thirty weeks in Ellel township. This time was remembered by Benjamin with very mixed feelings. The family was desperately poor, 'nearly naked', and yet the fresh air, fresh water and open space worked wonders for the health of the children – a damning indictment of the conditions in Preston at that time.

Benjamin was able to extract a regular pension, or payment from the Poor Rate, from Ellel during the long period after 1808 when he was unable to work and when the family was in danger of destitution. It is unfortunate that the overseers' records for both Ellel and Preston have been lost for this period, since the fluctuation in payments would otherwise have been more clear, but it is known from Benjamin's account that the Ellel overseers frequently attempted to reduce the amount which was paid.

Benjamin's unmarried daughters were also legally settled in Ellel township, even though none of them was born there and none of them had lived or worked there apart from their stay as children in 1808–9. When the girls had their illegitimate children they were compelled to go to lodgings in Ellel for the lying-in, to avoid any possibility of their claiming that the children should, on the grounds of birthplace, be relievable by Preston. Thus Bella and Hannah gave birth in Ellel, while Mary went to the township but returned soon afterwards with a 'certificate' – a settlement certificate – so that she could have the child in Preston. This somewhat more practical approach, whereby Ellel accepted in writing its liabilities and paid her a sum to support the child, reflects the reality of the situation. It was a rural township, without a workhouse, and did not want the day-to-day burden of the girl and her child. She had the baby in her father's house in Preston, a much more sensible solution.

There can have been few people courageous and determined enough to challenge the system in this way, and few who were sufficiently articulate and independent of spirit to take their – as yet hypothetical – case to the highest authority. Most people, uneducated and cowed by the threat of authority and power, submitted to the Poor Law system because they had no choice. Benjamin was of different mettle. His dealings with his employers and his comments about them confirm the impression given by the dealings with the Poor Law system –

that he was unusually uncompliant and inacquiescent. He had a clear idea of what he believed to be his rights, and was prepared to challenge those in authority and to use the law on his own behalf, to obtain redress or to find the answer which he sought.

Employment

Benjamin gives comparatively little detailed information about the nature of his work. He probably did not feel it necessary to explain the minutiae of his trade since much of that information would be familiar to his potential readers, but it is also likely that he did not consider his daily routine to be of sufficient interest or relevance. There is, in contrast, extensive reference to the wages which he earned: such information was of historical interest even in 1826, when he wrote the first volume, and it was also a subject which had great and immediate significance in terms of the household economy.

Although as a small child Benjamin knitted stockings, a task given to most children in Dent in the late eighteenth century, he began to help his father from the age of ten. Joseph Shaw had given up full-time weaving in order to build up trade as a travelling repairer of clocks and other small pieces of machinery. He had an inventive and practical mind, and put his talents to good use, but odd-jobbing was not a steady or reliable source of income. On occasion he had to resume weaving for short periods to provide additional money. Working alongside his father, Benjamin soon displayed a special aptitude for the lathe and for turning small parts and pieces of equipment.

When, at the age of eighteen, he moved with the family to Dolphinholme, it was natural that Benjamin should go to the machine shop, where he did work with which he was already familiar. He was bound in a formal apprenticeship at the mill for only three years, because he was much older and more experienced than most apprentices. The mill underwent a succession of crises, and for long periods was working at well under its full capacity. His regular trade was therefore supplemented by arduous and demanding work, doing general repairs as required. The consequences of frequently being given jobs on the mill dam were dire for Benjamin. The Wyre was icy in the bitter winters of 1792 and 1793, and standing long hours in the freezing water exacerbated the existing injuries to his right leg. In the final year at the mill there was so little work that he was unable to continue his proper trade at all, and spent his time keeping the machinery rust-free and in working order.

By the time of his dismissal in January 1795 he had completed his apprenticeship. The master, Thomas Edmondson, wrote a testimony on the reverse of the indenture document. His words, inscribed perhaps without great thought at a time when Benjamin was still only twenty-three, are remarkably accurate in their description of his character: 'Honesty, Industery, & Soberiety', and it is impossible to doubt the assessment of Nathaniel Booth, the mill manager, who wrote that Benjamin had over his time at Dolphinholme 'behaved with the greatest Properiety [*sic*]'. Benjamin kept the indenture, and transcribed these tributes in his autobiographical account over thirty years later – and no doubt recognized their accuracy with pride.[85]

After fruitless searches for work in Lancaster and the mills in the Lune valley around Caton, he set off for Preston, which was then just beginning its boom as a cotton town. In March 1795 Benjamin obtained work at John Horrocks's new 'Yellow Factory' at the eastern end of Church Street. During that summer his former master, Thomas Edmondson, opened a new factory at Hebden Bridge in Yorkshire. He went to Preston and asked Benjamin to go to work for him at Hebden Bridge. Ben did not accept, telling himself that to become unemployed in a small town, with little alternative employment, would be worse than losing his job in Preston. His experience of fruitless searching for employment in the rural areas near Dolphinholme was still fresh in his mind. He stayed in Preston, and never again worked anywhere else. His changes of work in Preston after 1795 are faithfully recorded, and are summarized in the table below:

1795 March	Working at John Horrocks's Yellow Factory, Dale Street
1796	Periods off work seeking medical treatment at Whitworth near Rochdale
1799 January	Paley & Riley (foremen at Horrocks's) set up on their own at Spittals Moss: Benjamin offered job but instead goes to work for David Ainsworth at the Lord's Factory in Dale Street
1800 March	Dispute with Ainsworth; leaves his employment; goes to work for Frank Sleddon near the Syke
1802 March	Shifts to Sleddon's new shop in the Brick Croft
1807 Autumn	Off work for ten weeks because of lameness, during which time Sleddon separates from his partners
1807 Christmas	Returns to Frank Sleddon, at the shop rented from Thomas Crane near the Brick Croft
1808 July	Forced to give up work completely because of leg: assists Betty in winding twist at home.
1810 April	Amputation of right leg
1815 December	Resumes work after seven-year interval; employed by Hope & Park, machine makers, in Stanley Street
1816	Working 'part-time' (a ten-hour day)
1817 spring	Full-time work starts
1817 August	Hope & Park separate; Benjamin loses his job and goes to work for John Welch, a hard and unpopular master, in the same building in Stanley Street
1817 October	Welch moves to former Sleddon's shop in the Syke
1818 September	Another move, to a larger shop

85   ibid., p. 33.

1822 February	Discharged from Welch's shop in trade depression; unemployed for three weeks, then goes to work for Frank Sleddon near Friargate
1825–6	Repeated wage reductions and part-time working at Sleddon's
1828 November	Off work for a month for health reasons
1830 December	Crushes thumb in lathe; off work for about four months
1835	Benjamin and some other 'older' employees do not receive a general wage increase at Sleddon's

This was a world which was at the same time intimate and unstable, close-knit yet uncertain. Preston was growing very rapidly as a cotton town, and between 1791 and 1831 many new mills were established. In the early years there were no large-scale commercial suppliers of equipment, and no existing firms which could produce, install and maintain machinery for the mills. To cater for the demands of the mill-owners there sprang up numerous small businesses which made equipment for very local markets, sometimes for a single specific contract. Many of these businesses were located in more or less temporary workshops and sheds within the mill yards, and they were often run by men who had previously been employed in the mills and had seized the opportunity to capitalize on the new business.

Because of cyclical changes in the economy and the cotton trade, demand fluctuated alarmingly and the trade was often precarious. The facilities and machine shops were often rudimentary. When Benjamin went to work for David Ainsworth in 1799 he and his fellows had not only to make the patterns for the equipment they would be producing, but also had to make their own tools. The better workshops, often within mill yards, had equipment powered by the mill steam engines, but others still used hand-operated lathes and were in inadequate, ill-lit, badly-ventilated (or sometimes excessively well-ventilated) and unheated buildings. Benjamin's description of one such place is vivid: 'a great wide place, and so cold that we were nearly Starved, in winter, & Scarce could keep a candle or lamp in, when the wind Blew hard . . . the floor was wet, & when it rained . . . we were flooded'.[86] The ending of a major contract often meant that the business closed down and the workforce was dismissed, while any fall in the fortunes of the cotton trade resulted – as it did for well over a century afterwards – in immediate hardship and depression in the ancillary and dependent trades.

The close-knit character of the business is clear. Skilled and trustworthy mechanics such as Benjamin were in short supply, and were regarded as a valuable commodity. The masters knew each other and knew each other's workers. Most men had worked for several of them at different times, and the

---

86 ibid., p. 56.

masters often formed short-lived partnerships and business ventures with each other. Many of the masters had themselves been workers at the lathe only a few months before, and some continued to work on the shop floor as well as managing their businesses. Preston was still a small town, and the mills and attendant workshops were geographically concentrated, in the belt between Spittals Moss and the Brick Croft at the eastern side of the town centre. Benjamin was therefore able to find work comparatively quickly when laid off by employers, and very soon had a network of contacts within the trade which stood him in good stead on many occasions.

The close ties among employers and between at least some employees and employers, and the comparative ease with which individuals could move between levels in the hierarchy and between different jobs, were greatly reinforced by the common bond of religion. The extent to which the employers in the machine-making trade were adherents of the Baptists and other nonconformist denominations is striking. The Methodist and Independent (Grimshaw Street) chapel registers show a remarkable number of entries relating to the employers in the trade – Frank Sleddon, Edward Salisbury, Thomas Crane, Thomas Munday and David Ainsworth among them. There is no doubt that these associations played an important though undocumented role: Benjamin's religious conversion was the result of lengthy discussions and debates with Francis Lambert and William Summerfield, members of the congregation at the Baptist chapel who were his superiors at Frank Sleddon's works. Thus religion added another dimension to the intricate network of contacts which was so fundamental to the operation of the machine-making trade in the town.

The familiarity meant that Benjamin was not in awe of his employers, in the way he might have been when, as a young apprentice, he worked at Dolphinholme. There he worked for the mill-owners, who were grand and powerful figures, not directly involved in the day-to-day work of the machine shop. In Preston, under such men as Frank Sleddon, John Welch and Thomas Park, he was working for people who were his contemporaries and who had an immediate contact with, and specialized practical knowledge of, the trade. They undoubtedly respected Benjamin and he had a distinctly undeferential attitude to them. His use of the term 'master' does not imply that he felt subservient, although naturally he was in a subordinate position and depended on their good opinion for his continued employment.

This is illustrated by the incident in 1800 when David Ainsworth, without warning, imposed and tried to enforce, contrary to contract, a new rule forbidding the men from taking 'tea breaks' during the long working day. They had their wages stopped, and instead of giving in they took Ainsworth to court. Unpaid wages were restored, but the men were threatened with dismissal. Benjamin and some others went, rather than submit – his disdain for the remainder is indicated by his account of them: 'Some submited & Beged their work again'. Ainsworth was greatly disliked by Benjamin, for this incident and for cheating him of money in the previous year. In his account of the cheating

Benjamin's contempt is clear: 'D Ainsworth, the manager gave me 5 Shillings, pretending he was sorry that there should be any misunderstanding between us'.[87]

His dislike of another master, John Welch, was perhaps even stronger. He only went to work for Welch, in August 1817, because his shop was nearby: 'this Shop was near to wheare I lived, or elce I should not [have] engaged with him, for I did not like him before, or ever had cause to like him after, for I was Badly [used] all the time I was with him . . . the worst master that I ever had . . . the most disagreeable man that I ever wrought for'.[88] The smallness of the world is apparent, for Benjamin knew Welch beforehand and knew his reputation. Only the fact that, with a wooden leg or crutch, he could not walk far forced him into taking this job. In the autumn of 1821 when trade was very bad and Benjamin was getting no work, Welch refused to dismiss him or to give him a share of the limited piecework available – he no doubt hoped to keep on this skilled but slower worker on the expectation that times would improve. Benjamin actually had to ask for his discharge.

The other side of the coin is displayed by Frank Sleddon, Thomas Hope and Henry Park. In the autumn of 1815 Benjamin was well enough to contemplate a return to work, after the seven-year interval caused by his lameness and later the amputation of his leg. Thomas Hope and Henry Park, machine makers, were setting up a new shop in Stanley Street. It was only a few hundred yards from Benjamin's house, and he asked for work: 'as I was well aquainted with both of them, they agreed to give me an envitation to come and work for them'. The personal relationship – perhaps even friendship – which is described here produced a form of employment significantly removed from that which conventionally existed between employer and employee. Its benefits to Benjamin are sharply revealed by his next phrase: 'they Promised to indulge me in any way'. In an unusual tribute he records their kindness to him, and how they allowed him special hours, giving him 'work Suted to my State'. The benefits to Hope and Park were also clear. Kindness was a good investment, for 'as the masters had been so kind to me, & they wanted work getting on, I Strove to obliege them'.[89]

Frank Sleddon was similarly generous. Though a markedly unsuccessful businessman, of great financial and managerial ineptitude, Sleddon had many merits. Above all, to Benjamin, he was a loyal and sympathetic friend who was tolerant of his disabilities and tried to accommodate them. Sleddon was on first-name terms with Benjamin: he could not have attempted to distance himself socially, at least in the first two decades of the century, since too many people knew too much about him. In 1800 his project to build a factory was 'wondered much at . . . for he was lately so poor that his family was in want of Bread' –

---

87   ibid., pp. 40, 38.
88   ibid., pp. 55–56.
89   ibid., pp. 53–54.

something that could probably not have been said of Benjamin's family even in the worst times in Preston.[90]

Frank Sleddon served Benjamin well. When Welch finally gave Benjamin the sack in 1822 he went to work for Frank, and remained there for the rest of his life. It was a valuable connection, and its significance was emphasized by Benjamin: 'if I had not been well known Both to him & foreman James Birkett, I should not have got work now, trade being so bad, & work so much Sought after'.[91] The old acquaintance and friendship, and Benjamin's excellent reputation, stood him in good stead at a very difficult time.

These were special circumstances. Benjamin was a particularly good and skilled worker and, despite his disability, his services would have been at a premium when industry was doing well. But there is no reason to suppose that men who were so generous to him would have been bad employers for their other workers. Likewise, it is apparent that Welch and Ainsworth were not disliked by Benjamin alone, but were generally unpopular with their workers – one had a reputation which went before him, the other provoked, by his harshness and unfairness, a courageous attempt to enforce the law against him.

Crucially, though, all this took place within that intimate world, the machine-making trade of Preston. It was in very marked contrast to the world in which his children, and the majority of his other relations, found themselves. Benjamin was in the fortunate position of having a skilled trade which was much in demand so that, except in times of acute depression or, in his case, of major health problems, finding work and keeping it were not too difficult. His wages were, by the standards of the time, respectable, and with piecework he could take home an adequate income. Such employment was not available for most of the others. All but one of his children went into the mills when nine or ten years old: the exception being Hannah, who was delicate and stayed at home until she was fourteen. They followed the standard path from the cardroom, which required small and nimble workers and where they stayed until thirteen or fourteen, to the winding frames. The girls almost inevitably ended up there, for it was 'all the work nearly for young woman here at Preston'.

Joseph, the eldest son, was apprenticed as a carder with Horrocks's, while the other two sons, William and Thomas, were destined by Benjamin to follow other trades. He sought opportunities for William to learn a trade, but without success because this period coincided with a trade depression. William therefore did a little training as a weaver with Edward Salisbury, and remained a weaver for the rest of his short life. Thomas was given particular attention by Benjamin. Although, like the other children, he began at the mill when he was nine, he wanted to learn a trade. Benjamin tried hard to get somebody to take him on, but times were again bad and business in depression. He worked for a few

90 ibid., p. 42.
91 ibid p 59

months as a weaver with Henry Pearson and with Horrocks's, and then served only eight months of a six-year apprenticeship as a moulder in Thomas Munday's foundry. In this case he left because 'some differance happened with the masters son & him'.[92] Eventually he ended up, like his father, as a mechanic, but seemed unable to stay in one job for any length of time.

Yet in the long term it was Thomas, alone of the children, who achieved a position and status which would have given Benjamin satisfaction. Despite his early difficulties and his somewhat impetuous nature Thomas eventually became a skilled mechanic, and his training in the foundry stood him in good stead. He was able to set up in business on his own, running a small foundry and machine shop which prospered in the second half of the nineteenth century, and lasted until Thomas's son Joseph sold the business in the early years of this century.[93] That Thomas was able to make this step is not only a tribute to his own resourcefulness – and perhaps to lessons and attitudes passed on from Benjamin – but also reflects the mobility within the machine-making trade which had been so useful to his father.

Nowhere does Benjamin condemn the employment of his children in the mills from such an early age, and he presumably understood that it was, in most circumstances, inevitable. There is, however, reason to believe that he did not accept that such employment was intrinsically a good practice, no matter how necessary it was financially. He notes that the deafness which afflicted both Hannah and Mary could have been the result of the noise in the factories. More disturbingly, he had before him the distressing example of his own little brother, Joseph, who in 1791 at Dolphinholme had been 'catched in the wheels' of the mill and horribly mangled, losing two fingers and dying not long afterwards. Of Joseph, he notes that 'he was employed in the factory, though he was a very little one', which implies, if not disapproval, at least a sadness that such small children should be put to that work.[94]

There must have been constant anxiety about the young children when they went to work. With Joseph's experiences in mind, Thomas was a particular worry, for he 'came home nearly every day, with his fingers or hands or cloaths torn'.[95] Benjamin tried to make it possible for both William and Thomas to avoid employment in the mills, by seeking places for them as mechanics, and it is probable that, had he been in a position to do so, he would have given the children a better education. With his strong views on the desirability of learning, Benjamin must have regretted the fact that the children had to be sent out to work when young, rather than spending more time at school. Two of them are specifically noted as having gone to school when little, but there is no evidence that they shared their father's interest in, or facility for, reading and writing. In

92   ibid., p. 93.
93   Personal communication from Mr Henry Shaw, 15 April 1991.
94   *Family Records*, p. 82.
95   ibid., p. 93.

any case, their employment was essential to the family income in the period from 1808 to 1815 when Benjamin himself was earning little or nothing because of his poor health.

A particularly useful feature of Benjamin's work is the coverage he gives to the employment of women. It is apparent that this was almost universal, both in the rural valleys of the Dent district and in the industrial town. The women of Dent were employed in knitting and spinning. Benjamin notes how his grand-mother's sisters 'all lived to a great age, they followed knitting Stockings gloves, gamashes, mittons, &c &c, for a living which was the common employment of the poor at that time, there'.[96] A woman could do these tasks – particularly knitting, which could be carried around – as well as looking after the house and family, so that every spare moment could be gainfully occupied: Benjamin's mother, Isabella Noddle, 'had of corse a Principle Care in the family – She lived with her mother, and was employed in Sewing & Knitting at every vaquent time from other more important business'.[97] Adam Sedgwick records a rhyme which told how the 'Dent lasses' could do four things at a time:

> 'She knaws how to sing and knit,
> And she knaws how to carry the kit [milkpail],
> While she drives her kye to pasture'[98]

Women might also work in trade. Peggy Noddle, Benjamin's grandmother, worked on Dent market, measuring meal for the farmers and selling vegetables. His formidable cousin, the dark-haired hard-drinking Nanny Watson, drove the coal carts from her husband's coalpit on the fells down to Sedbergh. Such evidence emphasizes the importance of women in the local labour market and in the household economy. It also points to the breadth of the range of work which they performed.

The earnings of women were also quite essential to the households in the eastern suburbs of Preston where Benjamin lived for the whole of his adult life. The destination of most working women was the mill, as it was to be for generations to come. All of Benjamin's daughters worked in the cotton industry, and even those who stayed at home because of physical infirmity or being tied by children were generally employed in winding twist or other domestic stages of the cotton trade. The evidence of Benjamin's family is supported by other contemporary sources, such as the 1841 census, to show that a non-working woman was a rarity.

In the domestic context it was possible for women to manage very small and informal businesses to supplement the income which the family derived from

96 ibid., p. 10.
97 ibid., p. 12.
98 Sedgwick, p. 82.

waged employment. The example of Benjamin's sister, Hannah Jackson, reveals a woman who was in comparatively secure circumstances, but who took advantage of opportunities to increase family income further. She made good use of the money which her father, Joseph, was prepared to give for his keep, so that although a member of the family he was in financial terms a lodger. She also used his payments in kind to add to her stock of household goods and to the non-monetary income. On several occasions he brought his own pots, pans and other small items of household ware with him when he came for an extended stay at her house, and she kept them when he left. He made furniture for her, tended an allotment and grew fruit and vegetables for the Jackson family, and performed a wide variety of domestic chores. She was thus relieved of a considerable proportion of the burden of domestic duties, and was free to develop a tiny business of her own – she took in washing and, as Benjamin noted in 1826, 'She hath kept a Mangle some time'.[99]

The Jacksons were clearly improving themselves by hard work, by careful management of their money and by making good use of opportunities such as Joseph's generosity towards them. Hannah was probably a good deal more like her brother than he would have cared to admit: although she seems to have lacked his strict regard for honour and honesty, she had the same attitude to respectability and the need to improve. It is possible that Benjamin's dislike for her in later years was in part a frustration at his own failure to make such improvement.

Betty Shaw, like her sister-in-law, ventured into private enterprise in a small way, when she baked oatcakes for sale. The fundamental difference between the two cases was that this venture was forced upon Betty by dire necessity. Whereas in Hannah's case the business was a supplement to the basic family income, in the Shaw family Betty's earnings from bakings *were* the basic income. Benjamin was unable to work, and the poor relief allowed by Ellel township was quite inadequate. For several years the family depended on the income derived from baking (of which Benjamin evidently disapproved) and on the earnings of the children.

Illness and death

Benjamin's adult life was clouded by his own ill-health and by the illnesses of his family. The most detailed descriptive passages in his writings are reserved for the harrowing and lingering deaths of his wife and his daughter Hannah, while the growing lameness which was eventually to lead to the amputation of his own leg is a theme which runs through seventeen years of the account. Much other information about health is given in a more incidental way – references to disease and illness are found in many of the shorter biographical sections.

99   *Family Records*, p. 79.

Benjamin himself suffered, with the rest of his family, from a smallpox epidemic in his childhood – they all recovered, but his brother George was dangerously ill and was heavily pocked as a result. Thereafter he makes no mention of his own health until the incident at Dolphinholme in 1792 when a boy threw a stick at him and injured his leg, but the deaths of his little sisters and brothers are recorded, as are the fevers which laid the family low at Dolphinholme in 1792. The injury to his leg seems to have involved serious internal damage – there was a 'hard lump or knott deep in the flesh' – and as a result the leg soon became ulcerous and agonizingly painful. Its deteriorating condition, including what must have been circulatory deficiencies, was greatly exacerbated by Benjamin's having to work waist deep in the icy river at Dolphinholme, repairing the mill dam. Once he had gone to Preston he had to stand long hours at his lathe, and by the late 1790s he was suffering acutely.

Visits to the celebrated Whitworth doctors failed to give any respite, and in the autumn of 1807 his lameness forced him to stop work for many weeks. He made himself go back early in 1808, but in July could carry on no longer. Without his income the family was almost destitute, and was removed by the Preston overseers to Galgate in Ellel. Benjamin thought that he had little chance of recovery, and expected to die. The opening of the Preston Dispensary was therefore an almost miraculous good fortune since it brought the opportunity of surgery, in itself an extremely hazardous undertaking but one which represented a last chance. In April 1810, during a forty-minute operation attended by seven doctors, Benjamin's right leg was amputated.

His strong constitution enabled him to survive the post-operative fever, and convalescence at Blackpool must also have helped – with remarkable speed his health returned, and for the first time since the autumn of 1793 he was well. Benjamin specifically refers to his use of a crutch while at Blackpool, but it is not clear whether he eventually had a wooden leg. Regardless of that, the loss of his right leg was ever after a major burden: he found getting to work troublesome, especially in bad weather, and was inevitably more restricted in what he could do. As he noted, he was 'nearly Cut off from the world, was quite like a Prisoner'.[100]

There are several references, apart from those which relate to his own lameness, to visits to the doctor. Benjamin's brother, Joseph, was taken by his father to the doctor at Lancaster after his hand had been mangled in the machinery at Dolphinholme Mill, and one or two of his fingers had been torn off. The mill management did nothing to assist, and there was probably no doctor in the district. Such accidents were, noted Benjamin, a common occurrence, and were presumably regarded as 'one of those things' by those in charge – not their problem or responsibility.

Benjamin's daughters were also attended by the doctor. In the fatal illness

100 ibid., p. 50.

which followed the birth of her second child, for example, Agnes was visited by the physician to the Preston workhouse. In the case of the 'first Mary', a child of ten months, the blistering which was administered for measles produced convulsions (which is not to be wondered at), and Betty Shaw ordered the treatment to be stopped. She suspected that it was making matters worse: in Benjamin's account of the episode there is some hint that his wife was merely being foolish and emotional, and that the treatment should have been continued. Hannah, too, was blistered, and received a variety of medicines from the doctor, none of which she could stomach. Although Benjamin evidently had great faith in these doctors, Hannah was unable to take the quack remedies which must have been prescribed – no doubt the side-effects were so unpleasant that she refused to take any more.

Benjamin's apparent faith in the medicines is perhaps surprising in view of the failure of those which he took himself. The ointments prescribed by the doctor at Lancaster who first looked at his injured leg, and the drugs administered by the Whitworth doctors, were equally ineffective. The Whitworth doctors, who were famed throughout the land, were an extraordinary dynasty of medical men, and there has been a substantial amount of research into their methods. That they began as animal doctors explains a great deal. Their basic remedies were effective and they were particularly skilled in the setting and repair of bones – their mechanical skills were undoubtedly great, their treatment of disease less so. The psychological impact of their treatment may well have been of considerable significance. They were highly regarded, they had a remarkably enlightened attitude to treatment of the poor, and the mere fact of being treated must have had a beneficial effect on many of their patients. But their ability to cure disease and infection, rather than mend physical injury, was naturally limited – Benjamin's ulcerous leg did not respond to their ministrations.

The underlying impression, from the references to illness and sickness, is that usually there was nothing to be done. The doctors were consulted because people in such trouble would try any means available, but cures were few. People suffered, often for years, and died in helplessness and pain, for want of adequate medical care. That was partly the consequence of their poor circumstances, but their more prosperous contemporaries had little better fortune. Few illnesses were curable, few treatments scientifically sound, and few doctors understood the true nature of the problems they tried to remedy. The almost inevitable result of any serious illness, and many which would no longer be regarded as such, was a long period of distress followed by death. The graphic and detailed accounts of the deaths of Hannah and Betty, and the rather less complete description of his father's death, show just how heartbreaking this could be, and emphasize the helplessness of those involved. Benjamin did not shirk from describing the distressing details, such as the peeling of Hannah's skin, and we may be confident that these are accurate accounts of the events. The courage of Hannah and Betty is striking. Both wished fervently to die, to put an end to their miserable state: a religious belief, in such circumstances, was their only consolation.

The whole question of Benjamin's attitude to death is a complex one. In the case of those closest to him – his children, wife, father and mother and one or two of his other relatives – he gives extensive detail of their sickness and deaths, and it is immediately apparent that their dying affected him a great deal. The deaths of other relations, including grandchildren, were more distant and had less personal significance. But it is necessary to bear the purpose of this work in mind. The autobiographies and biographies were not written primarily as a means of recording Benjamin's emotions and feelings, but specifically as a factual family history. In some instances his recording of deaths seems cold, even callous, lacking in any hint of emotional involvement but reading as a straightforward piece of detached reporting. Yet other descriptions of deaths and verdicts on those who had gone make it clear that Benjamin had warm and emotional attachments to some people, and felt their loss keenly. It could be, perhaps, that in many instances he deliberately avoided expressing emotions, in order to maintain the coherence and purpose of his writings, while in the cases of those closest to him he felt able to be more expressive and revealing of his feelings.

The descriptions of the last illnesses of Hannah and Betty show how acutely he observed their decline, noting the symptoms at each stage of deterioration, and recording their own feelings and religious testimony. There are still those who argue that the Victorians and their predecessors had a more casual or detached view of death than we do, and that because parents frequently had large families they were less affected by the deaths of children. Much evidence has been brought forward to contradict this view, and Benjamin's writing confirms the strength of feeling and the sense of loss and grief. Frequently he appears cold and harsh, but this was perhaps because he could not easily and freely express his own inner emotions, either in writing or in his relationship with those around him. But it is clear how much he suffered from the loss of those close to him.

The most poignant and telling expressions are those which are slightly oblique, referring not to death but to the waste of life. Writing twenty years later of his only child to die in infancy, the first Mary (1806), the pain is still clear: 'this was the loveliest Child of all the other^s, healthy & good Humoured, & in all respects a lovly creature . . . But her good Qualitys was not long enjoyed by us' – those are not the words of one to whom the death of a small baby had little significance. The phrasing of this passage echoes that used to describe his little sister Isabella, who died at Dolphinholme in 1792, aged about three: 'this was a very [fine] Strong Sharp & healthy Child . . . this was a lovly child, & greatly valued by the family, but this could not Sheild her from disease'.[101]

After Betty had died he felt her loss keenly, missing her companionship despite the stormy nature of their relationship, and feeling lonely and dejected

101   ibid., pp. 45, 92, 83.

at home on his own. He noted this loneliness in forlorn terms, and this goes some way to countering the predominantly negative impression of their relationship given by the rest of the work. Among the verses which he composed was one written on 24 February 1835, the seventh anniversary of Betty's death. It begins, 'This is a day I never can forget, A day so fraught with consequence to me', and is a moving testimony to the loss which he continued to feel.[102]

The tender side of Benjamin's nature is exemplified by the moving request which he made to the sexton of St John's parish church, to make Hannah 'a very deep grave, as they some times shift them two soon, I thought She might rest undesturbed'.[103] It is difficult, too, not to be moved by the simple, gentle and unaffected obituary which he wrote for his son William, who died suddenly in 1830 aged only thirty-five: 'had he been in good Circumstances [he] might have been a Stout man (But he was poor) & had to live upon a little . . . was a plain man simple & honest well meaning man – he enjoyed but little of this world's good, wrought hard – lived poor & died without much atention from docters or others'.[104] There is an underlying sense of grievance there, not only against death but also against the injustices of society.

This evidence shows that Benjamin could be emotionally affected by death, by the loss of those close to him and by the sense of injustice that their lives should have been ended with little achievement to show. It goes a long way towards redressing the impression of a cold and unemotional man which his writing might otherwise give: it would appear that he deliberately played down his own feelings to highlight the factual family history. It is clear, though, that the deaths of those less close to him had less effect. This is especially striking with regard to his grandchildren, none of whom appears as a personality in his or her own right. It is indicative of the smallness of Benjamin's circle that he does not appear to have had much interest in or pride in his grandchildren, and their deaths are recorded laconically and without much apparent concern – simply 'for the record'. By the time many of these children were born and died Benjamin was getting old and tired, and losing interest in his family as a whole, but there is an uncomfortable matter-of-factness about such phrases as 'nothing remarkable in our family happend this year – bellow had a child died at manchester in november' and (of his son Joseph) 'in the year 1821, 3 of his Children died in about 3 weeks time'.[105]

Daily life

Benjamin Shaw's writings do not include any systematic account of daily life, for this is not a diary but a retrospective autobiography and biography. Neverthe-

---

102   LRO: DDX/1554/13.
103   *Family Records*, p. 66.
104   ibid., p. 108.
105   ibid., pp. 111, 88.

less, there are scattered references to what might be considered the 'ordinary' routine, and these are of some interest. Particularly attractive is the rare (for Benjamin) poetic image of a romantic rural past conveyed by the description, brief though it is, of haymaking. A man in his fifties living in an industrial town looks back to his youth, when he lived in the Dales and had leisure and was without burdens: 'at noons when the haymakers rested, I took a Can & went to gather Rassberries, or Strawberries, then got Some milk and Sugar on them instead of resting (my grandmother used to say that is the stuf for daubing soul & boddy together)'.[106]

Contrast that with the bitter times following his marriage, and the vividly conveyed impression of dire poverty in a cruel winter: 'I made each of us a knife and fork . . . we got a pan . . . the winter was now set in and coals were very dear here then, as the cannal was not yet finished, and turf was dear . . . Betty used to go into wire, the river close to, & gather sticks, & sometimes go to Caulas mill . . . to fetch seeds to burn'.[107] That contrast, between the quality of life before the move to Dolphinholme and the misery and poverty which followed, is constantly apparent. It is rarely explicitly stated, but the difficulties of mere existence are indicated throughout the post-1793 account.

The diet was dependent upon bread, the basic foodstuff, and on oatmeal. Betty Shaw, although accused by her husband of financial mismanagement and domestic inefficiency, was compelled by circumstances to bake oatcakes for sale to neighbours during the long period when, after the amputation of his leg in 1810, Benjamin was unable to work. He describes this as a 'very disagreeable Business in a house, & very ingurious to health'. It is not entirely clear why this should have been so, but it certainly disagreed with Betty's constitution. Furthermore, to have made any sort of adequate living from such an occupation would have required an endless effort, with baking morning, noon and night to make enough oatcakes. It is not surprising, perhaps, that Betty – not a particularly strong woman in her adult years – found the work a great strain, and was left complaining 'heavely of growing weakness'.[108]

Insofar as it is possible to ascertain details from Benjamin's account, the family's diet was typically unvarying and limited, although perhaps less so in his rural youth than in urban adult life. His grandmother, Peggy Noddle, had worked in Dent market selling vegetables – potatoes, carrots, peas and beans – but when she was old she relied largely on the parish charities for her subsistence. There was a small dole of fourteen 2d loaves given out to the old people every Sunday, and she benefited from that. In the summertime Peggy subsisted largely on bread and milk, the latter being easily available in the pastoral valleys of Dentdale and Garsdale, and also cheap – a gallon of milk for a penny. Benjamin records that she did not drink tea: although it has been said

106   ibid., p. 25.
107   ibid., p. 32.
108   ibid., pp. 50, 52.

that tea-drinking did not become widespread among the lower classes until after 1815, the implication of Benjamin's view is that not to drink tea was slightly unusual even in his grandmother's day.[109]

Benjamin's father, Joseph Shaw, 'was fond of a garden' and the move away from Dent involved a particular wrench, for their last home in the valley, a cottage at Hallbank, had a large garden with its own well and a good-sized yard. The move to Dolphinholme in the summer of 1791 is eloquently recorded in relation to this garden: '[he] delved it & sowed it but never reaped it'. Earlier, in the mid-1770s, the family had had another cottage at West Bank where Joseph had 'Plenty of Berry trees' and a hive of bees, which he tended with such care that within three years he had four hives.[110] The loss of the garden was a double blow: apart from the pleasure and satisfaction which Joseph derived from gardening, there was the immeasurable benefit of free, or almost free, food grown on the spot, with fresh vegetables and fruit. There can be little doubt that the diet of the family when it lived in Dent was a great deal more balanced, nutritious and, not least, enjoyable, than in later years.

When Joseph had moved to Preston he was able to use his horticultural skills to advantage. He and the other members of his family lived on the edge of the town, in the areas of industrial housing which were springing up beside the new factories on the eastern side. Here there was still a substantial amount of vacant land, and around 1820 Joseph rented and cultivated a plot for some years. It was a source of grievance to Benjamin that he did this to assist Hannah and Henry Jackson, Benjamin's sister and her husband, who were comparatively prosperous and did not – so Benjamin felt – need such help.

Benjamin was well aware of the problem of water supplies, and in the late 1820s and early 1830s he recorded the progress of the Preston Waterworks Company venture, which in 1835 brought piped water supplies to the town from Grimsargh. In his childhood he had – unwillingly – been sent on errands from the cottage at Hallbank into the town of Dent (a distance of over half a mile), and also had to go to fetch water. At Hallbank there was a stream which ran down the fellside close to the house and was used for water, but when they moved into the town their supply was probably the copious spring in the very centre which is now the fountain which forms the memorial to Adam Sedgwick. Irrespective of source, country water was likely to be vastly better in quality and reliability than the town supply. Benjamin, describing the forced move to Ellel in 1809 when the family was evicted from Preston by the overseers, noted how their thirty-week stay in the country worked wonders for the children's health. One of the advantages was 'good water'.

Benjamin's family suffered because of the irregularity of his work between 1805 and 1818, and from Betty's seemingly incorrigible mismanagement of the

---

109   Burnett, pp. 4, 13–14.
110   *Family Records*, pp. 25, 21.

domestic finances. He tried on several occasions to introduce a thrifty planned regime into her food purchasing, by buying in bulk, but his attempts ended in failure. During his short-lived experiment Benjamin bought 'loads of meal, & packs of flower, pots of Butter & Chees &c. and pottatoes'.[111] Such a policy was extensively advocated in the nineteenth century by those who sought to make the poor improve themselves, but it was usually impractical since it required a large initial outlay, which was not only difficult to accumulate but often meant long weeks of even greater deprivation beforehand.

Moreover, in the damp, dirty and verminous conditions which prevailed in many homes, even those where every effort was made to ensure cleanliness, the storage of large quantities of perishable goods was well-nigh impossible. The flour and meal might be attacked by mice and insects, the butter and cheese turn rancid and rotten, the potatoes sprout and blacken, the bacon become green and inedible. He also bought coal by the load: that was more realistic, but it still required storage even if it would not deteriorate, and for many households fuel, too, had to be purchased in penny packets. For many the attractions of long-term economy were far outweighed by the convenience and practicality of purchasing small quantities for immediate use – a universal phenomenon, and one which is graphically portrayed in accounts of working-class life in the later nineteenth and early twentieth centuries, such as Robert Roberts' *The Classic Slum*.

The information which Benjamin gives concerning housing is disappointingly limited. As with his work, he seems to have seen no need to describe circumstances in detail. The house in Dale Street, where he and Betty went to live in March 1795 and which was his home until a few days before his death in June 1841, was a back-to-back property. It had been built in 1793 as part of a speculative development of workers' houses immediately adjacent to John Horrocks's new factory. The surviving photographs of the street show that the building had four storeys – a cellar, two full floors forming the major part of the house, and a low attic storey. The main entrance was, in the typical fashion of houses with cellar dwellings, approached by a half-flight of steps at the front.

Benjamin and Betty rented two rooms in the house, but from his scanty references it is not possible to say which these were. The references to 'coming downstairs' – in connection with the fatal illnesses of Hannah and Betty – show that there was a single room on each of two storeys, but whether these included either the cellar or attic is not certain. The most probable answer is that the family lived in the two middle storeys and shared the common staircase. Although Benjamin refers on several occasions to the paying of rent, he nowhere quantifies this and neither does he name the landlord of the property. There were other people living in the house, but he is completely silent on these fellow-residents of 1 Dale Street.

111   ibid., p. 44.

He is equally uninformative about the conditions in the house and the furniture and facilities which the family had. When he tells of the first home which he and Betty had after their marriage, a room at Dolphinholme, he makes clear their poverty and the scantiness of their furnishings – the vivid phrase, 'I made each of us a knife & fork, & 2 Stools, we got a pan, & a looking glass' produces one of the most powerful images in the whole work.[112] In Preston, though, the family seems to have lived in relative comfort. When Betty died in 1828 she distributed her possessions among the family: these included a large tea tray and tea canister, a spinning wheel, a clock and a bed quilt. With two rooms they had a great deal more living space than a lot of their neighbours, while Benjamin's good wages and skill at making furniture meant that, although they were by no means well-off, they enjoyed a better standard of living than many millworkers nearby.

Benjamin's attitude to alcoholic drink is somewhat ambiguous. In keeping with his practice of rarely referring to his own personal views he nowhere mentions whether or not he himself drank. However, his collection of epigrams suggests that in this, as in so many other aspects of life, he believed strongly in moderation and avoided excess. Three pertinent moral remarks from his collection undoubtedly reveal his thinking:

> Drunkennes what a fruitfull source of grief, –
> of every size and form beyond belief

> Drink like a Beast, but drink no more –
> than nature want, and then give o'er[113]

> O how I hate Drunkenness, A Nasty Pig
> With Snuff-Staind neckcloth without hat or wig[114]

He was sixty when, in 1832, the Temperance Movement was founded in Preston by Joseph Livesey, but there is no mention of this event in his writing – which perhaps indicated the limited local impact of the movement in its first few years. He would, however, have been sympathetic to the idea: another epigram states alarmingly that 'Intemperance is the greatest cause of Shortening life', which might apply to excess in all its forms, but would be quite appropriate to alcohol.[115] That he may have bought beer himself is suggested by references to its price in 1830, after the new regulations governing its sale at licensed premises had been introduced, although it is possible that he had obtained the figures from a newspaper. Whether or not he did drink, he had strong views on the subject.

He appears to have frowned particularly upon women who drank. Men were

112 ibid., p. 32.
113 LRO: DDX/1554/14.
114 LRO: DDX/1554/13.
115 LRO: DDX/1554/14.

not condemned out of hand: his own grandfather, for example, 'loved a little Ale – yet [was] not a drunken man', while his mother's brother, William Noddle, is described as 'a great drinker' with no suggestion of condemnation.[116] It is only when as a consequence of drink men behaved badly that Benjamin is moralistic: his uncle William Shaw, who led a colourful life in his forties, is obliquely criticized because he became 'very wild & drunken'.[117] Several female relations, however, are specifically referred to unfavourably because they indulged in alcohol. Thus, of his cousin Agnes Watson, he says 'I hear she has turned out a drinker this is a great fault in a wife'.[118] His aunt Mary Davis was the subject of family gossip: 'it was whispered that she would drink privatly, & I rather think this was too true'. With such views Benjamin clearly found a great dilemma when it came to describing his own mother, who also enjoyed ale, and he is forced to emphasize that although a drinker she was of moderate habits: 'she was fond of ale, But She was not drunken . . . in the later part of her life she had a Pint every night'.[119]

Politics and religion

Benjamin's fascination for politics and current affairs is immediately apparent in the extensive coverage of them in both volumes of his family record. What is less clear is the nature of his personal political beliefs. The most obvious likely source of such information, other than his writings, would be the poll books for the various contested elections in Preston after he came to Preston in 1795. However, these are of no assistance, except perhaps negatively. Preston enjoyed a very generous franchise, which allowed most adult males to vote. There were eight contested general election and by-election campaigns in the borough between 1796 and 1831, after which the franchise was substantially reduced as a result of the 1832 Reform Act. Study of a sample of poll books, recording the names of those who voted and the candidates for whom they cast votes, shows no reference to Benjamin Shaw, and it thus appears that Benjamin – who had the right to vote – chose not to exercise his right.[120]

Other members of his family did vote. In 1807 there was a contest in which Joseph Hanson, a comparatively radical Mancunian, was brought in by those who opposed the comfortable coalition between the Whigs, represented by Lord Stanley, and the Tories represented by Samuel Horrocks. Benjamin's father, Joseph Shaw, clockmaker of Horrocks Square, and his father-in-law Edward Leeming, carder of New Preston, both voted for the victorious coalition candidates. In 1820 Joseph again voted for the coalition candidates, but

116   *Family Records*, pp. 4, 19.
117   ibid., p. 14.
118   ibid., p. 15.
119   ibid., pp. 12–13.
120   The poll books analysed were those for the elections in 1807, 1820, 1822 and 1830.

Benjamin's son Joseph, a labourer of Walker Street, and his brother-in-law Peter Leeming, weaver of Willow Street, both voted for the independent liberal, John Williams, and the celebrated radical, Henry 'Orator' Hunt, the hero of Peterloo.

The family was divided in its political beliefs. In the by-election of December 1830 Peter Leeming, Joseph Shaw (grinder, of Bowram Street) and his brother, Thomas Shaw (mechanic, of Friargate) all voted for Henry Hunt, who was elected: these three were, presumably, recipients of the silver victory medals issued by the Radicals to each of the 3,370 Prestonians who had voted for Hunt. But the other brother, William, a mechanic of 39 Pole Street, and Bella's husband William Roberts, a mechanic of 34 Pole Street, voted for Lord Stanley, the sitting member who had had to stand for re-election after accepting a Cabinet post. Even Benjamin's daughter Agnes might be claimed to have had political views – though in her case the shouting of the name of the Radical candidate while the Tories were canvassing Horrocks's works might well have been a product of her 'pert & saucy' character. Her espousal of the Radical cause did her no good – she lost her job.

From all this Benjamin apparently remained aloof, not joining his sons and in-laws at the polling booths. This is in keeping with his character, for the healthy independence of spirit which he displayed in his dealings with the Poor Law officials and his employers was strengthened by a generous measure of cynicism. Although he does not expressly say so, he surely considered most politicians to be the same under the skin, and to have been motivated by considerations other than altruism. His comments on the actions of governments, especially concerning taxation, indicate that he was not enamoured of any authority. The consequence is that while he did not support the status quo, he did not overtly sympathize with the Radicals either. There may have been elements of their philosophy which accorded with his own, but he viewed their quest for political power with deep suspicion. He was not that popular figure, the Lancashire working-class radical, but that common figure, the ordinary cynic.

The generally dispassionate, unemotional tone in which he records political events is in keeping with his attitude to much of his daily life – he was not an over-emotional man. The account of his religious beliefs shows that he was, for many years, lacking in interest and enthusiasm, in keeping with his general character. He was baptized an Anglican and retained that nominal faith until 1799, during which time religion apparently played no part in his life. All this was to change, and he describes at length a religious conversion which produces one of his rare examples of emotional writing. In 1799, talking to the Baptist preacher, Frank Lambert, and working for and among men who were adherents of Nonconformism, he began to think about religion and faith. With characteristic dryness he records how he 'pretended to defend the Church of England [and] prated much though I seldom went to church, but was much atatched to it for all that'.[121]

---

121 *Family Records*, p. 38.

This was a difficult period in Benjamin's life. Lameness and loneliness were growing, his marriage was troubled and he and Betty frequently disagreed about the running of the household. It was also the period in which intellectual interests were becoming more important to him. Since he could not get about easily he stayed at home, and passed his time with reading and thinking, so that he was especially receptive to the stimulation of religious debate. In the summer of 1799 he – 'an intire stranger to real religion' – began to attend Baptist meetings and to think deeply about his own sinfulness and lack of hope. He gave the Church of England a fair trial, attending St George's and other churches, but 'I found nothing that I wanted there'. He resolved, in October 1799, that even if he was to be lost as a sinner beyond redemption, he would be 'lost calling for Mercy'.[122]

This conversion was of profound importance, for his outlook on life was completely changed and he attained a peace of mind about his troubles. He 'read the Scriptures with great delight' and talked of religion with his father and wife, both of whom themselves 'received the . . . precious Blessing'. The account of the process of conversion indicates just how powerful the feeling must have been. Yet, writing about it a quarter of a century later, he includes a strong undercurrent of cynicism and questioning, and an implication that much of that feeling was by then in the past. Though Benjamin retained his religious beliefs, he was far less committed and enraptured than he had been. He notes how religious conversion does not necessarily mean a change in day-to-day behaviour: 'the person that is chainged in mind as to religion is nearly the same as to the managment of his [temporal] affairs'.[123]

This attitude derived specifically from observing how Betty, after a period of enthusiastic devotion to the new way, returned to her old financial fecklessness and how their relationship resumed its turbulent and unhappy course. It is iikely that Benjamin himself became disenchanted with organized religion, and with his new Nonconformist brethren. After his conversion in 1799 several of his children were baptized at the Methodist Society in Preston, but the last child, Agnes, was baptized at the parish church in 1813. The implication is that for some reason he no longer considered the Nonconformists to be satisfactory or appropriate. Further supporting evidence for a waning of enthusiasm is found by comparing his accounts of the two Preston Guilds. In 1802, a fervent devotee of the faith, he did nothing, 'such was my deadness to pastimes & austontation . . . such was my contemp for these things, that I would not pertake in the folly as I considered them to be'.[124] In 1822 there was no such condemnation, and details of the Guild and its events are given without any criticism. Benjamin no longer held the views of twenty years earlier: he had mellowed, or become disenchanted – perhaps both.

122 ibid., p. 39.
123 ibid., pp. 40–41.
124 ibid., pp. 43–44.

Introduction

His religious faith, after 1811 or 1812, appears to have become personal, albeit serious and genuine, rather than one which involved adherence to a particular church or group. He makes no further reference to his own participation in the Nonconformist churches in Preston, although he records in some detail the devotion of his daughter, Hannah, to the Methodist Society, and tells with great sympathy of how this served her well in the long and heartbreaking months during which she lay dying. A similar story was told about the death of his wife, Betty. She found immense comfort and consolation in the Bible and her prayer book, and the words which Benjamin reports her saying to her assembled family include the directive, 'above all get reliegion this is what can suport us in health & in Sickness without this we cannot die happy & life is uncertain'.[125] In this, as in other parts of her farewell speech, Benjamin probably puts into Betty's mouth sentiments which he himself believed.

Benjamin thus appears to have lost his commitment to an organized religion, while retaining a strong faith. That is in keeping with his character, for as an independent-minded and cynical individualist, solitary and introspective in his ways and wary of authority in any form, an organized church would have been uncongenial to him, while any church might itself have found Benjamin Shaw a very awkward member of its congregation.

Chronology of the life of Benjamin Shaw

Dec	1772	Born at Dent, West Riding of Yorkshire, son of Joseph and Isabella Shaw
	1773	Moves with family briefly to Kendal
Nov	1774	Birth of sister Hannah
Nov	1776	Birth of brother George
		Begins schooling with Peggy Winn in Dent
May	1779	Birth of brother William
Oct	1782	Birth of brother Joseph
		(approx) finishes school and begins to work with father
Apr	1786	Birth of sister Margaret
	1789	Birth of sister Isabella
May	1789	Last haytime visit to his grandparents in Garsdale
May	1790	Spends haytime at Ingleton with aunt Agnes Slinger
May	1791	Family moves to larger house in Dent town
Jul	1791	Moves with family to Dolphinholme
Aug	1791	Apprenticed as fitter and turner at the mill
		Meets future wife Betty Leeming
Aug	1791	Family leaves Dolphinholme after disagreement with manager, leaving Benjamin behind

125   ibid., p. 99.

	1792	Family returns to Dolphinholme
Apr	1792	Death of sister Isabella
May	1792	Death of brother Joseph
		(winter) leg injured by boy throwing stick
Oct	1792	Quarrel between Benjamin and Betty: she goes to live in Preston
Feb	1793	Benjamin visits Preston to see Betty
Mar	1793	(approx) Betty tells Benjamin of her pregnancy
Apr	1793	Death of brother George
May	1793	Family moves to Milnthorpe
Jun	1793	Death of sister Margaret
Sep	1793	Marries Betty Leeming at Lancaster
Nov	1793	Birth of eldest child Joseph
Jan	1795	Loses job at Dolphinholme and seeks work in local mills
Mar	1795	Moves to Preston to work for Horrocks's
May	1795	Parents move to Preston
Jul	1795	Birth of second child William
	1796	Unsuccessful visit to the Whitworth doctors
Apr	1798	Death of mother Isabella Shaw
	1799	Meets Frank Lambert, Baptist preacher, and is converted
May	1799	Birth of third child Isabella (Bella)
Mar	1800	Goes to work for Frank Sleddon
	1802	Father-in-law Edward Leeming moves to Preston
Jan	1803	Birth of fourth child Hannah
Sep	1805	Birth of fifth child Mary
Jul	1806	Death of baby daughter Mary
May	1807	Birth of sixth child Thomas
	1808	Lameness results in long periods off work
Nov	1808	Removed with family to Ellel by overseers
Jun	1809	Returns to Preston
Jan	1810	Registers with Preston Dispensary and is visited by subscribers and by doctor
Apr	1810	Right leg amputated
May	1811	Birth of seventh child Mary
Jul	1813	Birth of last child Agnes
Dec	1813	Marriage of son Joseph to Ann Walker
	1815	Son William has two illegitimate children by different women
Dec	1815	Resumes work part-time for first time since 1808
Apr	1817	Begins full-time work again
Aug	1817	Goes to work for John Welch, 'the worst master that I ever had'
Aug	1817	Marriage of son William to Sarah Coyle
Nov	1819	Daughter Bella has illegitimate son by William Roberts
Feb	1821	Daughter Hannah has illegitimate daughter by Samuel Whittle
Jun	1821	Death of father-in-law Edward Leeming
Jun	1822	Marriage of daughter Bella and William Roberts

Feb	1823	Death of father Joseph Shaw
Mar	1823	Daughter Hannah gives up work because of illness
Feb	1824	Death of Hannah after long decline
	1826	Writes first volume of *Family Records*
Aug	1826	Wife Betty falls ill
Oct	1826	Secret marriage of son Thomas and Ann Richardson; they live with Benjamin and Betty for some weeks
Aug	1827	Begins to sleep apart from Betty
Feb	1828	Death of Betty Shaw; Benjamin widowed
	1828	Frequently ill, with long periods off work
	1829	Begins writing second, annually updated, account of events
Jan	1829	(approx) Daughter Mary pregnant by Bob Smith
Sep	1829	Birth of Mary's child
Nov	1829	Marriage of daughter Mary to Bob Smith
Jan	1830	Mary and Bob Smith separate: she lives with Benjamin
Apr	1830	Daughter Agnes leaves home and goes to Manchester
Oct	1830	Death of son William, aged 35
Jun	1834	(approx) Bob and Mary Smith reconciled; he moves in to Benjamin's house
	1834	Benjamin off work for three months with ankle injury
Dec	1834	Bob and Mary Smith move out
	1835	Agnes returns from Manchester
Nov	1835	(approx) Agnes discharged from work because pregnant
Feb	1836	Birth of Agnes's daughter Betty
Aug	1836	Death of Agnes: Benjamin left alone with granddaughter Betty Last annual updating of second volume of *Family Records*
Apr	1841	Census records Benjamin living alone in Dale Street
Jun	1841	Death of Benjamin, aged 69, at son Joseph's house
Nov	1841	Joseph granted probate of Benjamin's estate

EDITORIAL NOTES

Abbreviations used in bibliography and footnotes

CRO   Cheshire Record Office
CROK   Cumbria Record Office (Kendal)
IGI   International Genealogical Index
LL   Lancaster Library
LPRS   Lancashire Parish Register Society
LRO   Lancashire Record Office
SDHS   Sedbergh & District History Society

Bibliography

The bibliography below gives secondary sources quoted, referred to or used in the introduction and footnotes.

Anderson, M. *Family Structure in Nineteenth Century Lancashire* (Cambridge Studies in Sociology, 5). Cambridge U.P., 1971.

Anon. *A Biographical Sketch of the Whitworth Doctors*. Rochdale, Rochdale Observer, 1876 [originally published in the *Rochdale Observer*, 22 April 1876].

Anon. 'History of Millthrop Mill' in *SDHS Occasional Newsletter*, 1, pp. 2–3 (Part 1) and 2, pp. 6–7 (Part 2), 1981.

Ashmore, O. *The Industrial Archaeology of Lancashire*. Newton Abbot, David & Charles, 1969.

Bingham, R.K. *The Chronicles of Milnthorpe*. Milnthorpe, Cicerone Press, 1987.

Boulton, D. 'Hallbank: the Story of a Country Workhouse' in *SDHS Occasional Newsletter*, 9, pp. 3–6 (Part 1) and 10, pp. 8–11 (Part 2), 1984.

Burnett, J. *Plenty and Want* (third edition). London, Routledge, 1989.

Cameron, K. *English Place-Names* (revised edition). London, Batsford, 1988.

Clark, C. *Historical and Descriptive Account of the Town of Lancaster*. Lancaster, Clark, 1807.

Crosby, A.G. *The History of Preston Guild*. Preston, Lancashire County Books, 1991.

'Cross Fleury' (R.E.K. Rigbye). *Time-honoured Lancaster: Historic Notes on the Ancient Borough of Lancaster*. Lancaster, Eaton & Bulfield, 1891.

Dakres, J. *The Last Tide: a History of the Port of Preston*. Preston, Carnegie Press, 1986.

d'Cruze, S. *Care, Diligence and 'Usfull Pride': Gender, Industrialisation and the Domestic Economy, c.1770-c.1840*. Unpublished working paper, 1990.

Hall, P.P. 'A History of the Dolphinholme Worsted Mill 1784 to 1867' in *Trans. Fylde Hist. Soc.*, 3, 1969.

Hewitson, A. *History of Preston*. Preston, Preston Chronicle, 1883.

Hollett, C.G. 'The Woollen Industry in Sedbergh' in *SDHS Occasional Newsletter*, 6, pp. 24–6, 1983.

Holt, G. *The North West* (Regional History of the Railways of Great Britain, volume 10) (revised edition). Newton Abbot, David & Charles, 1986.

Lancashire General Directory [T. Rogerson]. Manchester, 1818.

Lancashire Parish Register Society, 71 (1933): *The Registers of Ingleton and Chapel-le-Dale 1607–1812*.

Lancashire Parish Register Society, 73 (1935): *Warton Parish Church Registers 1568–1812*.

Lancaster, K.J. 'Mines and Quarries on Baugh Fell' in *The Sedbergh Historian*, 2 no. 4, pp. 15–20, 1989.

Morgan, N. *Vanished Dwellings: Early Industrial Housing in a Lancashire Cotton Town – Preston* (first edition). Preston, privately published, 1988.

Oakes, E.C. *Water Supplies Through Three Centuries*. Preston, Preston Corporation, 1953.

Pigot (J.) & Co. *National Commercial Directory for 1828–9*. Manchester, 1828.

Price, J.W.A. *The Industrial Archaeology of the Lune Valley*. University of Lancaster Centre for North West Regional Studies, Occasional Paper 13, 1983.

Sedgwick, A. *Adam Sedgwick's Dent* [reprint of *A Memorial by the Trustees of Cowgill Chapel* (1868) and *Supplement to the Memorial* (1870), with new Introduction and Notes by David Boulton]. Sedbergh and Dent, privately published, 1984.

Spencer, W.M. (ed.) *The Parochial Chapelry of Colne Burial Register 1790–1812*. Colne, privately published, 1968.

Spencer, W.M. (ed.) *The Parochial Chapelry of Colne Register of Baptisms and Burials 1774–1789*. Colne, privately published, 1969.

Textile Mercury. *'Mercury' Dictionary of Textile Terms*. Manchester, 1950.

West, J.L. *The Taylors of Lancashire: Bonesetters and Doctors*. Walkden, H. Duffy, 1977.

Whittle, P. *Topographical, Statistical and Historical Account of the Borough of Preston* (second edition). Preston, 1837.

Wilkinson, J. *Preston's Royal Infirmary: a History of Health Care in Preston 1809–1986*. Preston, Carnegie Press, 1987.

Editorial Conventions

The following conventions have been followed in the editing of the text of the two volumes of Benjamin Shaw's writings:

Paragraphs   The original texts are almost without paragraph divisions, and except in a handful of instances where there are logical breaks (such as the beginning of a new group of biographical accounts) the text is a continuous narrative. For this edition it has therefore been broken up into paragraphs of convenient and conventional length. Whenever possible these have been chosen to separate distinct sections of text, and particularly to emphasize the division between personal and local history, and the national and political dates and events. All paragraphs breaks which do not appear in the original text are indicated by an asterisk * at the start of the paragraph.

Punctuation Benjamin Shaw's punctuation is highly idiosyncratic and personal, with very extensive use of the characters '&c' instead of full stops, and with numerous dashes and ampersands. This style of punctuation is in itself important and of interest, and to render it in modern form would greatly alter the sense, character and feel of his writing. The original punctuation is therefore reproduced unchanged. The character of Benjamin's handwriting means that distinguishing between full stops and commas is often impossible. In ambiguous cases I have used commas, since these allow greater sense to be made of the text.

Spelling and letter forms All spelling conforms exactly to the original text, and no alterations or expansions have been made. Benjamin wrote in a very small hand with, for some letters, little differentiation between upper and lower case forms: c and s are the most difficult to distinguish. Some ambiguities and uncertainties remain, but doubtful cases have not been indicated since in no instance do they have any effect upon the sense of the word. The use of *sic* has been avoided whenever possible, but there are a number of words which Benjamin spells very oddly: in these cases *sic* has been added to make it clear that these are not typographical errors.

Inserted phrases In a few places I have inserted words where they must have been intended by Benjamin but were omitted by him. The insertions are necessary to make the sense of the narrative clear. In some places Benjamin himself went through sections of text at a later date, and added phrases or words. In both these circumstances the additions are marked by square brackets [ ] and a footnote has been included to indicate whether this is an author's or editor's addition.

Political and current affairs sections The material in the text which relates to political and national events is derived from published sources such as newspapers and almanacs. It was included by Benjamin because he was deeply interested in current affairs and politics. It may also have been his intention to provide a comparative chronology against which to set the events happening within his own family. This information is of only limited interest for its own sake in the present context, and it has not therefore been edited except where the events described relate directly to Preston and district and so to Benjamin's own experience. In the footnotes no explanation is given of the national and international events mentioned, except in a few cases where the spelling is so unclear as to make a note essential.

Record Office references   Full Record Office references to manuscript source material are given, but no list or bibliography of documents is included.

Family trees   The family trees have been compiled to show every member of the Shaw, Noddle and Leeming families who is mentioned in the text. In these, as in the footnotes, there has been no attempt to continue the story of these people beyond 1841, the year of Benjamin Shaw's own death. Thus, the 1841 census for Preston has been used to show the state of a number of families at that time, but no later material has been checked. Neither have the details of the deaths of, for example, Benjamin's sister Hannah or his daughter Mary been sought. The tracing of the families in previous generations has been limited to those people who are mentioned by Benjamin, and their children. I have not attempted to trace the earlier ancestry of these families since to do so would add nothing to the interpretation of the *Family Records* and is beyond the scope of this edition.

BENJAMIN SHAW'S FAMILY RECORDS

Benjamin Shaw's Family Records &c A Short Account of Benjamin Shaw and his Family &c with some Short Scetches of his ancesters written by himself in 1826

Partly for his own use & Partly for his Children

After his time

&c &c &c

Preston   May the 31   1826

No. 1 Dale Street

Lancashire

Preface

to know something of our ancesters, has allways appeared to have been a desirable thing to me, and if any records had been handed down to me, I should have considered it as a Vallueable treasure – but I have not been so fortunate as to know any thing of my family, but what I remember to have heard, by word of mouth, or seen, and as I have very few helps, my account must be very imperfact, but in the following Pages, I have put down a few broken, and imperfect hints, from memory partly, & partly from a few notes kept by me, for my own use, mostly of the latest dates, mentioned, &c – I have not attempted to deceive any that may read this account, by falsehoods or by selecting those circumstances that might make the most favourable appearance – but I have simply attempted to state facts, whether hounourable or shameful – as I consider truth the most valueble ingredient in any History or Biographycal account – and as all men have their weakness & failings when I see any writer give us an account of men all fair & faltless, & every thing that is good, and amiable, I allways suspect that the author has only toly [*sic*] us a part of the truth, through partialaty or a wish to set the person decribed in the fairest light &c &c
Benjamin Shaw June 7th 1826 Preston

1

Some account of my ancestors

What I know of my ancestors is either what I have seen or remember to have heard from some of our relations and as I never wrote any thing with any intent to preserve any records of any of them my account must be very imperfect – the farest that I can go back is to my great grandfather and of him I can say but little his name was Richard Shaw but when he was Born or died I cannot tell[1] he lived at a place called Smorthwate Hill[2] in the township of grassdale[3] in the Parrish of Sedburgh in the west Riding of Yorkshire – he lived in a pleasant place near the Center of the dale and close to the road that goes from Sedburgh to a town called Haws – it seems he was in the farming line & in easy circumstances as he gave his sons good Education – he had 3 Sons that lived in the same township untill they were old men[4] their Names was Benjamin & Joseph which were twins & Edward the youngest[5] – the twins were good Scollers Joseph got a part of his living by teaching writing & accounts & was Clark at the chapel a long time died in that office[6] he married & had too children which grew up the son Edward Shaw was Educated for a parson & got a place at Barbon near Kirby lonsdale & married a woman deaf & dumb or nearly so[7] – the daughter never married that I know of

1   Richard Shaw married Margaret Hodgson at Garsdale on 24 August 1696, and was buried at Garsdale on 5 June 1744 (CROK: WPR/60/1). He lived at several farms during his married life: Pinfold (1696); Paradise (1697); Woodend (1700); Roger Pot (from at least 1708, and where he was living when he made his will in 1737); and finally Thursgill (where he died). All these are within half a mile of each other, in the vicinity of Smorthwaite and the present hamlet of Garsdale.
2   Smorthwaite, on the north bank of the river just west of the hamlet of Garsdale.
3   Garsdale
4   Richard Shaw's will was made on 17 November 1737 and proved on 29 June 1744 (LRO: WRW(L) 1744 Richard Shaw of Garsdale). It names four sons – James, Edward, Joseph and Benjamin – and his wife Margaret; Joseph Shaw was the sole executor, although the administration bond also names Benjamin. The Garsdale chapelry register shows that Richard had other children, including John, baptized on 12 December 1696, and Richard, baptized on 13 November 1697 (CROK: WPR/60/1). John was still alive at the making of his father's will although he is not mentioned in it. James Shaw of Roger Pot and Joseph Shaw of Paradise administered the estate of their late brother, John Shaw, singing master, with probate granted 15 January 1742/3 (LRO: WRW(L) 1742 John Shaw of Garsdale).
5   The Garsdale chapelry register records the baptisms of John (12 December 1696); Richard (13 November 1697); James (5 February 1700); Edward (23 September 1702); Joseph and Benjamin (30 November 1708). Edward was therefore not the youngest of the sons, as Benjamin suggests (CROK: WPR/60/1).
6   Joseph Shaw was clerk of the chapel at Garsdale from approximately 1735 until 1795, when he was succeeded by John Watson, the husband of his niece Isabel Watson. Throughout the sixty years in which he served the chapel he appears as a signatory to documents, and witnessed many marriages after the introduction of the printed registers in 1754. He married Margaret Nelson on 26 April 1729. She was buried on 27 January 1740 and on 28 October 1744 he was married again, to Ann Raw. He was buried at Garsdale chapel on 11 September 1802, aged ninety-three, having outlived his second wife by thirty-four years (CROK: WPR/60/1 and 60/2).
7   There are few eighteenth-century records for the ancient chapel at Barbon, but Benjamin is correct in stating that his father's cousin had been a clergyman there. Edward Shaw was baptized at Garsdale on 20 September 1755 (CROK: WPR/60/1). He was ordained deacon by

Benjamin Shaw my grandfather the other twin &c was twice married his first wife[s] name was Jain or Jeny, they had 3 sons & 1 daughter which all lived to have familys – Richard & Benjamin & John & Peggy[8] – my grandfather made all three sons weavers which they followed all their lives for their living Richard & Benjamin settled in Kendal & Both died there Richard had a great family & Benjamin had only one daughter that servised him – John the youngest son settled in Kirby Stephen & I think died there this John had 4 wives 3 of which had no children the fourth had several[9] – Peggy marryed & Settled in Durham but I know little more of her[10] – my grandfather it is reported & I partly believe it was rather unhappy in his first marrige – it is sade that his wife was a very cleanly woman but not a mannishing[11] person so they were poor – his seccond wife (my grandmother) was born at Sedburgh her name was Hannah Handelow[12] the daughter of William Handelow of that town –

---

the bishop of Chester at the parish church of Ashbourne, Derbyshire, on 2 January 1780; and ordained priest at Chester Cathedral on 5 August 1781. On the same day he was licensed to the perpetual curacy of Barbon on the recommendation of Rev. Marwood Place, vicar of Kirkby Lonsdale and patron of the living. Edward Shaw's resignation from the curacy of Barbon, for reasons unspecified, was accepted on 1 October 1789, and there is no further reference to him in the Chester diocesan records (CRO: EDA/1/8 pp. 31, 61, 64 and 197).

The register of Killington chapel, four miles NNW of Barbon, records the marriage on 17 November 1784 of the Reverend Edward Shaw, Curate of Barbon, and Mary Sampson, spinster of the same place (CROK: WPR/34/2). The marriage licence bond gives the ages of the parties (27 years and 30 years respectively) but no other information (LRO: ARR 11/1784). Edward and Mary Shaw had only one known child: a son, Joseph, was born on 16 December 1784 and baptized at Kirkby Lonsdale on 17 January 1785 (CROK: WPR/19/3).

8   The Garsdale chapelry register records the marriage of Benjamin Shaw and Jane Plummer, both of Garsdale, on 3 May 1731. Their children were all baptized there: Richard (21 March 1732); Margaret (August 1733 – the day is omitted); John (11 September 1735); Joseph (15 November 1737, buried 15 May 1738); Benjamin (17 August 1741, buried 29 October 1741); Benjamin (12 February 1744). The burial of Jane, wife of Benjamin Shaw, is noted on 22 February 1746 (CROK: WPR/60/1).

9   John Shaw married Elizabeth Parkin on 2 June 1759, and Eleanor Edmondson on 9 June 1772, on both occasions at Garsdale (CROK: WPR/60/2). On 12 June 1780, a widower aged 44, he married Isabel Turner, a widow of thirty-five, at Kirkby Stephen (CROK: WPR/77/6). The only child definitely known to be theirs, Margaret, was baptized at Kirkby Stephen on 9 November 1783, and she and her mother were both buried on 14 November (CROK: WPR/77/7). A different John Shaw married Isabel Hutchinson at Kirkby Stephen in November 1780, and it is unclear, in the cases of Isabel (baptized 1781) and John (baptized 1782), which set of parents was involved.

John's fourth marriage was at Ravenstonedale on 30 August 1788, to Dorothy Haygarth of that parish (CROK: WPR/6/3). They had two children: Margaret (baptized at Kirkby Stephen 12 February 1791) and Mary (baptized 7 September 1794). In both baptism entries John is described as a weaver, and Dorothy is recorded as 'late Haygarth, formerly Parrington' (CROK: WPR/77/8).

10 Peggy Shaw did not marry in Garsdale or an adjacent parish, and her subsequent history is unknown.

11 managing

12 'Handley' in parish register entries.

* my Grandfather had by this wife 3 Sons & 2 daughter – their mames [*sic*] were Joseph (my father Born 1748) & William twinns Isabella – & Edward & Mary of which I shall say something hearafter[13] – my grandfathe [*sic*] followed manufactureing wooling good (that is Carding Spinning & Knitting Stocking, mittons, Socks, Scotch bonnets & Duch-hats, Calmanack[14] Caps &c &c, – my grandmother took an active part in this work & the Children were kept close to work & by their dilligence they saved a little notwithstanding their family,[15] they first Bought a Cottage & lived in it & after wards took a small Farm & Sald their House to Stock it &c & continued to farm as long as they were able to Manage it, my grandfather was born about the year 1712 his wife was younger he died about the year 1792 aged 80 years his wife lived a little longer[16] – he was in his person Strong built but not tall dark hair & a longish face &c my grandmother was but a Small weakly woman but healthy & very Spiritful in her Temper – when young very fair complectioned her Hair red or sandy Coulerd She died 1793

* my grandfather's Brother Edward Shaw was never married yet lived untill he was old this man lived a Soletery life by himself employed in Knitting mostly & labouring Sometimes – but was much given to gaming &c &c he lived very Poor & lied [*sic*][17] in the workhouse my grandfather was a Stanch churchman and a constant goer to church[18] – his Hobby was Books was a great reeder & writer – told a Story well – loved a little Ale – yet not a drunken man – he was not much of a Machanic or workman, had a poor notion of doing anything in this way &c &c – could not reconcile himself to poverty yet died poor chiefly on the account of old age & the bad management of his Childre – a bout a year or a little more before he died some sort of a fit took him and from that time he never recovered his reason was disposed to ramble away – was a deal of trouble to watch and keep at home &c

.

13   The marriage of Benjamin Shaw and Hannah Handley, both of Garsdale, took place there on 26 February 1747. Their children were baptized at Garsdale: Joseph and William (13 February 1748); Isabel (11 March 1750); Edward (23 May 1752); Mary (31 October 1754) (CROK: WPR/60/1).
14   *Calamanco* is a woollen material woven with one side plain and one striped or checked, often ribbed. The alternative, and more probable, interpretation is that the word is *Kilmarnock*. The phrase 'Kilmarnock caps' was employed in the local woollen industry to refer to flat caps which were knitted and then felted to render them waterproof (Hollett, p. 25).
15   notwithstanding the size of the family
16   The Garsdale chapelry register records the burial of Benjamin Shaw of Middlesmithy, aged 85, a pauper, on 21 January 1794. Hannah Shaw of Middlesmithy, aged 84, was buried on 29 August 1797 (CROK: WPR/60/1).
17   This could mean 'lived', or 'lied' in the sense of staying, but 'died' is almost certainly intended: the Sedbergh parish register records the burial of 'Edward Shaw out of the Poorhouse' aged 76 years, on 30 September 1776 (CROK: WPR/59/3).
18   In 1734 Benjamin Shaw served as a chapelwarden at Garsdale in substitution for Richard Nelson (CROK: WPR/60/1).

Of my father Joseph Shaw & family

Joseph Shaw Son of Benjamin & Hannah Shaw was Born January 17th 1748 in grassdale & at the same Birth his twin Brother William. Joseph was the older & fell to the care of his father as his his [*sic*] mother could not manage them both – they lived at a place called the Scarr end – I know but little of his youth but that he was employed in the family in the wooling work as soon as he could do anything when he was about 10 or 11 years old he was put apprintice to a weaver which was thought a good trade then – he served 9 years to this trade with Richard Cornthwate in Westmorland, he lived in differant townships but the last was Preston Richard & got his Settlement there[19] – when he was out of his time[20] he came into grassdale where he was Born and worked at his trade there – here he became a quainted with my mother who lived then at Dent about 4 miles from where he lived – her name was Isabella Noddle daughter of George & Peggy Noddle and they were married June 24th 1771[21]

* they went to House at Dent and 18 months after she brought forth her first born son in a Cottage at Hallbank $\frac{1}{2}$ a mile from the town of Dent[22] & called him Benjamin Shaw (the writer of this) on the 23rd of December 1772 at 10 oclock forenoon (and I dare say they never forgot this event for they had a good deal of trouble with me) and in nearly 2 year after my sister Hannah – the next was Gorge, about this time my father began to turn his atention towards Clocks, he bought one and pulled it in pieces & cleaned it & examined it & thought he

---

19 His legal place of settlement under the Poor Laws was at Preston Richard, a small township four miles south of Kendal in the parish of Heversham. The only village in the township was Endmoor, where Joseph's son William was to be apprenticed as a blacksmith a quarter of a century later. No apprenticeship record for Joseph Shaw can be traced.
20 had completed his apprenticeship
21 Joseph Shaw of Garsdale and Isabel Noddel of Dent were married on 24 June 1771 at Dent. The witnesses were William Shaw and Richard Tunstall; the groom signed, but the bride made her mark (CROK: WPR/70/3). The spelling of the surname Noddle in contemporary documents is extremely variable.
22 Hallbank was a farm which in 1733 had been hired by the overseers of poor for Dent township 'for the lodgeing, Dyeting, and Employing of the poor'. It was therefore the Dent township workhouse. Benjamin states that he was born in a cottage at Hallbank, although he later simply refers to it as 'a place called Hallbank'. By the time he was nine months old his family had moved from Dent to Kendal, to work in the weaving trade, but they returned shortly afterwards and when he was about four years old they again went to live at Hallbank. There they occupied what Benjamin calls 'a house in the same yard where I was born'.
    This confirms that there were other dwellings as well as the workhouse (the former Hallbank farmhouse). As Benjamin showed no hesitation in referring to such issues as poverty and illegitimacy it might reasonably be argued that he would not deliberately have concealed his being born in the workhouse. Conceivably he did not know that it *was* the workhouse, but that seems unlikely. It is therefore possible that the cottage in which he was born was not the workhouse itself but an adjacent building, part of the same farm hamlet. An account of the Hallbank workhouse is given by Boulton.

could manage to Clean Clocks got some tools set of in search of work in that line, – yet followed weaving some times afterwards he got a quainted with some men in the neibourhood that were curious & they first sceamed one thing then another my father after some time became noted for jobing in clocks guns-locks, locks & all sort of work he got a Vice & lathe & did turning & fileing work &c, he Shifted into the town, Sometimes he wove A Piece or too sometimes went of into the countery a clock dressing & Stoped 2 or 3 weeks at a time –

* his family still increased By this time William & Peggy was Born, my mother was employed in winding when he was weaving and in knitting Stockings or Spinning worsted for stockings or stuff gowns &c which was the common employ at that place she learned and kept us children to this work constantly this helped my fathers earnings a little – in this way things went on – my mother bringing a child every too years nearly so that about the year 1791 they had 7 children[23] – about this time some of our neighbours came to Dolphinholme in Wiresdale to a worsted factory there[24] & cotton mills begun to Spread all over the countery, at this time miles Burton a Carter[25] a native of our town[26] came over to Dent to seek hands [to go][27] to Dolphinholme and told a fine tale what good wages we could get, inclined many to go there to work – the master M[r] Edmonson[28] came to our town & hired many familys & among the number our family &c my father

23   The children of Joseph and Isabella Shaw were Benjamin (baptized Dent 23 December 1772); Hannah (baptized Garsdale 27 November 1774); George (baptized Dent 10 November 1776); William (baptized Dent 23 May 1779); Joseph (baptized Dent 27 October 1782); Margaret (baptized Dent 9 April 1786); Isabella (baptism not traced: there is no record of it at Dent or Garsdale – she was born circa 1789); and a stillborn child born at Milnthorpe, Westmorland, in 1793 (CROK: WPR/70/4 and 60/1).

24   Dolphinholme mill on the River Wyre, 5½ miles SSE of Lancaster, was originally a corn mill. In 1784 (Hall, p. 2 and Price, p. 22) or about 1787 (Ashmore, p. 266) it was converted for spinning worsted yarn, and is claimed to have been the first worsted spinning factory in the world. It survived, through numerous vicissitudes, until final closure in 1867. The mill was in the bottom of a deep steep-sided valley, and in the late 1780s a new village of millworkers' housing, 'the best early example of a local mill community' (Price, p. 22) began to develop on the flatter land at the top of the slopes north of the mill. Dolphinholme was the largest and earliest mechanically operated mill in north Lancashire, employing 1000 spinners and 200 outworkers in 1809.

25   A carter, in this context, was a man who carried the products of cottage industry, such as knitted goods or partly-finished cloth, to a factory or collecting point.

26   There were several people called Miles Burton in Dentdale in the mid-eighteenth century, but it is possible this was the one who married Jane Willan there in 1761. If so, there is a certain irony in the fact that, having persuaded his former neighbours to leave their homes and go to work at Dolphinholme, Miles Burton himself apparently returned to Dent. He was buried there in April 1807, when he was described as 'school-master' (CROK: WPR/70/2, 3 and 4).

27   Added subsequently by the author.

28   The mill at Dolphinholme was converted to textile production by three Lancaster men who formed a partnership: Edmondson, Addison and Satterthwaite (Ashmore, p.266). Thomas Edmondson was a prosperous Lancaster ironmonger who had substantial surplus capital, but little is known of his partners. They took a 61-year lease on the site and water rights from the

& family left our native town [& shifted to Dolphinholme][29] in July 1791 –, but some differance took place between my father & Edmonson in a little time after my father was discharged but the family was employed the master sent for me & told me that I must be aprintice or have no work I agreed with him for 3 years for 8 Shillings[30] for too years & 9 for the 3rd and was bound August 4th 1791 to be a filer & turner in the machene shop – my father got work again but not in the machanic[s] shop & we lived alltogether at this place about 18 months or perhaps 20 months

* this was the most troublesom part of my father[s] life in this short time his Son george Sickened & died of a consumption about 15 years old, my father had a bad Fever & was long down, my Brother Joseph got his hand Catched in the factory, lost one finger & was much Cut & mangled – after that he sickend & died aged 11 or 12 years – after this a little girl called Bellow[31] took the fever & died they were all buried at Cockerham[32] – all this time my mother had trouble enough, for she was oppressed with the Cronick rhumatism so that she had nearly Lost the use of her limbs, now the masters began to quarrel and the hands was turned of & my father[s] family among the number, they went to Aconthwaite green, near milthrop[33] & left me at Dolphinholme aprintice, I got Boarding with Hannah fleming – after this my Brother William was bound aprintice to Lenard gibson, then at the End-moor near Kendal to a Blacksmith, my father lived here sometime & had the 8th child born here, but it was dead – here his daughter Peggy died, and was buried at Heasom church[34] – he next shifted to Milthrop, & wove seccing for a living[35] here he lived untill may 1795 when he went to Preston

---

Duke of Hamilton, the lord of the manor, and built a mill which was upstream of the Dolphinholme road bridge (the post-1810 mill was below the bridge). The partnership failed in 1794 and the mill was sold to Thomas Hinde, a Lancaster merchant, who continued the business (Hall, p. 4 *et seq.*). That a number of Dent families went to Dolphinholme in 1791 is corroborated by the existence among the Ellel township records of a removal order dated April 1792 for Edward Robinson, his wife Jane and their three children to be sent back to Dent from Ellel (LRO: PR/2942/4/4).

29 Added subsequently by the author.
30 The rate of pay per week.
31 Isabella or Bella.
32 Cockerham parish register records the burials of Isabella, daughter of Joseph Shaw of Ellel (27 April 1792); Joseph, son of Joseph Shaw of Ellel (1 May 1792); and George, son of Joseph Shaw of Ellel (2 April 1793) (LRO: PR/1371).
33 Ackenthwaite Green, near Milnthorpe, Westmorland. The family moved to Milnthorpe between 2 April 1793 (when Benjamin's brother, George, was buried at Cockerham) and 28 June 1793 (when his sister, Margaret, was buried at Heversham).
34 Heversham, Westmorland. The parish register records the burial of Margaret, daughter of Joseph Shaw of Ackenthwaite, aged 6, on 28 June 1793 (CROK: WPR/8/20).
35 Joseph was weaving sacking. There were several mills on the River Bela at Milnthorpe, and this minor port and small market town was a centre for the production of rope, twine, canvas and sacking in the late eighteenth and early nineteenth centuries. It is likely that Joseph Shaw was employed by Thomas Huddleston, the licensee of the *White Lion*, who from the late 1780s

to live (where Benj[n] was living then[36]) here he ingaged for a year to learn to spin with Paul Catteral at the factory in moor lane[37] – at the years end he went to M[r] horrockes yard to spin & wrought there untill he was turned of he worked here about 18 or 20 months he lived in a room rear[38] horrocks gates at yard[39]

* in the Spring his wife died on good friday 1798 when he left Spining he began to travle in the countery dresing & repairing clocks which he did untill he died nearly[40] – he kept his room Sometime living by himself Sometimes his daughter hannah lived with him, & sometime, about the year 1797 while his wife was living, She lefft them & went to Dolphinholme to work, here she got married to one Isiac Walker, a wool comber, but he hired into the Lancashire Millitia, Soon after & She came home, by him she had a child, & about the year 1799 or soon in 1800 he died and the child in a while after & she got married again to Henry Jackson,[41] my father about the year 1799 I think began to feel & see his need of inward Religion, began to go more frequently to church & chapples & in 1800 found that peace with god that makes life more happy & death less dreadfull, after this he lived with his daughter hannah sometimes and sometimes by himself & followed traveling mostly – he joined the methodist Society in 1800[42] but some

---

was 'engaged in rope making, sacks and cloth weaving, in his two twine walks and a large weaving shed' (Bingham, pp. 156–65).

36 The author, Benjamin Shaw.

37 Paul Catterall, cotton master and manufacturer, was a leading figure in the business and industrial life of Preston for many years. He operated the factory at the junction of Moor Lane and Walker Street, the first cotton mill in the town, which had been opened in 1777 by Collinson and Watson.

38 near

39 John Horrocks, the most celebrated of all the cotton merchants of Preston, was born at Edgworth near Bolton in 1768. He came to Preston in 1791 and opened his first factory in Turks Head Yard, off Church Street. Through a succession of shrewd business dealings and a remarkable entrepreneurial flair he rose rapidly to become the most important and richest manufacturer in the town. Later in 1791 he opened the 'Yellow Factory' in Dale Street at the east end of Church Street. In the next ten years several other factories were built by him in different parts of the town. In 1802 he became M.P. for Preston, but died in March 1804 when still only thirty-six.
     Joseph Shaw went to work at the 'Yellow Factory' – apparently so called because of its yellowish limewashed exterior. It was alternatively known as the 'Yard Works', a name which was eventually applied collectively to all four great factories on the site. Horrocks encouraged the building of workers' housing around the factory, and it was this which led to the development of the first suburb to the east of the old town, the district known as New Preston which is referred to several times by Benjamin Shaw. The Yellow Factory itself was at the end of the same short street in which Benjamin lived, and the houses were literally in its shadow.

40 almost up to the time of his death

41 A detailed account of the life of Hannah Jackson (née Shaw, formerly Walker) is given by Benjamin later in the work.

42 The Methodist Society in Preston was founded in 1777 and flourished in the 1780s and 1790s. It outgrew the original place of worship and meeting (a house in the town centre) and in 1787 a chapel was built in Back Lane, the road which ran parallel to and east of Friargate to the north

years after he went to the Independants[43] & continued with them untill he died –
About the year 1816 his son in law Jackson[44] at the begining of this year got to be
Clark at a new church caled trinity church in Preston[45] & Joseph Shaw got the
office of Church Cleaner which he kept many years

* in the year 1822 hannah his daughter had saved as much money as to build a
house they got a piece of land in the park[46] & in may began to build Joseph took
the oversight of this house & wrought at it himself Sometimes above his strength
then sat down & rested & got cold & was ill & had been used to travel constantly
& now Stoping at home he began to be quite stiff in his joints & lame & from this
time declined dayly – in october he shifted to Jacksons[47] – Sold some of his goods
&c &c by december he could not go out he continued to live, untill the 10th of
February 1823 then died aged 75 years 3 weeks & 3 days,[48] he had lived in
Preston near 28 years & had been a widdower 25 years – Joseph Shaw was about
5 foot 8 inches high when young his hair light brown or dark flaxen his beard red
his eyes grey his legs not very well shaped & his feet spred out too much – he was
not very fluent of Speech – spook with some difequilty Read & wrote Slowly,
was rather Pationate, he was sober, frugal, & temperate, most but when he
made a feast bountiful to a Blome[49] &c

* my grandmother Hannah Shaw had 3 sisters, all Younger than herself, these all

---

43 of the market place. This chapel was itself replaced in 1817 by the present imposing Classical
chapel in Lune Street. Joseph Shaw joined the Methodist Society as a result of Benjamin's own
conversion in the same year.

43 The first Independent Chapel in Preston was built in 1772, although there had been
Independent congregations in the town for at least three-quarters of a century before then. In
about 1780 the congregation moved to a room in the Old Shambles, and in September 1790 a
new and purpose-built chapel was opened at the corner of Fishergate and Chapel Street. This,
in turn, became inadequate and was replaced in 1826 by a chapel at the bottom of Cannon
Street.

44 Henry Jackson, husband of Hannah (Walker) Shaw.

45 Holy Trinity Church, in Great Shaw Street on the northern edge of the town centre, was built
in 1815 and was sponsored by many gentlemen and notables of Preston society. It was 'at one
time the most influentially attended or patronised place of worship in the town' (Hewitson,
p. 476). Declining prestige and central area depopulation meant that by the late nineteenth
century the church was no longer required. It has now been demolished.

46 The 'park' was the area of undeveloped land which lay to the north of the eastern end of
Church Street, adjacent to the growing suburb of New Preston and south east of St Paul's
Church (opened 1825). The 'park' was gradually built over in the 1820s and 1830s, and Park
Road was laid out at the same time: this has now been transformed into the eastern end of
Ringway. Henry and Hannah Jackson lived at the end of Newton Street.

47 went to live with Henry and Hannah Jackson

48 Joseph Shaw of Park Lane, Preston, aged 76, was buried at Preston St John on 12 February
1823 (LRO: PR/1476).

49 The punctuation here is confusing. The sentence should read: 'he was sober, frugal and
temperate most, but when he made a feast, bountiful to a *blame*' (generous to a fault).

carried their maden name to their grave, for none of them were maried their names were, Mary, Ruth, & Denny Handlow, these all lived together the later part of their lives I cannot remember much about them but that they lived at Sedburgh where they were born, & died there,[50] Mary & Ruth uere spare & thin, but Denny the youngest was very fat, I think near 3 times the weight of my Grandmother, She had lived in Sirvice the greater part of her life, mostly a Cook, Ruth took the natural Small Pox when she was above 60 years old, & recovered, they all lived to a great age, they followed knitting Stockings gloves, gamashes,[51] mittons, &c &c, for a living which was the common employment of the poor at that time, there

my Mothers Parents george & Peggy Noddle

my mother, Isabella Shaw, whoes maden name was Noddle, was daughter of George & Peggy Noddle – George Noddle my grandfathe was was [sic] [not][52] a native of Dent for anything that I know,[53] however they Settled there, after my grandmother and him were married,[54] She was a Native of Swodale,[55] So called from the river Swow that falls into the Owse, & runs down by York into the Jerman Oceon at Hull, this Dale is in the north riding of Yorkshire (her name was Eleshaw &c) famous for lead mines &c, they had 7 children that grew up &

---

50 Although Benjamin states that the sisters were from Sedbergh, they were in fact baptized at Garsdale chapel. William Handley of Garsdale married Isabel Bousfield of Ravenstonedale at Garsdale on 17 November 1705. Their children were Anna (a form of 'Hannah': born 1706, died 1707); Mary (baptized 10 January 1708); William (baptized 22 August 1709, married Mary Morland at Garsdale in 1735); Ruth (baptized 3 November 1711); Hannah (baptized 21 November 1713, married Benjamin Shaw at Garsdale 26 February 1747); and Philip (baptized 11 May 1716). Benjamin makes no reference to his grandmother's brothers, William and Philip Handley. The baptism of 'Denny' has not been found, and it is not clear what her real name was (CROK: WPR/60/1).

51 Leggings or gaiters worn over stockings in inclement weather or in muddy places.

52 The sense of the text requires 'not' at this point.

53 George Noddle was a native of Garsdale. He was baptized there on 5 December 1715, the son of James Noddle. His brothers and sister were James (baptized 24 February 1703); John (9 June 1705); Agnes (25 May 1707) and Robert (4 December 1709) (CROK: WPR/60/1). The marriage of James Noddle has not been found: it was not in the Dent-Sedbergh-Kirkby Lonsdale district.

54 The Dent township records include the settlement certificate of George and Margaret Noddle and their eldest child, Marian. It was issued by the township of Garsdale on 27 April 1741, and in it George is described as a husbandman. Marian had been baptized at Dent in 1740, so George and Peggy must have moved to the neighbouring valley soon after their marriage in May 1739. The issuing of a settlement certificate, sent to the authorities in Dent, implies that the Dent overseer thought the family likely to become a charge on the poor rate, and he therefore required a promise of indemnity from Garsdale (CROK: WPR/70/04/27).

55 Swaledale, river Swale

married[56] – 3 of which are now living (May 1826) they might have more but if they had they died young, their names were James first William, Isabella (my mother) nanny, Robert & maryann & mally, (of thes I shall say something hereafter) George Noddle was a Badger as they called them there, or a dealer in grain &c he kepe a few Horses, & attended the Haws & Kirby lonsdale markets – he died about 40 years old[57] & left my grandmother with 7 children or more & some of them very young –

* however she did not marry again – but fought[58] them up &c the older lads went to Service,[59] & the younger to Scool, untill they were able to go to Service (for none of them got any trades[60]) She lived in the town of Dent, & Sold meal &c, after her children got up & married or went to Service She lived by herself, & knit Stockings & on the market day, used to measure meal for the farmers, or to sell pottatoes, Carrots, Peas, Beans, &c when she was old, She got the widdow toopence (as they colled it (that is 2^d per week) and on the Saboth there was a dow[61] made of 14 toopenny loves She got that constantly & Sometimes too she got sometimes shifts, Petticots, Bedgowns &c which was given to Poor wid-dows,[62] she got plenty of milk in the Summer time, 4 quarts for a penny, & as she did not use tea that was a good deal of her living & she lived untill she was above 70 years old, & was burried at Dent,[63] She was a Stout old woman, with Black

56 George Noddle of Dent and Margaret Elishaw of Garsdale were married at Garsdale on 8 May 1739. Their children were all baptized at Dent: Marion (14 May 1740); Isabel (8 May 1742); James (12 February 1744); Agnes (13 July 1746); William (5 November 1748); Isabel (3 March 1751); Agnes (17 June 1753); Mary (24 August 1755); Marion (25 December 1757); Robert (8 March 1761); Mary (4 April 1764) (CROK: WPR/60/1). Four of the children died in infancy.
57 George Noddle was buried at Dent on 20 April 1769, so he was actually fifty-three years old when he died, considerably older than Benjamin believed. His wife, Peggy Noddle, was evidently something of a character, and it is possible that George had faded into obscurity in comparison with her. She also lived long enough for her grandson to know her well and so his memories of her were personal ones, whereas he only knew of his grandfather from second-hand sources (CROK: WPR/70/4).
58 brought
59 Probably meaning farm service as labourers.
60 were not apprenticed
61 dole
62 Three tenements, called Birkrigg, Baines and Lockengarth, all within Dent township, had been given to the township authorities to provide a rent income which could be used to help the poor. On 23 February 1786 it was agreed that the lands should be sold, and the money used to purchase more convenient property, which could be adapted to accommodate the poor. The land and buildings at Hallbank, where Benjamin Shaw had been born fourteen years before and where the poorhouse had been for many years, were purchased for £650. The trustees of the property, on behalf of the township, were to make a weekly payment to twelve poor widowers or widows of 2d each out of the rents and profits, and the residue was to be used for the 'maintenance and support of the poor of Dent'. It was this 2d a week which Peggy Noddle received (CROK: ST/35/25).
63 The Dent register records the burial of 'Margaret Noddal of Town Widow' on 10 February 1793, and the letter P (for Pauper) is added in the margin. Assuming that she was about twenty

hair, a round face, & a very hollow-backed nose, She was a very Cleanly, manageing woman, very careful, & spareing, & all her care & labour was nessacery, as she had a numerous family to provide for, of her own, & She nurced & brought up a child of her Daughters (maryanns) untill her death, the child was then 10 or 11 years old &c my grandmother died about the year 1793 perhaps about 70 years, her maden Name was Peggy Ellishaw

My Mother Isabella Shaw

was the eldest daughter & 3 child of george & Peggy Noddle of Dent corn dealer &c – her father died when she was young – perhaps 15 years, & left her mother with 7 children, She being the oldest daughter She had of corse a Principle Care in the family – She lived with her mother, and was employed in Sewing & Knitting at every vaquent time from other more important business – She was Born about the year 1750, & Named after my grandfathes mother I Supose[64] – She was married to Joseph Shaw my father June 24, 1771. She had 8 children By him, the first was Benjamin, (the writer of this) and Hannah, georrge, William, Joseph, Peggy, & Bellow the last was dead born[65] – for the Places where they lived See the account I have given of my father, &c &c She was a woman that had not good health, was frequently ill, Subject to the Rhumatism, & Convulcive Spasms, so that she was frequently unable to do her work in the family, She employed herself with winding, sewing, & knitting, & Spining, when she was able & learned[66] & kept her Children to the same work, but as the most of her work was in the house she Soon became Lame, & stiff in her joints – So that before she was 40 years old, She was hardly able to walk atall, & for some years before she died she was confinded to her room, & was obleged to be carried to & from bed – yet in this state she used to wind twist nearly as long as she lived – after living in diferant places (See Joseph Shaw[67]) She died in a room in Dale Street, in Preston near horrocks factory – on good friday in the year 1798, aged 48 years[68] – She was a loving mother, & a careful wife She was a Strong Boned, Broad Set woman, with black hair, a round face & dark eyes – She was no Scholler this was a great loss in her family – She was fond of ale [But She was not

---

when she married in 1739, Peggy would have been over eighty when she died (CROK: WPR/70/4).
64 Isabella Noddle was baptized on 3 March 1751 at Dent (CROK: WPR/70/2). The name of George Noddle's mother is unknown, as his parents' marriage has not been traced and his mother is not named in the baptism records of her children.
65 There was a stillborn child after Bella.
66 taught
67 Phrase in original text.
68 The register of Preston St John records the burial of Isabel, wife of Joseph Shaw, aged 47, on 6 April 1798 (LRO: PR/1445).

drunken &c[69]] & in the later Part of her life she had a Pint every night, she eat
but little &c &c

My fathers Brother[s]

were William (Shaw) & Edward – his Sister[s] were Isabella & Mary – (of his half
Brothers & Sister I have spoken before) of these in order of William Shaw twin
Brother to my father was born in grassdale, in the parish of Sedburgh, in the
west riding or (triding[70]) of Yorkshire – January 17th 1748[71] he was sent early to
school, & kept there untill he went aprintice, which he served to a Shoe-maker,
(with Richard Shaw, in the same township[72] – when he was about 23 years old he
married Mary Winn, daughter of John Winn, of that neibourhood,[73] & followed
his trade, by this wife he had 7 Children, their names were first Benjamin John,
hannah, Thomas, Joseph, William, & Molly[74] – of these 2 only is now living
(June 1826) that is William & molly – William maried at Sedburgh,[75] a
timber-merchants daughter, & soon after shifted to North Shields, & is a
Book-keeper for his father in law &c &c molly is living in this town, (Preston)
She married a Spinner whose name was Antony Greaves, – she is now a widdow
with Several Children (1826),[76] my Uncle Set his wife up in Shop-Keeping, &
Sold grosery but soon he turned his attention to Clock dressing & repairing, &
traveling about the Countery for some time, he afterward Shifted to Otley, & set
up Clock making, after this he shifted to Cown,[77] here his sons John and
Benjamin died[78] – John had been very usful to him in the watch work business –

---

69   Added subsequently by the author.
70   The word 'riding' is from the Scandinavian word for *a third part*, which can be rendered in
     modern letters as 'thriding'. The initial 'th' was lost because of the awkwardness of the phrase
     'west thriding'. The use of the term 'triding' by Benjamin is an interesting occurrence of the
     modified ancient form (see Cameron, p. 57).
71   William Shaw was baptized at Garsdale on 13 February 1748 (CROK: WPR/60/1).
72   Richard Shaw was the uncle of William Shaw. He was born in 1697, married Agnes Guy at
     Garsdale in 1724, and was buried there in 1770 (CROK: WPR/60/1).
73   William Shaw and Mary Winn, both of Garsdale, were married there on 1 July 1772 in the
     presence of William Winn and Joseph Shaw (CROK: WPR/60/2).
74   The children of William Shaw, shoemaker of Garsdale, and Mary his wife, were all baptized at
     Garsdale: Benjamin (25 April 1773), John (18 December 1774), Hannah (23 May 1778),
     Thomas (22 March 1782), Joseph (6 May 1780), William (9 May 1784) and Molly (20 February
     1787) (CROK: WPR/60/1).
75   There is no record of this marriage in the Sedbergh parish registers.
76   Anthony Greaves, a mule spinner, and Mary Shaw, both of Walton-le-Dale, were married
     there on 14 May 1808 (LRO: PR/2948/1/9). Their first child, Elijah, was baptized at
     Walton-le-Dale on 2 October 1808 (LRO: PR/2948/1/3). The other children were baptized at
     Preston St John: William (28 March 1813); Betty (11 February 1816); Thomas (2 November
     1817); John (14 May 1820); and Margaret (17 April 1825) (LRO: PR/1461, 1462, 1463, 1465).
77   Colne
78   The Colne parish registers record the burial of John Shaw, of Colne, on 11 August 1788. No

* here his wife died[79] & left him with several Small children – how to cary on he did not know – however he got a neece to keep his house, Named mally Winn. She had not lived long with him untill she proved with Child by him. (this was a Shamefull affair) he sent her home & sold up his tools & furniture, & Sent his 2 Sons to his town,[80] & some of his wifes relations took another, & he became very wild & drunken – he began to woork at the machien Shops, first at Barrowfoard, then at Samsbury, & Moonmill – Roach-Brig[81] &c, about the year 1796 he married Easter Richmond, a woman from Scorton in Wiresdale[82] – She had had a child by chance before – by this woman he has had 3 Children,[83] which are all grown up & all live at home now Betty the oldest is married & Peggy & John live at home – John is Book Keeper at Catteral & Ainsworth & Co. Church Street Preston[84] & & William Shaw is now living, but is feeble yet works, still though he is now 78 years old,[85] his wife has about £10 of an anuety coming yearly in this is very usefull, – it was left to her by her father, & is paid twice a year & &c the Child she had by Chance died very young before they married. William Shaw has lived in Preston near 20 years, is now working for Catteral & Ainsworth Cotton Court, & lives in Shepherd Street – he is but a little man, a bout 5 foot 5 inches high & perhaps was never more than 9 Stone weight, with dark or Black

details of age or occupation were given at this period, so it is not possible to determine definitely if this was William's son (Spencer 1969, p. 144). The Garsdale registers record the burial of Benjamin, son of William Shaw, shoemaker, aged 19 and a pauper, on 16 July 1792 (CROK: WPR/60/1). William Shaw had sent his sons back to Garsdale, and Benjamin is therefore wrong in stating that both died in Colne.

79   Mary Shaw of Bradley (near Barrowford), aged 41, died in childbed and was buried at Colne on 23 March 1794. It is possible that this was William's wife, but by no means definite (Spencer 1968, p. 103). They were married in 1772, so a date for her birth *c.* 1753 would be feasible.

80   i.e. Garsdale. There is a possibility that the eldest son, Benjamin, may have gone back to Garsdale voluntarily, as he died there in 1792 which might have been before his mother's death (see previous note).

81   The mills at Samlesbury Bottom and Roach Bridge were in Samlesbury township. Moons Mill was at Higher Walton. All were on the River Darwen.

82   The second marriage of William Shaw was at Samlesbury. Although Benjamin writes that his uncle was by this time working in machine shops, William is recorded as 'clockmaker' in the marriage register: either he wished to be thought of as a craftsman, or he was actively working in that business. The marriage took place on 21 January 1798, between William Shaw and Esther Richmond, both of the chapelry of Samlesbury (LRO: PR/2883/9).

83   The first two children were baptized at Samlesbury: Betty (born 30 March 1798, baptized 17 June) and John (born 23 December 1799, baptized 1 January 1800) (LRO: PR/2883/5). The Walton-le-Dale registers record the baptism of Peggy, daughter of William and Easther Shaw, on 11 March 1804 (born 20 January) and of a second Peggy, baptized on 14 September 1806 (LRO: PR/2948/1/3). A fourth child, Hannah, who died in infancy, was baptized at Preston St John on 26 November 1815 (LRO: PR/1461).

84   A partnership formed by David Ainsworth and Paul Catterall: in 1818 Ainsworth, Catterall & Co. were cotton spinners of Church Street mills. These premises were in Cotton Court, off Church Street.

85   William Shaw, aged 87, of North Road, was buried at Preston St Paul on 26 November 1834 (LRO: St Paul's Burial Register Transcript).

hair & dark eyes he was a good reeder & writer & in acounts few common men Better & a Constant goer to Church & &

My Father[s] Sister Isabella Shaw daughter of Benjamin & Hannah Shaw of grasdale was the 3 Child, by a Second wife Born about 1750 or 51,[86] in her youth She lived at home, and followed the common employment of knit wooling goods, I dont know much about her in her youth – she married John Watson, Son of James & Nanny Watson a neighbour,[87] he was a tailor, but was allways a journeyman, as he was no Shaper[88] – they lived all their days in the same dale, & died in an advanced age[89] – they had only one Child whose name was nanny[90] – they enjoyed all the advantages of a married life without much of the care & labour common to rearing a family – She was a very hansom woman, of a midle size, with dark Hair, & Brown Eyes – She was but in a weakly state for some years before she died her husband was a good looking man, with red hair, & grey eyes – very fluent of speech, & a good Scoller, but recconed proud & vain – he was Clark at their Chapple many years,[91] and became very lame before he died – Nanny their daughter was a Hansom girl when young, with dark hair & a Broad mark on one Cheek, which had been burnt. She married a Collier, I dont know his name & they live in the same township[92] – but I hear she has turned out a drinker this is a great fault in a wife – She has many children – & she drives the carts with coals to Sedburgh &c now (1826)[93]

Edward Shaw my uncle, & Brother to Joseph Shaw, & Son of Benj[n] & Hannah Shaw of grasdale, was the 4th child & 3 Son of the above, born about the year

---

86 Isabella Shaw was baptized at Garsdale on 11 March 1750 (CROK: WPR/60/1).
87 John Watson and Isabel Shaw, both of the chapelry of Garsdale, were married there on 23 May 1774, in the presence of Benjamin Shaw and Joseph Shaw (CROK: WPR/60/2).
88 did not cut out and make clothing
89 John Watson of Low Smithy, aged 72, was buried at Garsdale on 20 June 1818. Isabel Watson of High Whitbeck, aged 72, was buried there on 27 March 1821 (CROK: WPR/60/6).
90 Agnes, daughter of John Watson, was baptized at Garsdale on 2 April 1775 (CROK: WPR/60/1).
91 John Watson appears to have been clerk at Garsdale chapel from the summer of 1795 until November 1805. It was only during this period he was regularly a witness at marriages (CROK: WPR/60/2).
92 Agnes (Nanny) Watson, spinster, married John Holme, collier, at Garsdale on 16 May 1795. The witnesses were John Watson, her father, and Joseph Shaw, her great-uncle (CROK: WPR/60/2).
93 There were numerous small coalpits on the high fellsides and plateau tops in the vicinity of Dentdale and Garsdale, where the gritstones, sandstones and narrow coal seams of the Yoredale Beds overlie the Carboniferous Limestone. Some of these pits continued to operate until 1878, when the opening of the Midland Railway across the head of the valleys brought cheap supplies of good quality coal to the area. The coal mined in Dent and neighbouring townships was used as far afield as Kirkby Lonsdale and Kirkby Stephen, but apart from purely local use the small town of Sedbergh was its main market (see, for example, Lancaster, pp. 15–20).

1757[94] he was brought up at Home, & employed in the land, as they had a little farm, & in the wooling[95] at times in winter & when there was no work without, this man had no trade, & lived with his parents while they lived, & then with his sister mary even untill now, (1826 for any thing that I know[96]) this man was never married, (nor ever had a child to keep) and yet has been very poor mostly, he never could be prevaled on to leave home – he went with his sister mary to Kendal to live after his parents died, & then they came to this town after they left Kendal & lived some years, but they went back to grasdale many years since – Edward Shaw was a tall man perhaps 5 feet 11 inche, Strong & active but not fat – dark hair & eyes – a long face & a very good walker – it is rather remarkable, that Edward Shaw his uncle was never married after whome he was named, & Both of them lived very poor all their days led a life of Liberty without much care &c &c

Mary Shaw my fathers Sister, & daughter of Benj[n] & Hannah Shaw, was the youngest Child, Born in grasdale about 1759 or 60[97] – She lived with her parents all the time they lived, She was employ in the house & in kniting & spining &c She married when she was about 30 years old one John Davis, son of Jacob & Nanny davis of their town a waller, (as they call them) or builder & flager & Slater plasterer &c by him she had 2 Sons, the first Jacob & 2d Benjamin,[98] the first died in this town Preston about the year 1804 – the other went for a Soldier & never returned – after her parents died they went to Kendal to live, with an intent of getting a better living, this might be about 1796, then they shifted to this town, (Preston) about the year 1801 and lived several years, John following mason work & her Brother Edward who allways lived with them sometimes turned a laith wheel, Sometimes Strook[99] for the Smiths, & Sometimes tented[100] a Steam Engin &c while they were in Preston their Son Jacob died about 14 years old,[101] & Benj[n] went to be a Soldier, & never came back – after this they went back to their own countery and are living yet for anything that I know

94   Benjamin says 1757, but Edward was in fact baptized at Garsdale 23 May 1752: this is probably an indication that Benjamin used rough notes in the compilation of the autobiography, since he has evidently miscopied '1752' and written '1757'.

95   'woollen' – in weaving, spinning or knitting

96   He did in fact live for another ten years. The Garsdale registers record the burial of Edward Shaw of Low Smithy, aged 84, on 31 January 1836 (CROK: WPR/60/6).

97   Mary Shaw was baptized at Garsdale on 31 October 1754 (CROK: WPR/60/1).

98   John Davis, mason, and Mary Shaw, spinster, both of Garsdale, were married there on 14 May 1786, in the presence of Benjamin Shaw and Joseph Shaw (CROK: WPR/60/2). Jacob, son of John and Mary Davis, mason of Whatehead, was baptized at Garsdale on 25 March 1787 (born 25 February). Benjamin was baptized on 22 May 1791 (born 17 October 1790), when his father was described as a mason of Rogerspot and a pauper (CROK: WPR/60/1).

99   struck: wielded the hammer

100   tended

101   Jacob Davis, aged 17, was buried at Preston St John on 8 March 1804 (LRO: PR/1445).

(June 1826[102]) this mary was of the midle size, with Black Hair & Brown Eyes – But not so Hansom as her Sister Isabella – John her Husband was tall & Slend[r] not Hansom, had a big belly, & very small legs, was a drunken man, & it was whispered that she would drink privatly, & I rather think this was too true &c &c – this John davis had his leg broken before they came to Preston, & was very lame on it ever after &c &c

My Mother[s] Brothers & Sisters &c

were James, William Isabella (my mother) & nanny, marionn, Robert & Molly (Noddles) – James Noddle was son of george & Peggy Noddle of Dent, born about the year 1744,[103] he was grown up when his father died, he was brought up in the Husbandry line, and has followed it all his life,[104] he married Else green[105] and by her had a numerous family the Names of the 3 oldest was george, Peggy, & Ellin, the other I dont remember[106] – he has lived in Dent mostly, but is now living near Coatla,[107] 2 or 3 miles from Sedburgh, (june 1826) this man has been a Sober, Steady, & industerous Person, had a great family to bring up, & , has had but a small farm mostly – he must be now about 82 years old &c[108]

William Noddle, the Second Son of george & peggy Noddle, was born at dent about 1747 or 48,[109] this man was brought up in the agraculteral way, & has

---

102 John Davis of Low Row, aged 64, was buried at Garsdale on 31 October 1824. Mary Davis of Garsdale was buried there on 28 August 1842, aged 78 [*sic*]: the latter is probably the entry which relates to Benjamin's aunt (CROK: WPR/60/6).

103 James Noddle was baptized on 12 February 1744 at Dent (CROK: WPR/70/1).

104 In 1780 the register entry for the baptism of his daughter Agnes records that James was farming at 'Womenland' – Woman's Land, on the south side of the dale just over a mile south east of Dent town. By 1786 he was living at Woods, and was still a farmer (CROK: WPR/70/4). It is possible that he was the James Noddal of Deepdale who in 1788 undertook, for £135 per year, to maintain and clothe the poor belonging to the township for three years, and to occupy the estate at Hallbank. This was the place where Benjamin had been born, and where his family had lived for two separate periods between 1775 and 1785 (CROK: WPR/70/04/27).

105 Her name was in fact Alice Greenwood.

106 James Noddel and Alice Greenwood, both of Dent, were married there on 27 June 1768 (CROK: WPR/70/3). Their children were baptized at Dent: George (11 June 1769); Margaret (25 December 1770); Ellen (30 August 1772); Joseph (3 July 1774); Joseph (20 April 1775); Mary (20 April 1775); James (11 August 1776); Betty (21 June 1778); Agnes (30 April 1780); Edward (13 January 1782); William (7 January 1784); and Robert (24 September 1786). Of these twelve, the first Joseph was buried on 22 July 1774; Mary on 3 May 1775; and William on 17 January 1784 (CROK: WPR/70/4).

107 Cautley, on the road between Sedbergh and Kirkby Stephen.

108 James Noddle was buried at Dent on 14 March 1832, aged 88, when he is described as being of Ravenstonedale. This suggests that he had gone in old age to live in that township, but it is possible that he was still living near Cautley, which although within the parish of Sedbergh borders on Ravenstonedale (CROK: WPR/70/4).

109 William Noddle was baptized at Dent on 5 November 1748 (CROK: WPR/70/1).

followed it all his life, this man married one Ann Hutchison, a native of ravenstanedale, about the year 1770 – by her he had 4 children, which are all but 1 living now (june 1826) the first Peggy, William, Ann & Bella[110] – soon after he was married he managed a farm for a gentleman of that place, many years &c – afterward he wrought at the coalpits, sometimes at the sinder ovens, & sometimes in the land – about the year 1790 he took out an octioneres licence,[111] & held this many years, then he turned Bumbaley[112] &c, his wife died about 1806, & he has been married many years to a Second, & is now living, (June 1826) he must be near 80 years old[113] – his first wife took the Small Pox when she was above 30 year old and recovered (it was whispered that this woman was unfaithful to the marrig contract), Peggy his oldest daughter married one Parinton, a labourer, & is now living at lancaster, & has 3 or 4 children[114] – William went for a Soldier, & came home with a Pention, &c he died last winter & has left a wife & several Children – Ann married William Thistlewood of dent, a talor She has 2 Children & lives at Caton[115] – Belle is married to a coachman at Hornby & has several children[116] &c, his Name is Wilson &c This William

110 The marriage of William Noddle and Ann Hutchinson, both of Dent, took place there on 15 June 1771 (CROK: WPR/70/3). Their children were all baptized at Dent: Peggy (30 August 1772); George (3 December 1775); James (18 January 1778); William (22 October 1780); Ann (29 June 1783); Bella (21 June 1789). George and James were buried on the same day, 30 May 1782 (CROK: WPR/70/4).

111 William Noddle was described as a labourer when his son William was baptized in 1780; as a husbandman on the baptism of Ann in 1783; and as an auctioneer when the last child, Bella, was baptized in 1789. In each instance his abode is given as Dent town. The last entry is annotated in the margin with the 'P' which stood for 'pauper' (CROK: WPR/70/4).

112 bum bailiff: a man who assisted the constable to make arrests

113 There is no record of William's second marriage at Dent or the adjacent parishes. No burial for William Noddle was recorded at Garsdale or Dent in the period 1826–1846, so the date and place of death are also unknown.

114 The marriage of William Parrington and his wife Peggy/Margaret Noddle has not been traced. Their children, all baptized at Lancaster St Mary, were Peggy (7 April 1799); Thomas (1 May 1803); William (29 June 1806); George (23 April 1809) and Ann (5 December 1812). In 1799 they were living at Skerton, just outside the town of Lancaster, but in 1803–12 they were described as being resident in Lancaster (LRO: PR/3262/1/6).

115 The surname of Ann Noddle's husband was Thistlethwaite, not Thistlewood as stated by Benjamin. It is a common name in Dent and adjacent areas. At the marriage of Ann's parents the witnesses were John Thistlethwaite and M. Thistlethwaite, so William may well have been a cousin. William Thistlethwaite of Lancaster, tailor, and Ann Noddle of Quernmore, spinster, were married at Lancaster St Mary on 3 November 1803, in the presence of Joseph Dickenson and Samuel Thistlethwaite (LRO: PR/3262/1/21). Their children were baptized at Caton: Agnes (15 April 1804); William (16 June 1806, buried 26 June); Ann (14 August 1808); James (23 November 1810) (LRO: PR/494).

116 John Wilson, husbandman, and Bella Noddle, spinster, both of Melling in Lonsdale, were married there on 28 December 1812 (LRO: PR/2898/1/6). The baptisms of their children were as follows: Charles (11 July 1813 at Melling); Isabella (21 May 1815 at Arkholme chapel); Ann (11 or 17 February 1816 at Melling); and, at Hornby, William (9 May 1819); John (27 May 1821); Joseph (12 December 1824); Mary Jane (9 December 1827); George (5 September 1830). The baptism entries show that John Wilson had a varied career before becoming a

Noddle has been a healthy man, and a great drinker – Broad Set, & Strong, with dark hair & eyes, & very red round face & good teeth &c &c &c

Nanny Noddle, was the Daughter 2nd & 4 Child of george & Peggy Noddle of Dent, Born about the year 1752,[117] She mostly lived in service, she had the small Pox very ill, & was much Pitted, & her eyes was rather tender, She kept the House of one James Shaw a Quaker, widdower with 2 children many years, & while she was with him She turned quaker. She lived with him untill he died – after this she came Home – & She married an old man Called Simon Slinger, when she was above 30 years old, and went to live with him in Ingleton fells, near Ribblehead[118] – she had but ill health after, and it is said he was a cross old man, & behaved ill to her – however he lost her soon, for she died soon after[119] – She was a broad set woman with Dark Hair & eyes like all the family –

Robert Noddle (My mothers Brother) was son of george & Peggy Noddle, was youngest son that grew up, this Brothe of my mother[s] lived mostly about midleton & killinton,[120] in Sirvis, & he got married when he was about 24, to one Ann Middleton[121] – this woman had had a child by one dixon, & is said to have been to much atached to him after her marrig with my uncle – it seems robert Noddle had very Poor health after he was married, having got a Surfeit in Service – he however did not live long after, but left his wife to her dear dixon[122]

---

coachman (presumably at Hornby Castle): he was a weaver of Hornby in 1813; shoemaker of Arkholme 1815; husbandman of Hornby, 1816; and coachman of Hornby from 1819 onwards (LRO: PR/2898/1/4 and PR/3321/1/1).

117 Nanny Noddle was baptized at Dent on 17 June 1753: her given name was Agnes (CROK: WPR/70/1).

118 Simon Slinger, husbandman, and Agnes Noddle, spinster, both of Ingleton Fells, were married in 23 December 1789 at the chapel of Ingleton Fells (now called Chapel-le-Dale) between Ingleton and Ribblehead (LPRS vol.71).

119 They lived at Intack in Chapel-le-Dale, where they had two children, both baptized at Ingleton Fells: John (26 September 1790) and Alice (27 October 1793). Simon Slinger died on 8 May 1820. His will names four living children: John, of Chapel-le-Dale; Edward; Elizabeth, wife of James Lawsley; and Alice, wife of John Swindlehurst of Marshaw in Wyresdale (LRO: WRW(L) 1820 Simon Slinger of Chapel-le-Dale). Edward and Elizabeth were his children by a previous marriage. The burial of Agnes Slinger is not recorded at Ingleton, Chapel-le-Dale or Dent before 1812, suggesting that her death was not as soon after her marriage as Benjamin had supposed.

120 Middleton and Killington, near Kirkby Lonsdale

121 Her maiden name was in fact Nelson. Robert Noddle and Ann Nelson, both single persons of Dent, were married there on 27 May 1793 (CROK: WPR/70/3). Benjamin gives Ann's surname as Middleton, but as he refers to this as a placename in the previous sentence he was presumably confused when writing out these lines.

122 Robert and Ann had a child, Peggy, who was baptized on 19 January 1794 and is not mentioned by Benjamin. Her father was described as a labourer, of Hollins (on the north side of Dentdale, $2\frac{1}{2}$ miles east of Dent town); the subsequent fate of this child is unclear. Robert Noddal of Hallbank was buried at Dent on 13 November 1794 (CROK: WPR/70/4).

&c this man was not so Lusty as his Brothers, James or William – was a good servant & a very careful man, frugal, temperate, & sober remarkable fond of Bird catching, fishing &c &c he died about the year 1794, having beed [*sic*] married about 2 yeare &c

Mariann Noddle, 3rd daughter & 5 Child of george & Peggy Noddle of dent, was born 1754 or 55[123] – She mostly lived in Service, in differant Places – when she lived at Mrs. Turners at Barbon near Kirby Lonsdale,[124] she came Home with Child by one Thomas Bains[125] – the child lived & she left it at home with her mother & went to Service again, to a Place on Bowland forrest, here got aquainted with one Clason,[126] a farmer & Beast Jober, & soon after got married to him (But it is sade she was with child again)[127] they Settled in that Countery but I know little more about her – nor do I know what Came of her first Child after her mother died[128] – this marionn was a good looking woman Broad Set & rather inclined to be fat – with a red face, Black Hair & dark eyes – a very Chearful Smiling woman

Molly Noddle, the younges child of george Noddle of dent, this woman was Born about the year 1766,[129] She was brought up at home, & employed mostly in knitting & spining She married young to one Frank Allen,[130] this mans father was a man of Property but had many children – however he took him a farm, & Stocked it, gave him a good stock of sheep, as he himself kept sheep – but this frank was a mean man, wild & drunken – of turbelent bad tempers – he traded in cattle &c, she had many Children by him but [he][131] died young & left her with a Small family,[132] and not much Property, for he was wild & extravigant and,

123 Marian Noddle was baptized at Dent on 25 December 1757 (CROK: WPR/70/1).
124 Agnes Turner was the wife of George Turner of Barbon, gentleman, who died in 1782 (LRO: WRW(L) 1782 George Turner of Barbon).
125 The Kirkby Lonsdale registers record the baptism of Thomas, son of Marian Noddle of Barbon, illegitimate, on 13 April 1783. No father's name is given (CROK: WPR/19/3).
126 His name was James Clarkson.
127 Benjamin is correct in noting that his aunt was pregnant when she married. The marriage took place at Dent on 19 May 1787: James Clarkson, bachelor, of Pendleton in the parish of Whalley, and Marrian Noddal of Dent chapelry, spinster, by licence (CROK: WPR/70/3). They had a large family, all baptized at Whalley parish church: in each case the father was described as a farmer of Pendleton – Ann (2 September 1787); Peggy (3 October 1790); Robert (25 November 1791, buried 12 February 1792); Elizabeth (19 May 1793); Mary (24 May 1795); James (7 May 1797) and Alice (10 March 1799) (LRO: PR/7 and 8).
128 The subsequent fate of Thomas Noddle is unclear: the Dent parish registers give no clue.
129 Molly Noddle was baptized at Dent on 4 April 1764 (CROK: WPR/70/1).
130 The marriage of Francis Allen and Mary Noddal, both single persons of Dent, took place there on 21 May 1785, in the presence of Joseph Sykes and James Allen (CROK: WPR/70/3).
131 Added subsequently by the author.
132 i.e. a family of young children. The children of Francis and Mary Allen were all baptized at Dent: James (9 June 1786); George (16 May 1788); Thomas (27 December 1789); William (29 July 1792); Sarah (2 November 1793); Peggy (12 May 1797); Nelly (3 December 1798) (CROK: WPR/70/4).

nothing prospered with him[133] – She is living yet,[134] but she is very lame, her family are mostly got up – this woman was not [so][135] Stout as her Sisters, But far from being a little woman, She was a managing woman, & very careful, but She could not be happy with such a man &c

having given some account of my parents, & their relations, I now proceed to give some account of myself, & family as well as I can from the few notes that I have by me, from my Birth untill the presant time – Benjamin Shaw Son of Joseph & Isabella Shaw, was their first child, born december the 23rd – 1772 – at a place called Hallbank, in the township of dent, in the Parish of Sedburgh, in the west riding of yorkshire, at 10 o'clock forenoon[136] – my parent has often told me that I was a remarkable cross child, the first year of my life – however that does not seem to have had any bad effect on my health, for my mother has often told it, that she lost me when I was only 40 week old, for I could walk at that age, & she had left me at the back door, I went out of the yard door, & the wind Shut the door, & I was lost &c – we lived at this time in Kendal, my father being a weaver and wrought for that town – this was about the middle of the Americam war, the Inhabitants of Boston this year rose & destroyed by throwing overboard 342 Chists of tea, sent thither by the east india company, because the English government had laid a duty of 3d per lb on tea – which now pays here 10s & excise duty beside –

* my parents did not live long at Kendal but came to dent, it seems that my mother was very Partial to the Place of her nativity – in about 2 years after my sister hannah was born – my father began to feel the efects of a growing family, for the times times [sic] were very bad then on account of the war, and stagnation of trade – this year (1775) was fought the battle of Bunker Hill – Charlstown was burnt to ashes, & the Siege of Quebeck &c – was caried on &c – my parents lived at a Place called the West Banks at this time, & before I was 4 year old my Brother george was born – my father shifted to a house in the same yard where I was born (Hallbank) here we had a good garden, with Plenty of Berry trees &c, and soon after they got a Hive of bees, this Hive increased fast and in about 3 years, they became 4 hives – I now began to go to School to a

---

133   Francis Allen of Stonehouse, aged 48, was buried at Dent on 22 September 1813. The suggestion that 'nothing prospered with him' may be supported by the circumstantial evidence of the register entries for the baptism of his children. These show that he moved frequently from farm to farm: 1786, farmer of High Thistlethwaite (a remote farm high on the fellside in the upper valley); 1788, labourer of Kirthwaite; 1789, farmer of Cow Dub; 1792–3, farmer of Willans; 1797, farmer of Slack; 1798, yeoman of Stonehouse. All these farms are in the same part of the dale, near Cowgill, but the evidence suggests that Frank could not or would not settle (CROK: WPR/70/4).

134   Mary Allen of Stonehouse, aged 75, was buried at Dent on 28 May 1838 (CROK: WPR/70/11).

135   Added subsequently by the author.

136   Benjamin Shaw was baptized at Dent on 23 December 1772 (CROK: WPR/70/4).

woman called Peggy Winn, this woman was the only Person that I ever went to School to, either to read or write.[137] She had a great name up for a good School mistres, but was very sevear with the Scollers, but it happend very favourably for me, that she had a Son the Same age as me, who died a little before I went to School,[138] and when she saw me it brought to mind her Son this was a favourable circumstance for me, for this Prejudice never wore off &c –

* from the time that I could walk I used to go to my grandfathers[139] in the Christmas week & a month in the Hay harvest &c as they had no children, you may think they Paid no little attention to me, (it seems I was the darleng) &c was marred[140] as we say very much – I can remember that they had a lodger called gilbert Bleathorne,[141] & he was a fiddler (for his own amusement) and used to fiddle me asleep at night, while I lay in a box &c by the fire – the neighbours that came in used to bring me something nice, & when I went home I allways had a good deal of money to take with me, & other nice things, this gave me a great Pleasure in going to this place – & continued to go constantly as long as they continued to Keek[142] land, which was untill I was about 17 years old –

* but to return, when I was about 5 years old, my father began to turn his

---

137   Margaret (Peggy) Winn was married to John Winn, a butcher of Dent town. The entry for the baptism of her daughter Margaret in 1778 is one of the few which record the occupation of the mother as well as the father. No specific record of her school seems to have survived: the Chester diocesan records have no reference to the granting of a licence to teach, perhaps because they are very incomplete for the period, and the parish bundle among the Ripon diocesan records at Leeds is also uninformative. By 1789 Peggy had become a pauper: the overseers' accounts for that year include payment to her of £1 5s in poor relief (CROK: WPR/70/W2).

   Connections between the Noddle, Shaw and Winn families were more than merely academic. John Winn, Peggy's husband, had fathered an illegitimate son, John, on Agnes Noddle, the cousin of Benjamin's mother Isabella Noddle, in the autumn of 1753, and the Dent overseer had served a filiation order upon him (CROK: WPR/70/14/O6). Agnes Noddle was excommunicated for 'Adultery, Fornication or Incontinency' on 13 February 1766, and the indictment stated that she was 'already before excommunicate' for the same offence (LRO: ARR/3/62). She had further illegitimate children in 1755, 1757, 1764 and 1767.

138   Thomas, son of John and Margaret Winn, was baptized on 15 January 1773 and buried on 20 August 1775 (CROK: WPR/70/4).

139   Grandfather Shaw, living in Garsdale.

140   spoiled

141   Gilbert Bleathorne or Blaythorn was a local man, who lodged with Benjamin's grandparents in the years before his marriage to Ann Parkin at Garsdale in August 1777. In the subsequent baptism entries for his seven children Gilbert is described as a husbandman. He was soon widowed, and was married for a second time at Dent in September 1785, to Anne Hodgson (CROK: WPR/60/2 and WPR/70/3). He lived all the rest of his life in Garsdale and when he died in 1809 was the owner of three properties (Far End, where he lived; Hard Ing; and Mudbecks) at the head of the valley, close to the summit of the road into Wensleydale (LRO: WRW(L) 1809 Gilbert Bleathorn of Garsdale).

142   keep

atention toward Clock work, he was a weaver by trade, but weavers dond like it alltogether,[143] and as they are more at liberty than most men, they frequently Saunter away their time when they should be at work – my father bought a clock, & pulled it in Pieces, & put it up & tried fances[144] untill he thought he could manage to clean any Clock, he got a few tools & set off to try his luck in the Country, & he got some work, & from this time untill he died he followed this work – but at the first he had but few tools, but kept makeing, & buying, untill he was able to do any sort of work. I continued to go to School, & learned to knit Stockings as was the fashon of the place, & day, & nothing remarkable that I can remember happened – the war in america continued, and people complained of hard times, as they have allways done ever since I can remember – as I was the oldest of the children I had to nurce, & to run errands, & was kept bussyly employed – we continued to live at Hallbank 4 years I was Better than half a mile of School[145] & frequently had to go to the town errants – to fetch water &c, that it was no wonder that when I went to my grandfathers I should think it the happiest part of my life, for I got Clear of all this hard work – and every one was giving me something, besides I lived like a prince, & the young folk were continualy giving me money or something, so that I went as often & staid as long as I could –

* when I was 8 years old we Shifted near the town^s end,[146] here I had more play fellows, & I was nearer the School – the first year that we lived here we all of us Children took the natural small Pox, and near all at one time, I had not very many but I was very ill long, my brother george had them very ill, we expected he would die long, but he got through – about this time Wilks the famous Patriot was much talked of, and every Boddy was shouting out Wilks & liberty, as they lately did Hunt & liberty – about this time Admeral Rodney was the nations darling. Pots were marked with his Portrait & name, & dogs were called Rodney &c – at this place we lived but one year, & then shifted into the Center of the town, where we lived 9 years, here my father followed all sorts of jobing, clocks, Jacks, waches, guns, locks, Buckles, Reels &c. he fit ut[147] a laith, & did many sorts of turning wort [sic] &c –

* when I was 10 years old, (that is in 1782) a peace was concluded with america, and that country was declared free & independant, from this time trade revived, and there was better times for a little time, & soon after this I began to work a littl with my father – I was very fond of turning, but as that trade was not much known at that time, we were badly of for tackle, but we continued to improve by

---

143   do not like the same sort of work all the time
144   fancies: experimented with different examples to repair
145   more than half a mile from school
146   the eastern end of Dent town
147   Probably 'up' is intended.

little & little, (as they say Roome was not built on a day) so we improved as we saw what we wanted & our means would allow &c – 1783 this year Peace was contluded with france & Spain – the year before the Spaniards made an unsuccesful atack upon gibraltar. 1784 peace made with Holland –

* about this time the cotton trade in this countery spred very much – there was a factory built at milthrop[148] near Sedburgh & 4 miles from dent this was the first Factory in that part,[149] & they came to dent to put out Cotton batting,[150] this was a change of employment for the woman, & was rather better wages than kniting, & spining – ginnes & roving billies[151] about 24 spindles began to be common in Houses, for both Cotton & wollen – my fathe made many Batting frames,[152] worsted reels, & twisting frames – some of his reels were of quite a new construction, to count what was put on &c – he made Clock Chains & Cords – laces & brat[153] strings, weavers bobbins, wharles,[154] & batton breeds,[155] &c &c in all these things I wrought sometimes[156] –

* I still continued to go to my grandfathers in Haytime & Christmas, & as I grew Biger I went often on the Saterday afternoon, & came back on the Sunday, These Visits was the happiest part of my life – our family was now increased to Six children, & all at home, their mames [*sic*] was Hannah, george, william, Joseph & Peggy (of these I intend to speak of hearafter) – when I was 15½ years

---

148 Millthrop, half a mile east of Sedbergh (not to be confused with Milnthorpe, which Benjamin spells in the same way).
149 The Millthrop factory was a water corn-mill which was rebuilt in 1796 as a cotton mill by William Sidgwick, Peter Garforth and Peter Garforth junior, three cotton twist-makers from the Skipton area. They were highly successful, and in 1812 were able to sell the mill for a substantial profit. By 1816 it had almost 5,000 spindles, 5 pairs of mules, 24 throstles and 10 carding engines. It continued manufacturing cotton until 1864, when it was converted to production of woollens (see Anon. 1981).
150 Cotton batting, a preliminary stage in the preparation of the spun fibres for weaving, involved the production of a soft, twisted strand which could be spun onto a bobbin. It was frequently undertaken as outwork by the rural cottagers in their homes. As it was part of an industrial process it was more regular and better-paid than knitting or spinning, but the work had to be systematically organized and, unlike those two occupations, was not a spare time activity to be carried on in odd moments.
151 A roving billy was the frame on which roving, the attenuated strand of fibres from which yarn was spun, was twisted as the next stage after cotton batting.
152 In the late eighteenth century the frames for cotton batting were installed in cottages, for domestic production. Subsequently this became a factory process.
153 apron
154 whorl, a small pulley by which the spindle on a spinning machine was driven
155 A batten was the moveable bar which closed the weft on a handloom; 'breeds' probably means boards.
156 The machinery described in this paragraph is typical of the first stages of the mechanization of the textile-making process. Whorls, for example, originally meant the weights on the thread in hand spinning, but in this context were part of an early spinning machine.

old my grand father bought me a Scyth, & I learned to maw, though I was too weak for any sort of ground,[157] I was favoured with mawing in the best places, & seem to please greatly – at noons when the haymakers rested, I took a Can[158] & went to gather Rassberries, or Strawberries, then got Some milk & Sugar on them instead of resting (my grandmother used to say that is the stuf for daubing soul & boddy together &c) but about this time I saw a new rival Spring up, my aunt mary was got married, & had a son,[159] & Both her & Husband lived with the old folks, this son partly took my place, as favourite – this was an unfavourable circumstance to the old folks, for they[160] were Both lazy & extravagant, & they soon reduced the old people who were now old, & unfit to manage the farm the Conciquence was, they soon became poor.

1789 this was the last Haytime that I went to work for them & I now found my Happines to consist in other things, than formerly it did. I now found my mind desturbed with thoughts of the lasses, & to spend my time among young folk &c was constantly wishing to spend my time at Home, with my Comeades [sic] – Soon after this (that is at may 1790) they gave up their farm, & retired to a cottage, & I seldom saw them after, – about this time (1789) the french Revolution began, and they took the Bastile &c. things began to be in an unsettled State, & trade much worse – in 1790 I went at Haytime to my aunt Nanny's, She had married a man called Simon Slinger, in Engleton fells,[161] I stoped about 5 weeks &c,

* by this time my sister Bellow was born, & my mother became very lame, She was very subject to the Cronic rhumatism, & Cramp fits or Spasms, so that her hands were drawn up so that she could not use them for many days some times, & She becam quite lame, so that she could scarce walk atall – at mayday 1791 we shifted to a larger house in the same town, (dent) here we had a large garden, a draw well, a good yard, &, a pleasant prospect into the Countery, my father was fond of a garden, & delved it & sowed it but never reaped it, for about this time, some people were come to a factory at dolphinholme in wiresdale 3 miles from golgate[162] in Lancashire, – from our town – there was a man named Miles Burton, a carter, this man was a native of dent & employed at this factory, & there happened to be a want of hands there,

* this miles informed the master that he could get them hands at dent, so he was authorised to come over to dent to hire hands, & trade being bad, some families

---

157 learned to mow, though I was too weak for some sorts of ground
158 A cylindrical vessel, usually of earthenware, used for drinking.
159 The son was Jacob Davis, born in 1787 at Garsdale.
160 Mary Davis and her husband.
161 Ingleton Fells: the Slingers lived at Chapel-le-Dale.
162 Galgate

went thither & seamed to like [it[163]] well, & being in want of more hands, Mr Edmondson the managing master came over to dent to engage hands, several more families hired, & among the rest my father & family – we were 7 childrer & they liked large families the Best, for the Chidrers[164] sake[165] – my father engaged for him & me to work in the machanic shop, at our trade &c – so my father sold the greater part of his goods, & some he left unsold, & came to Dolphinholme with some others in July 1791 this year there was a dreadful riot in Birmingham, in consequence of some gentlemen meeting to commemorate the French revolution &c –

* this leaving our own Countery was a great cross to my mother, for she was greatly atached to her Native town, & had she known what would follow, I am sure that she never would have left her relations & countery on any account. I think this was the most troublesome part of my Parents life, for at the end of the first Pay (for they only Paid once in 3 weeks) the master & my father disagreed about wages, & my father & all his family was discharged – however the children were employed again soon after, my father went into the north where he was known, a Clock dressing – soon after this my master sent for me, & told me that if I would go apprintice he would ingage me for 3 years, as I could work well at the Vice – I consented to be bound for 8 shilling per week for the first 2 years, & 9s for the third, we set our hands to an agreement august the 4th 1791, and I begun work again, we wrought from 6 o'clock in the morning, to 6 in the evening, had 1 hour at noon, and went to our drinking &c, Sometime after this, my father got work again at the factory, to piece rovings,[166] & we settled here, & thing went on smoothly for a time. here I got aquainted with Betty leeming, daughter of Edward leeming, who wrought at the mill here, & we soon began to be warmly atached to each other, as we were near Both of one age, & lived near each other, We begun to Court Strongly, though I was only begining my apprintiship, (so thoughtless are young people) & she as unfit for a wife, as I was for a husband, for we were only about 18 years old &c – some time after this my little Brother Joseph, got catched in the wheels in the factory, and got his hand ill crushed, & cut, one finger taken off, & the other Broken & Sadly mangled, nothing very remarkable happened, (that is of intrest to be told) this autumn or winter I continued to keep company with my new Sweetheart, (afterward my

163   The sense requires 'it' here.
164   children's
165   This is a clear expression of the preference of the mill-owners for families with several children, who could be employed in the mill at lower wage costs. Price (p. 22) notes that in the case of rural mills, such as Dolphinholme, the bringing of whole families was especially important because of the lack of a local reservoir of labour.
166   'Rovings' were the attenuated strands of loosely twisted fibres from which yarn was spun: piecers were the workers who joined together the threads or rovings which had snapped or come apart, by twisting the strands together manually.

wife) Sometime in, Sometimes out,[167] but on the whole we could not part – great uneasiness in france about this time –

* in the Spring of 1792 my Brother george began to be ill, & continued to be of work long, his complaint was a consumption, & in the course of the year he died – our family Suffered much through sickness this year – my Brother Joseph soon after his hand got well, Sickened & died, & my sister Bellow, likewise died – my father had the fever & wass long down, & reduced to the greatest weakness – we buried 3 of our family in the course of this year, I was also ill awhile & my mother was lame & unable to atend on her family – my brothers & sister was buried at Cockeram &c –

* in march this year, peace was made in the east Indies, between Lord Cornwallis & tippoe Sultan, in which the Sultan gave up half of his dominion to the English, & gave his 2 Sons as Hostiges untill the treaty was fullfilled, &c &c &c – in this year Thomas Pane, having been in this country, had published several Book on politics, (his Rights of man & age of Reason &c) which was thought to enflame the Public mind against goverment, they were cried down forbid to be read or sold &c and he was Burned in Effigee, in most of the towns in England – &c we at dolphinholme were as loyal as any &c, we made an Image, & got a cart & set of with the Image to Scorton, & then to golgate, with such a crowd with it, Shouting & laughing &c – at last the Image was tried, cast & executed on a gallows, erected at Croft Height, near the crag in Ellel, & then burnt to ashes while the Cannon roared, and the mob Shouted &c[168] this was all for Laying Something against that Sistom of goverment, then in its infantcy, that has now loaded us with a Debt of £800,000,000 – and which now requires £57,000,000 of Revinue – besides 10,000,000 of Poor taxes – besides Poliece & Church taxes, tithes & highways &c taxes –

* in the Autum of this year, my Sweethart & I quarreled, & after Sometime she

---

167 sometimes they were together, sometimes they quarrelled
168 The diary of Timothy Cragg, a Quaker farmer of Ortner near Dolphinholme, relates this event:
  '1793, January 16th There is going to be a great hullabulloo about Thomas Paine. Cawthorne [M.P. for Lancaster] will give something to drink on the top of Croft Height and make a great fire and burn the effigy of Thomas Paine and sing God Save the King and Lillaballearo and burn heretics . . . This disturbance is to be on Friday night next. They are making the effigy of Thomas Paine at Dolphinholme Factory. Lord help such fools.
    January 18th, Friday This morning a set of Tom Paine fools went with the effigy of him all through the country a begging to all the gentlemen's houses far and near but I suppose got not much [he then describes the hanging and burning of the effigy] They shot a deal of powder away which had better have saved till the French came . . . Many of the fools got drunk and then departed home without doing any mischief. It is to keep the people quiet and to keep them from making any disturbance and from talking treason. ?Is this a likely way to make people silent' (LRO: DDX/760/1).

detirmined to leave dolphinholme, so another young woman and her set of for Preston, but before she went she promised Volontearly that she would be true to me &c, this was in October 1792. So when she got work which she did at the factory in moor lane, then belonging to Watson & C⁰[169] She wrote to me, & let me know where she lived &c and envited me to come to see her at Christmas &c – (this was about the time the french convention tried, & condemned their King Leuis the 16ᵗʰ–) at Christmas I went to Preston, with Samuel Winn my cousin,[170] & staid a few days &c She sent me letters by the waggon from dolphinholme, & I frequently wrote to hir – this was the begining of my writing, for I never went to any school to write in my life[171] – and wanting to send to her I was ashamed to let anybody know my secrets, I set about writing love letters &c, (it is an ill thing that is good for nothing) –

* She left hir lodgins Soon after, & the busy[172] folk sent for me sometime after, pretending they had something to tell me – (on the 21 of January 1793 the King of France was beheaded, & all Europe engaged in war against them, this war lasted 22 years – trade now began to be very bad, & a great army raised & sent to france &c, – the last winter I got hurt by a lad throwing a stick on the backsid of my leg, and having to work at the Cow or Dam, or wear in the water,[173] in very cold weather,[174] I found it began to be very Painful, I went to lancaster to the doctor, and he gave me something to rub it with, & Salts to take &c, this did it a little good, but it was still a hard lump or knott deep in the flesh, & put me in some pain in walking –

---

169   The Moor Lane factory, opened in 1777 by Collinson & Watson and, upon the final bankruptcy of John Watson in 1808, taken over by Paul Catterall.
170   No baptism for a Samuel Winn is recorded at Garsdale or Dent 1750–85, and the identity of this 'cousin' is unclear.
171   Benjamin had learned to read and to knit at Peggy Winn's school in Dent, but had never been taught to write. It seems likely that Betty could write, although it is nowhere categorically stated. The Charity School in Lancaster taught writing to its girl pupils, and Benjamin here says that she sent letters (although it is possible that somebody else wrote these on her behalf). She signed the marriage register in 1793 with a mark, but studies of literacy using such sources have indicated that the signing of a name or making of a mark is not entirely reliable as evidence of ability to write.
172   interfering; busybodies
173   *Cow* is probably 'cowp', meaning 'cop', an embankment; *wear* is weir.
174   Benjamin's job as an apprentice was in the turning shop, but the times were hard and he had no choice but to undertake whatever task he was given, including the repair of the weir. Maintaining the dam was a perpetual problem at Dolphinholme, for the River Wyre was subject to flash floods resulting from cloudbursts in the hills, and the weir was regularly damaged. The diary of Timothy Cragg of Ortner records three major stoppages caused by damage to the weir in the second half of 1793 alone. The dam was 'broken down in the middle 4 or 5 yards in length and the Factory water-wheel broken' on 22 August; 'another great flood on October 3rd burst the Dolphinholme Factory weir out' and 'on the 26th [October] it was again riven up and washed clear away. Not above half of it was left standing'. He notes that after the first of the October floods the factory was stopped for eight days while repairs were carried out (LRO: DDX/760/1).

* I went to Preston on Shrove Sunday februy 10th 1793 to hear what these folks
had to say of my Betty, they told me many things not so pleasing, but there was a
young woman that lodged with them, which told me not to mind them, that it
was not true; &c this woman told Betty that I was come to Preston, & what they
had told me &c – (this was a Creitical time) I stoped all night & never went to see
her that night – the next morning I thought I would go home, without seeing her,
but this woman went down friargate with me & when I came to the Bottom
where the lancaster & kirkham road part,[175] She stoped me & urged me to go &
see her, (She lived in a House about the nearest end of Kirkham Street),[176] and
at last I went we spent the day together, & things were ajusted, (the neighbour,
& her aquaintance all coming to see me &c) –

* I stayed all night with her, and went home the next morning &c – (this 11th of
february I had cause to remember, for she soon after let me know that she was
with child, & recconed from this time &c) we wrote to each other frequently, but
I saw her no more untill about the middle of July, when she came to
dolphinholme, the Offisers in Preston would not let her stop any longer[177] &c –
this spring (1793) trade was very bad, & goverment raising all the men that they
could for the war, the duke of York went over with an army to Holland, to join
the allied armys &c – about this time many familys was discharg'd at dolphinholme, and among them my father^s family, they went to aconthwate green, near
milthrop,[178] and left me a bed and Box, & a few odd things, & I went to live with
Hannat fleming &c, I now began to feel the want of my mother, who had been
very kind to me, though I did not Prize that kindness as I ought – about this time
I began to practis accounts, I Bought a Book, & Slate, and got somebody to set

---

175   North Road, the present main road northwards from the town centre, had not yet been built,
      so the Lancaster traffic followed what is now Moor Lane. The Kirkham road was the modern
      Fylde Road, and the parting of the ways was at the present *Lamb & Packet* public house next
      to the Polytechnic roundabout. Kirkham Street still exists, running westwards from Fylde
      Road opposite the former St Peter's Church, but all the late eighteenth-century housing in this
      district was demolished in the 1930s slum clearance programme.
176   Kirkham Street, a short street of back-to-back houses with cellar dwellings, was built by John
      Horrocks in 1796 next to his new factory at Spittals Moss. It was therefore not yet in existence
      when Betty was working in the Moor Lane factory nearby. She must have lodged in a house
      close to where Kirkham Street was eventually built, and Benjamin, writing more than thirty
      years later, uses the latter street as a point of reference for his readers. The precise location of
      Betty's lodgings remains unclear.
177   The Poor Law authorities were particularly watchful in preventing unmarried pregnant women
      from remaining in townships where they had no settlement. This was because in some
      circumstances place of birth might be used in assessing the responsibility for the maintenance
      of illegitimate pauper children. Betty was therefore removed from Preston. She had her
      settlement in Lancaster, but came to Dolphinholme in Ellel township en route, because
      Benjamin was there. As she was a single woman advanced in pregnancy the Ellel officers would
      have been equally unwilling to allow her to remain there.
178   Ackenthwaite Green, near Milnthorpe, Westmorland

me agate[179] at the beginning of a Rule, & then wrought by my book &c, and in a while got forward in arethmatic &c –, about this time my Brother William was bound apprintice to Lenard gibson, a Blacksmith at the end moor, 5 miles from Kendal – (in june 1793) the Siege of Valencennes comenced, by the duke of York &c, – ,

* July, my Sweet Heart Betty Leeming come to dolphinholme, in her way from Preston to lancaster, for her fathers family had been discharged, and shifted to that town, where they came from, I was now in a Sad Predicament, left in a Strainge place, & aprintice with only 8 Shilings per week, & my parents shifted away, I had 13 months to serve of my time, & trade very bad & the lass quite big, (alass for Poor Ben) I did not know what to do, for I loved her still, though there was no Prospect before us but extream Poverty, I thought many things, but could fix on nothing, I sometimes thought I would not have her, but then this came to my mind, how must She do,[180] &c She went to lancaster to her fathers, & I went to see her Sometimes on the Sundays, we continued on in this way a while – on the 4th of august I was raised to 9s per week, this was a little better, &c – about this time Admeral Hood took Tolon, with the Ships in the Harbour &c, in September the duke of york made an unsuccesfull attack upon Dunkirk, (Sometimes called dunkirk races &c) and was near being taken Prisoner &c, – after this he retreated into Holland &c, –

* at the beging of this month I put up the exings[181] as they call it, or Published the Bans &c, at Cockeram, & Lancaster, & on the 21st of September,[182] we were married at Lancaster old Church,[183] I had saved about 30 shillings, so they perswaded me to make a dinner at her fathers House, for the guests, this with the other expences of the day left me nearly without a penny &c, though we had nothing to go to house with – Before we were married, Betty told me she would live at home, untill she got her bed,[184] & it would save us some expence, for we

---

179   started or going [started working on arithmetical formulae]
180   Even if he had not married Betty, Benjamin would still have had responsibility for the maintenance or partial maintenance of their child. Betty would have filiated [sworn that he was the father]. A bastardy order would almost certainly have been issued, and payment thus required.
181   askings
182   Benjamin is in error about the date of his own wedding, which actually took place on 23 September (see below).
183   The parish register of Lancaster St Mary ('Lancaster old Church') records the marriage of Benjamin Shaw of Ellel in the Parish of Cockerham, whitesmith, and Elizabeth Leeming of this town and parish, spinster, by banns, on 23 September 1793: the witnesses were George Allen and Thomas Denham. The day was not that stated by Benjamin in this text. A whitesmith was a worker in tin and tinned metals, and it is quite unclear why Benjamin was described as such, since he was still an apprentice mechanic. The register uses the name 'Elizabeth' for the bride, although she had been baptized as Betty (LRO: PR/3262/1/20).
184   gave birth

had neither furniture, or monney, nor friends, & but fue cloths & she had her little clothes to provide &c, – but very soon after we were wed, She came to dolphinholme, & would not go back any more to lancaster,[185] &c – this autum a Convention met in Edenburgh, semelar to that in france, & many of the members being apprehended, were tried, & sentanced to bottany bay for life &c – about this time Hood was driven out of Tolon & they Burnt 10 Ships of the line, & did other damage, before they left it, &c, & Hood soon after took the Island of Corsica, Some Islands in the west Indes &c –

* after my wife came from lancaster, we lived with Hannah fleming, a widdow where I had boarded before, & we found our own vituals, & were poor enough, & to make ill worse, She was Delivered of a child November 4th 1793[186] – (14 days before the time but she as if conscious that there might bee some suspition, had a good Story to tell, She said that having to go to lancaster, on Business she hired a galliwa[187] of a neighbour, & it being an uneasy trotter, & She wanted to be at home, she pushed it on too fast & it Shaked her so that she was never well after till she was delivered &c) (& you know that young woman claim as a Privelege, a month on either side of the time, So what could I say – I owned it as mine on hir word of honour &c and called him Joseph, after my father[188] &c –

185 Having married Benjamin, Betty acquired his place of settlement. At this stage, before he had completed his apprenticeship, Benjamin was probably legally settled at Preston Richard in Westmorland, his father's place of settlement (Joseph Shaw had completed *his* apprenticeship in that township). When Benjamin eventually completed his time at Dolphinholme he obtained settlement in Ellel, and retained it for the rest of his life. Even though he lived his last forty-five years in Preston he could do nothing to earn settlement in the town where he lived for so long.
186 The parish register of Over Wyresdale records the baptism of Joseph, son of Benjamin and Elizabeth Shaw, on 1 December 1793 (LRO: PR/2955/1).
187 galloway (a small pony)
188 Modern methods of reckoning give an average pregnancy length of 266 days. Assuming that conception was on 11 February, which seems undoubtedly the case, the birth of the child on 4 November would have been exactly on time, to the very day, and Betty's honour would have been unquestioned. However, Benjamin clearly had some doubts about the paternity of the child, and seems to have had reason to suppose that Betty had not been faithful. The gossip of her neighbours in January and February is referred to in guarded and imprecise terms, but it would appear that Betty was known to have been involved with someone else – or at least that Benjamin was not entirely convinced by her claims to the contrary and those of the young woman who shared her lodgings.
   Since the autobiography was intended to be read by his children it is possible that Benjamin did not wish to be too explicit about his suspicions of Betty's pre-marital exploits (it is evident from references to others that he was unsympathetic to women who were 'unfaithful to the marriage contract'). The lingering doubts about Joseph's paternity might explain an otherwise puzzling feature of the accounts of Benjamin's children. Although Joseph was the firstborn, and although he seems to have been the only one of the surviving children to cause Benjamin no trouble or pain, he is given surprisingly little attention and his character – unlike those of his siblings – is not described. This suggests a possible coolness towards Joseph, or lack of interest in him.

she had a very hard time in labour, (& so had I) for Sometimes I thought how foolish I had been – & wished that she might die I think that if she had died, I should have greatly rejoiced, for we were so poor, & such a dark prospect before us, that it was quite discourageing however it was not so to be –

* the masters began to be at variance among themselves, Edmondson the manager, had begun to build a factory in yorkshire, at Hepton Brig,[189] where the greater part of their trade lay, and wanted the other masters to join him at it but they being Both rich, & not wishing to go any further into trade, they would not consent, & he thought to force them, Stoped the works by degrees &c – we went to House by our selves & had nothing to put in it, But a bed that my fathers & me at dolphinholme, & Betty had a Box for Cloaths, & a pair of tongs, & a fue pots, &c I made each of us a knife & fork, & 2 Stools, we got a pan, & a looking glass, & a few trifles the winte was now set in and coals were very dear here then, as the cannal was not finished,[190] and turf was dear, & the house was very cold, we were nearly Starved,[191] Betty used to go into wire, the river close to,[192] & gather sticks, & sometimes go to Caulas mill,[193] (a corn mill about half a mile of) to fetch seeds[194] to burn &c[195] (we were wed now indeed)

* however time went on, and the winter got over, and we got a few mor things &c, – trade continued bad, & the war went on &c, in the Spring about march, we took Several of the west India Island – but the french were driving the allies out of france &c as Spring came on we did some better, we could do with less fire, & we got plenty of milk &c – and we still hoped that trade would revive, but thing went worse at dolphinholme, folk kept shifting away to other places, so that there was very few now left on the spot. on the 1st of June 1794, Lord Howe got a glorious Victory over the french fleet of Brest, he sunk 1, Burnt 2, & brought 6 Sail all of the line, into Plymouth &cr on the 4th of agust (1794) I was loos from my apprinticeship, but this was no good news to us, for trade was so bad, I could not tell where to get work, indee [*sic*] I was glad to stop on without any advance

189   Hebden Bridge
190   The Lancaster Canal was started in the winter of 1792, but the section between Preston and Tewitfield (south of Kendal) was not opened until 1797 because of delays in completing the aqueducts over the Wyre at Garstang and the Lune at Lancaster.
191   frozen
192   The River Wyre, which runs through Dolphinholme and provided power for the mill.
193   Corless Mill, half a mile downstream from Dolphinholme
194   chaff or spilled grain
195   Timothy Cragg confirms that in the bitter winters of the early 1790s fuel was short. The main local fuel was turf, dug on Abbeystead and Catshaw Fells: when the cutters went onto the fells in midsummer they found the peat still frozen solid in its lower layers, so severe had the frosts of winter been. The workers at Dolphinholme, including Benjamin, had no turbary rights and so could not go onto the moor for turf even if they had been able to do so. They were therefore dependent on coal or turf sold locally, or on gathering firewood from the valley slopes and water's edge (LRO: DDX/760/1).

of wages, for the mill was now Standing,[196] & we expected it to be sold, I continued to stop here repairing, & keeping the machienery from rusting &c I never Spoke of wages raising &c &c – this autum, Several great men were tried for treason &c and the french driving their enimies out of france, the duke of york came Home with the remnant of his army, –

* we continued at this dreary place, untill I was turnd of work[197] in January, 1795, then I was forced to try my fortune, but Still unwilling to leave this place, I went first to lancaster, then to Caton,[198] thinking to go back to dolphinholme when it begun again, but I could geg [sic] no work. So I set of to Preston, with little money, & a sorrowfull heart to Search work – but before I set of, I went to me old master for a Caracter, & he took my Indenture & wrote on the Back of it – Benjamin Shaw has fullfilled this his Indenture with Honesty, Industery, & Soberiety &c Signed Thomas Edmondson

I like wise got a note from the maneger, which ran thus, Benjamni [sic] Shaw, the Bearer, has been in our employ Several years, during which time he has behaved with the greatest Propotiety, & is intirely at liberty from us, to get work wherever he pleases &c – he has Served in the filing & turning Business, Signed, Nathaniel Booth – I went to Preston, & soon got work at Horrocks' Yard, & at the weeks end I got 14 shillings per week, I might have got more, if I had asked more, but I was so afraid of differing with them, that I durst not ask more – in about 3 weeks my wife came to Preston, and we took 2 rooms at the corner of dale Street, where we have lived 31 years[199] –

196 idle
197 turned out of work
198 Caton, five miles north west of Lancaster and seven miles north of Dolphinholme, was a locally-important textile centre in the late eighteenth and nineteenth centuries, specializing in silk and cotton. The mills were on the Arkle Beck, a tributary of the Lune. The same trade depression which had afflicted Dolphinholme was affecting the Caton mills, and Benjamin was over-optimistic in hoping to find work there (see Price, pp. 14–22).
199 Dale Street was at the eastern end of Church Street, at the edge of the old (pre-1790) town. It was laid out as part of a speculative housing scheme in 1794: Whittle, in the chronology of events included in his *History of the Borough of Preston* (p. 309), records that on 27 August 1793 'proposals [were] made for building thirty houses in Dale-street, Thos. Leeming the builder, and George Bolton, Esq, the treasurer'.
    The houses were immediately adjacent to the huge 'Yellow Factory' of 1791, which completely overshadowed them. They were back-to-back cellar dwellings, and although Benjamin does not give a detailed description it is probable that he and his family rented the ground floor and first floor rooms, linked by a staircase, while another family presumably occupied the cellar. Benjamin came to Preston, and to Dale Street, in February or March 1795. In May 1795 his parents also came to live in Preston, and they soon moved to Dale Street from their first home at Friargate Brow – an excellent example of the proximity of related migrant families noted by Anderson in his study of Preston in 1851. Later, other members of the family also lived in Dale Street, including Benjamin's sister Hannah Jackson and his son Joseph.
    The houses in Dale Street were demolished as part of a slum clearance scheme in 1939–40.

* our Betty was now with child of the Seccond, Joseph by this time could run about, & – this Spring I suffered a great deal in one of my feet, in coming to preston,[200] I got the skin of by blisters, & the wether being very frosty, & not taking care of it, the frost got into it, and having to stand to work constantly made it worse, so that it was nearly may before it got well, & at the same time the hard knot in the back side of my leg, which had been there above a year was still worse, & more painfull &c – our Betty got some winding[201] into the house, & we got a few things into the house, But Bread was now very dear, the quarter loaf $3\frac{1}{2}$ pound was a 1ˢ 3ᵈ in London this year, & great disturbance in many towns, by rioting &c – about this time, my old master, Edmondson, came to see me, & wanted me to go with him into Yorkshire, but I thought if I was out of work here, I was more likely to get work with less trouble, than I should be there, & I did not consent to go &c – on the 29ᵗʰ of July this year, my wife brought me another son, we named him william, after my brother,[202] now her hands was compleatly tied, & I had 4 to keep with 14ˢ a week, and few good in the house, & bread very dear, &c

* as my wife had never been shown the way to manage household afairs in the best way,[203] our money did not do us the good it might, had it been in some hands we were allways in Debt, & traded in Shops, & this is a bad prictise, but it was her way, I could not prevail with her either by fair, or fowl means, to change this plan, She began this way, & we have continued in this way, do all I could to prevet [sic] it – there never too persons, I think, were more at varience in our plans, of conducting household affairs, than we were – I allways wanted to stand clear of debt, to buy our goods for ready money, & if possible to have a little money by us to make a good bargin when there was a chance, (as there often is) (my maxim was a peny saved is a penny got) but this was not her way – this caused us endless trouble, & contentions &c, She was soft and easy, & if she could carry on without much care & trouble, that was all she wanted, was quite indifferant about cloaths or furniture, or caracture, &c –

Benjamin lived at No.1, which was on the south side of the road at its junction with Stanley Street. The site is now occupied by warehousing and light industry (see also Morgan, p. 40).

200   Benjamin walked to Preston from Dolphinholme, a distance of sixteen miles. It is not clear whether Betty, who was five months pregnant with their second child, and Joseph (with their few possessions) went by the carrier's cart which is known to have made the journey more or less regularly.

201   The winding of yarn onto bobbins was a process not yet mechanized in the factories and so let out for domestic work.

202   The Preston St John register records the baptism of 'William, son of Benjamin and Elizabeth Shawe' on 23 August 1795 (LRO: PR/1444).

203   Benjamin attributes what he considered to be Betty's financial incompetence to the fact that she had never had a mother to show her the correct way of managing money and budgeting. It is more likely that her casual, perhaps over-generous, spirit, in such marked contrast to Benjamin's own cautious ways, was the cause, and that no amount of training would have altered her – Benjamin certainly failed to do so in thirty years of marriage.

* this autumn Subscriptions was made & provisions sold at a cheaper rate, to some poor familys that could get a recomendation from the Subscribers[204] &c – at the begining of this year, the stadholder, prince & princess of orange, escaped from Holand to England, & had appartments asigned in hampton court &c and in april the Prince of Wails was married, to Caraline of Brunswick – this Spring Warren Hastings, Esquire, governor of Bengal, was aquitted, after a trial which lasted 146 days & in the summer there was insurections in many towns, on account of the high price of Bred – the Cape of Good Hope was taken by Admirals Clarke & Elphinstone – his majesty was asulted in his carriage, on his way to the parliament house, & in January (1796) the princess of wales, delivered of a daughter &c

* this spring my leg became much worse, & broke out into holes,[205] in this spring, & in April, I went to Whitworth,[206] & stayed untill the Election, which took place in may (1796) when John horrocks, stood Lord Stanley & S[ir] Henry Hoghton, when Horrocks failed at that time, but stood them so hard that the next Election, Stanley coalesed with him, & this coalesietion, lasted 30 years &c – I went again to whitworth, & stoped about 7 week, but got little better, & as I saw how they dresed it, I thought I would come home, & buy the drugs that the used &c, it continued incureable, & I wrought in misery constantly. could not sleep at night, & in the day had no ease, in this way I went on, sometimes a little better, & sometimes worse, & all the means I could use was ineffectual – Some times one hole would heal, but soon it broke out in another place, &c – in may

---

204 The more prosperous townspeople subscribed money for a special poor relief fund, because of the great suffering caused by the trade depression.

205 became ulcerous

206 Whitworth near Rochdale. Benjamin visited the Taylors (generally known as 'the Whitworth doctors'), a family of surgeons and medical practitioners widely famed in the late eighteenth and early nineteenth centuries. John Taylor (1740–1802), a farrier and amateur horse doctor, achieved a reputation for special skill in his craft and then turned his attention to human patients. Several generations of his family, trained in a combination of minor surgery, bonesetting and the preparation of patent medicines, followed in his footsteps.

The special characteristic of the Whitworth doctors was that they would treat anybody irrespective of class and financial status, and with equal care and attention. Of John Taylor it was said that 'if the poor never paid him, as many never did, he never asked them for it; they staid as long as they pleased, and they went when they pleased . . . There was a subscription box kept to help such of the poor as could not support themselves' (Anon. 1876, pp. 3–4). Taylor is said to have treated duchesses and even Princess Elizabeth, daughter of George III, as well as Benjamin Shaw and his ilk.

The Taylors had a reputation for extraordinary powers of healing, and they were undoubtedly gifted in surgery and bonesetting. But modern opinion suggests that their patent medicines were of little value, and the unkind word 'quack' has been used of them. In Benjamin's case it is apparent that his leg was already becoming ulcerous and that the skills of the Whitworth doctors were not appropriate. As his account indicates, he made a second visit but it was useless, and the leg 'continued incureable'.

1795, my father, & mother, & sister hannah, came to Preston, my fathe learned to Spin at friar gate factory,[207] & lived on friargate Brow, &c

* this year a duch fleet was taken by admiral Elphinstone, near the cape of good hope – general washington, resigned the Precedency of America – Spain declared war against England this year, & Cathrine 2rd of Rusia died &c – Corsica was evacuated this year – the french land[ed] at Bantry Bay in Irland, & great fear lest they should land in England &c – (1797) & great preparations was made, in case an invation should take place, However they did not stop long in Irland, till they were taken –

* in the sumer of this year, I got my wages raised to 16 shilings per week about this time, Spindle & fly frames[208] came into use in this town, they began at Horrockses, & factorys increased fast, the last year (1796) Spining by Steam on the mules,[209] or spining wheels likewise began, & the hand Spiners thought that their trade was ruined,[210] & there was great murmerings among the Poor &c, the throstle spining frame was much improved about this time, &c, the old factory at Spittles mos was built, & french wood[211] about this time[212] – the first steam factory in Horrocks yard was burnt dowwn, Soon after it was finnished &c this year my Sister Hannah went to dolphinholme to work, that place had got agate[213] again, Soon after got married, to Iciac walker, a wool comber & soon after he went into the Militia, & toward the end of the year she came home again,[214]

* this year (1797) Sir John Jervice got a great Victory, over the Spanish fleet of Cape St Vincent, in february – in April & may, there was an alarming mutiny, in the fleet at Sheerness, & Spithead &c – & in June, Parker, the ringleader of the

---

207   Friargate factory, close to the junction with Heatley Street, was not opened until some years later. Joseph Shaw learned to spin with Paul Catterall at his Moor Lane factory, as noted by Benjamin in his account of his father.

208   Fly frames drew out the sliver, or partially twisted fibres, and wound it onto bobbins, giving it a further twist which allowed it to be wound off the bobbins during further stages in the spinning process.

209   The spinning mules were a major advance in the technology of the industry. They were so called because, like mules, they were the result of crossbreeding. Spinning mules combined the best features of Arkwright's water frame and Hargreaves' spinning jenny.

210   They were right.

211   Frenchwood, on the eastern edge of Preston: see note following.

212   Spittals Moss lay just to the north of the old town of Preston, in the vicinity of the present Lancashire Polytechnic: it derived its name from the medieval leper hospital at nearby Maudlands. The 'old factory' was the first Spittals Moss factory (opened by John Horrocks in 1796); a second, the 'new factory', followed in 1799. In 1797 Horrocks opened the Frenchwood factory, which was just south of Dale Street and the earlier 'Yellow Factory'.

213   going or started

214   Hannah Shaw was married at Churchtown in October 1797.

mutiny, was Hanged &c – in October, Duncan got a complete victory over the dutch, & took 9 ships of the lile [*sic*][215] – in december, the king, & both Houses of Parlement, went in Procession to St Pauls, to return Public thanks to god, for the 3 grand victorys, of Howe Jervice & duncan &c,

* in the autumn this year my father began again to travle a Clocking, & in the Spring, this year (1798) my mother Sickened, & on good friday died, aged 48. She had been confined to her room many years, through lameness. She could knit, Sew, & wind twist, but could not walk &c, this is a great affliction where it happens, both to the Sufferer, & to the family in which it happens &c, my fathe kept his room on,[216] & my Sister lived with him, Soon after this She went to Sunderland, to see her husband, & came home with Child – I continued still very lame on my leg, trying various thing, but all in vain – & excercised my spare time in reeding of which I was very fond, & as I was always tired with my work, & not able to take any more active divertions, I became Soletary, & was mostly at home, I sometimes Practised drawing Machinery &c, and other things of the like nature, by this time I had got a few Book, of my own &c. I likewise often helped my wife, to wind twist when she was bussy &c,

* this year 1798, Sir Henry Houghton lade down his place in Parlement, & John Horrocks was put in without opposition – this year (1798) a rebellion Broke out in the South of Irland – & in may our army capitulated with the french, in Holland – in July the rebels defeated in Ireland – in august Nelson got a Complete Victory over the french fleet, at the mouth of the Nile, in Egypt, where he took 9 ships of the line, & Burnt 2, the same month the french landed some more troops in Irland, soon after JB:Warren got a victory over the french fleet of Ireland, where he took I Ship & 3 friggats &c, decemb^r. Sirdinia given up to the french, the same month, the king & Queen of Naples fled to Cisaley, on the aproach of the french &c, and the french took it over soon after –

* the last summer, Riley & Paley, went into Partnership in the Machien making Business, and took a Shop at Spittles moss, in Horrocks factory,[217] & me and the

215 line
216 Benjamin's parents were living in one room in Dale Street at the time of his mother's death.
217 Richard Riley was a foreman at Horrocks's 1796 factory at Spittals Moss. In 1799 he and John Paley went into partnership to make machinery, but eventually they progressed to cotton manufacturing. In 1802 Paley & Co. built the mill at Heatley Street in conjunction with Riley, but they retained their interests in the Spittals Moss mill and (later) the Canal Bank mills. Paley also became involved in an iron foundry on the Heatley Street site. Richard Riley developed, in his own right, the Banktop Mill at Fishwick, in east Preston.
        It was customary for the various ancillary trades associated with textile manufacturing (such as the making and repair of machinery) to be undertaken by small firms, partnerships or individuals, who rented space within the factory yard or buildings. Thus many of the early nineteenth-century mills spawned a complex of sheds and workshops, and it was in these that

men in the Shop at the yard had notice to leave, or go to the new Shop, at the beginning of the year 1799, Riley Had been the foreman in the yard, so he & John Paley, took as much Machinery of horrocks as they could do &c – I did not like to go to the moss, & I had an offer of a Shop in the dale Street, at the lords Factory, as they wanted to have some Spindle & fly frames, which were lately come into use, in this town so I ingaged with them, & James Kay went at the same time,[218] we were to have a guinea a week, but to draw only 16 Shilings untill the first frames were made, & if they answered[219] to be paid the arrears the week they were done – we went in January 1799, & we had all the Patterns to make, & tools for it was a very rough Shop[220] &c, it was 16 weeks before the first frame was finished, & when we came to settle our account they cheated me out of 16 Shillings, aledging they agreed with me for 1 Pound a week, however D Ainsworth, the manager gave me 5 Shillings, pretending he was sorry that there should be any misunderstanding between us, &c

* at this place I got aquainted with Frank lambert, a Spining master, he was of the Baptist Religion, & was frequently talking of religion,[221] I likewise pretended to defend the Church of England &c I prated much though I seldom went to church, but was much atatched to it for all that &c – May the 7th my wife

---

Benjamin spent his working life. Many such ventures were small in scale, financially precarious, and short-lived – some only lasting as long as the fitting out of the mill to which they were attached.

John Paley was a member of the unreformed (pre-1836) Corporation of Preston, and was elected for the St George's Ward on the reformed Borough Council on 7 January 1836. He was made an alderman in August 1838, and served as Mayor of Preston in 1838–9. He died in January 1855.

218   The factories at Spittals Moss were a mile from Benjamin's house in Dale Street, and his increasing lameness made this a major disadvantage. The offer of work almost next door to his home was too good to miss. The Lord's Factory, in Dale Street, was opened in 1796 and was eventually acquired by David Ainsworth, another of the new breed of cotton entrepreneurs: in 1799 he worked for Riley and Paley, but by 1818 he had gone into partnership with Paul Catterall and was a cotton manufacturer, part owner of the Church Street mill (*Lancashire Directory* 1818, p. 10). A pillar of the local Methodist church, Ainsworth was very highly respected within the town's establishment, but Benjamin's account of his business methods (later in the text) gives another perspective.

219   answered the requirement – were satisfactory

220   an unfinished shop, without equipment

221   Francis Lambert, spinning master at the Lord's Factory in Dale Street, was a leading member of the Baptist Chapel in Leeming Street. In the mid-1820s he became associated with a Scotch Baptist group which separated from the existing Baptist organization in the town, and held its own meetings over a smithy in Church Street. He and the temperance pioneer, Joseph Livesey, were two of the ministers of the Scotch Baptists. Most of this group eventually reunited with the main body of Baptists after the opening, in 1858, of the Fishergate Baptist church (Hewitson, p. 534). Lambert eventually became a partner in Lambert, Stephenson & Co., cotton spinners and manufacturers of Brunswick Street (Pigot's 1828 *Directory*, p. 439). He had a very important effect upon Benjamin's life, since it was through his influence that Benjamin joined the Methodists, but it is not clear whether they remained close.

brought me a daughter, we called her Bellow[222] – this year Bread was very dear, &c, this Summer my oldest Child Joseph, had Some sort of a Blood Vessel burst with in him, or an impost,[223] &c we never expected him to recover, & for several days I thought veary [sic] thing that came by the Shop window, was coming to inform me of his death &c –

* this Sumer Frank lambert, invited me to go to his Chapple with him, which was at the corner of leeming Street, & Queen Street,[224] I promised I would, but did not intend But he came to call on me, & I went with him, I liked the Sermon very well, & thought there was something more in religion than I had thought of, I went again, & the Preacher Preached from Job the the 14 Chap & 10 Verse,[225] this Sermon came home to my Concience, I now was fully convinced that I was a sinner, & if I died in that state I should be lost – I now began to pray for the first time – I had constantly Sade my Prayers, & repeated the appostles Creed &c but was an intire stranger to real religion, but I was dreadfully tempted that my day of grace was past, and it was too late for me to pray now &c, in august I went with frank to the Vestery, to Sit & talk with the Preacher, but I did not join in the discourse, for I had Broken up my mind to frank, & he brought forward such discourse as suted my state, I was much pleased & incouraged by this discourse &c, the preacher sade that none need dispair that found any wish to come to the Saviour, for that was an evidence that he was under grace, & ought to come, & put in his clame for Salvation &c

* however, I continued full of doughts & fears &c long after I now went constantly to some place of worship, often to St George' Chapple,[226] for I was still Prejudiced in favour of the Church, but I found nothing that I wanted there, I now about october, was still doubtful & fearfull lest I shoud be lost for ever, I came to this resolution, if I must be lost Eternally, I will be lost calling for Mercy – Soon after this god was Mercifull, & spoke Peace to my Soul, & now I found that Peace with god which Passeth all understanding, & rejoiced all the day long,

222 Isabella, daughter of Benjamin and Betty Shaw, was baptized at Preston St John on 9 June 1799 (LRO: PR/1445).
223 an abscess or large septic swelling
224 Leeming Street Baptist chapel was opened in 1783. In 1854 the membership split, and the site was eventually sold to the Church of England (St Saviour's church was built there). In 1858 the remaining 'official' Baptists built the present Fishergate Baptist chapel.
225 Job 14, 10: 'But man dieth, and wasteth away; yea, man giveth up the ghost, and where *is* he?'
226 St George's Church, now incongruously situated next to a 1970s multi-storey car park in the middle of Preston, was opened in 1725 as a chapel of ease for the parish church of St John. It was technically a chapel only until the creation of a separate parish in 1808 although Benjamin, writing in 1826, used the old term. The church was popular with the 'middle class and "better end" people' (Hewitson, p. 471). It is possible that Benjamin, with his intellectual tastes, preferred the sermons and service to those at the parish church, which was much more conveniently situated.

& saw every thing in a new light, I wondered that I never saw them before, my heart was now Chainged, & my life was Chainged of course, I now read the Scriptures with great delight, & recomended them to my wife, & my father, who was my constant companion &c, my father soon after this received the like precious Blessing &c, we now constantly conversed together on devine Subjects, & our lives went on Happaly together,

* the last year was remarkable for the following occurrances, in may 1799 Siringapatam was taken, & Tippoo Killed, in the east indies – in august the pope died at Valence – do[227] the dutch fleet taken by admiral Mitchel, & Suranam taken from them &c October this month Bonaparte arives in france, from Egypt where he had been a long time, & chainges the form of the Goverment of france – he was appointed first Consul &c, in November, a secret expedition against holand the duke of York at the head of it, when the whole of the fleet was taken without the loss of a man –

* there was great scarcity of Corn this year, & many subcriptions made for the poor, & Soop shops appered &c[228] (1800) in february, this year, the master david Ainsworth, order us that we should not go out to our drinkings, (or Baging as some call it,[229]) as we had done, and at the end of the week stoped 2 Shiling of our wages for not complying, with his order – we all combined together about this trifleing thing, & sent him a Summans, and had it tried before the mayor,[230] & cost him for our wages, but not for the new regulation of our time,[231] he being much offended with our conduct discharged us all together – Some submited & Beged their work again, but I and another got wort [*sic*] with Frank Sleddon, lately begun his Shop was at the Bottom of Bolton Court, near the Sike, I agreed for a guinea a week &c,[232]

---

227   ditto
228   Whittle (p. 311) notes that in 1799 'soup-houses' were erected in Friargate and that oatmeal was selling at the remarkably high price of £6 per load in the town.
229   short breaks for refreshment during working hours
230   John Grimshaw, the Mayor in 1799–1800, was the brother of Lt-Col. Nicholas Grimshaw, the most powerful man in Preston politics between 1790 and 1830. The Grimshaw family, lawyers and landowners, were closely allied with a powerful group of manufacturers in sustaining the strongly Anglican and Tory complexion of the Corporation against the attacks of Radicals and Whigs.
231   They did not succeed in having the new regulation overturned.
232   Francis (Frank) Sleddon was a key figure in Benjamin's adult life. In 1799 he began a machine shop in Bolton's Court, off Church Street, and in 1801 took a lease on land in the Brick Croft near Stanley Street, where he built a workshop of his own. As Benjamin notes, Sleddon was a poor man but full of ambition. In 1804, in partnership with his brother William, he began to produce machinery with the aim of setting up his own cotton manufactory, but quickly over-reached his slender resources, ran into serious financial trouble, and had to go into partnership with Robert Buxton, a prosperous corn dealer who (unwisely) saw this as an opportunity for a profitable investment.

* about this time I began to meet in one of the Methodist Classes, with William Summerfield, & this was a great Blesing to me my Soul, I was truly alive to god, & I delighted in Religious meetings, & conversation, I had gained the consent of my wife, to attend the chapple & She likewise got convinced of her need of a change of heart & life, & in march found the Pearl of great Price, this month we entered into the methodist Society & now our Strife & Quarreling ceased, we prayed with & for each other, & not withstanding she had 3 Children she got frequently to the Chapple, & I now thought that we should be throughly Happy, & our tempory[233] concerns Better managed than formerly,

* but I am convinced that there is a great likeness between the old & new Creater,[234] or the person that is chainged in mind as to religion is nearly the same as to the managment of his terpory[233] affairs, my wife continued still to conduct her concerns in the same way &c, trading in Shops, & Still in debt sometimes chainging Shops – paying off at one Shop, & Scoreing on at another, trading with Scotch men,[235] & often going to the Pawn Shop &c – though I allowed her more money that the most of men, for I was reguror at my work, & Spent nothing but in Books &c, I alowed her 20 Shilling per week &c when I had anything, and saw the children want any thing, or her, I bought it &c But I was doomed to Poverty from the time that I was married – She had no Shifty[236] management about her, as a poor woman ought to have, and would not change

---

A year later Buxton, apparently realizing the precariousness of Sleddon's activities, withdrew. Sleddon was forced to return to rented workshop space, leasing a building from Thomas Crane. He remained in the machine-making business, and in 1818 had premises in Back Lane (which ran parallel with Friargate near the present Orchard Street) (*Lancashire Directory* 1818, p. 56). His career of misjudgment and ill-luck continued. In 1822 his factory blew down – an indictment of early nineteenth-century jerry-building – and in 1825 he went bankrupt: there was a forced sale of his housing properties, but his factory mysteriously burned down before its sale went ahead.

By 1828 he had re-established himself in Snow Hill as a brass-and iron-founder and also had a small cotton mill in Hanover Street (Pigot's 1828 *Directory*, pp. 438–40). He was elected to the Borough Council for Trinity Ward in January 1836, and served until 1844. In the latter year he again went bankrupt in spectacular fashion (see Morgan, pp. 9–10). His connection with Benjamin Shaw was undoubtedly reinforced by their shared religion. Sleddon was a member of the same Methodist chapel as Benjamin, and his children were baptized at the Methodist Society between 1804 and 1815. Like Benjamin he seems to have turned against the Methodists thereafter, and the children were rebaptized at Holy Trinity in 1820.

Had Sleddon enjoyed greater success in business, and been less subject to extremes of fortune, Benjamin's own working life might have been different. He seems to have enjoyed consistently good relations with Sleddon, with whom he was on first name terms (LRO: DDX/1554/2), and pays a rare tribute in the section dealing with 1822 when he describes him as a 'good master', and points to Sleddon's kindness in giving him work despite his disabilities.

233 temporal
234 creature
235 'Scotch drapers': pedlars or credit traders
236 clever, adaptable or thrifty

her plann, She kept Company with the lowest, & poorest of the neibours, & & hearing their tales of destress, was often imposed on to help them. & I think was often cheated at the shops in her accounts, for she was easy, & Honest, & thought everyone so &c,

* this year Bread was very dear, & Soup Shops opened &c, but work was not so scarce as formerly &c – at the begining of the year (1800) Bonaparte proposed peace to England, but it was rejected – in febr^y Pope Pious 7th was elected, to the papel chair, april general Sewarrow, of Russia died – at this time the french gained many Conquests, in may Hadfield Shot at the king (george 3) in drury lane theater, was aprehended, tried & aquitted, Verdict Insanety &c, in august an unsuccesful attack was made upon ferrol in Spain – in Septemb^r Malta taken by the English – & in the same month the Russians ly an embargo on our Shiping, Octob^r, a conspiracy in france to kill Bonaparte, but it failed – November, Russia, Sweden & Denmark, all unite against England – d^o England, & Ireland, united by an act passed in Both Kingdoms –

* 1801 this year work was more plentifull, but provisions very dear, the Shop in which I wrought was very Bare of tools, and the road to it was allmost impassable, the nearest way from us which was down Shephard Street, & by the old poor house, (which is now a very good road) I went in the dark round by the Turkshead yard,[237] &c, in the Summer this year, Sleddon Bought a piece of ground in an old Brick croft,[238] which is now Stanley Street, & began to build the factory now in the Possesion of Bleasdale,[239] we wondered much at this, for he was lately so poor that his family was in want of Bread – but we pushed work on, & he got another floor on when a pair of Mules went out &c – & before winter got it covered in, this year as usial I continued lame, but wrought constantly &c,

---

237   The old workhouse stood on the north side of Avenham Lane at the corner of Bolton's Court (Hewitson, p. 399). It was closed shortly after the opening of a new workhouse on Preston Moor in 1788. The area south of Church Street, apart from the courts themselves, was still largely undeveloped in the first decade of the nineteenth century, and the stream, Avenham Syke, which ran at the foot of the slope was still an open watercourse. The area was therefore semi-rural, with muddy tracks which were troublesome for Benjamin, who was now very lame.

238   The Brick Croft was a field on the east side of the high road (now London Road) leading from Preston to the Ribble bridge at Walton, and on the south side of what was later to be New Hall Lane. As the name suggests, the land had been used for clay extraction and a small brickworks, but it was close to the growing town and adjacent to several new mills, and so was ideally situated for industrial development. Frank Sleddon and James Bleasdale, among others, built workshops and sheds there. Part of the site was cleared in the early 1820s and Stanley Street, a widening and realignment of the old high road, was laid out across it.

239   The Stanley Street mill, owned by James Bleasdale in the late 1820s, was acquired by him from Frank Sleddon during the latter's bankruptcy in 1824–5. Bleasdale was the owner of the land on which Sleddon had built his mill, and the acquisition had probably been in payment of debts.

I got a job of my master by the Piece, which made my wages a little better,[240] & toward the end of this year, the master got more hands & seemed to prosper – as to religion, I continued to Clieve[241] to the lord, & my Heart rejoiced in Jesus Christ above all things &c –

* I think there was an Election this year, at the Union of the Kingdom of Ireland but there was no opposition &c here – the Political occurances of 1801) January, the first Parlement of England & Ireland united met feb[y]. Peace Signed between france & germany at lunaville march the minestery Chainged, & Mr Pit retires from office, do Victory over the french in Egypt, and General abecrumbie was wonded & died in a few days after – bread at 1[s] 10½[d] the quarter loaf &c, &c march, Paul Emper of Russia asasinated in his own Palice &c, Succeeded by Alixander 1st do the Danes take possession of Hamburg &c, april Sir Hide Parker, & lord Nelson, destroy the daneish fleet at Copenhagen, and make a Peace with the Danes – Conquest of Egypt compleated by general Hutchinson – August, Lord Nelson fails in an atack upon the flottila at Bologna – October prelimeneries of Peace signed between France & England, but this Peace was of Short continueance, & Scarce like peace

* 1802) this Spring, the Poor were full of complaints, on account of Bread, it was so uncommon dear, but work was plentiful, which made it more tolerable – in March this Spring, we Shifted our Shop, the factory in Stanley Street was in that State that we went into it, but it was in a rough Condition, the windows were not got in we were ill Starved,[242] but we wanted more roome. I was now much nearer my work, & had more lazure time of Cource, which I constantly employed in reading, or doing Something for my family – makeing or repairing some thing, Constantly, this Spring, my father in law Edward Leeming, come to preston, & his family, &c, he got 2 Sons, John & Christopher[243] to the weaving trade, the Steam Engin was not ready when we went in to the new Shop, & we had wheel turners to turn our laiths, untill the Engin was ready, which was not before autum –

* this year, Preston guild was Held in august,[244] but Such was my deadness to

---

240   Piecework was better paid than a weekly rate, but inevitably less predictable. Benjamin tried to do piecework whenever possible, to supplement his regular income.
241   cleave: adhere or stay close
242   bitterly cold, frozen
243   Benjamin gives a detailed account of the Leeming family later in the work.
244   The Preston Guild, 'our greatest carnival', was held every twenty years, as it still is. The core of the Guild was the medieval ceremony of the renewal of burgess membership, which had originally been obligatory for anybody who wished to conduct a trade in the town. Around this ceremony had grown a great festival of entertainment, processions, balls and masques, sideshows and banquets. By 1802 the ancient commercial role of the Guild had lapsed, but the celebrations were continued as a great popular festival, and have grown in scale ever since (see Crosby, chaps. 4 and 5).

pastimes & austontation, that I never went up the street,[245] or saw any thing belonging to the guild all the time, for such was my contemp for these things, that I would not pertake in the folly as I considered them to be &c, in the autum, the Engin started, & all things went on Better, trade continued good, & we got more hands, & more tools, & all things seemed to prosper &c I now got more wages, and had Piece work some times &c, Still I continued lame, but Still put the bes Construction on it, & seemed to be easy, but no one knew what I suffered – when our sufferings are some sudden attack of sickness, or some late acedent, many will enquire of us with seeming concern, but if the complaint continue long, the simpathy goes of, & they give us up to our fate, they tire with enquirey &c,

* – I have little to say of Politics for this year, the prelimeniares of Peace agreed upon in october last, was Signed this year on the 27th of march at Amiens, &c – the Seas now being open, the french strived to reduce the Island of S[t] domingo, to the obediance of france, but after much loss of money & lives it was found imposible, the peace was soon at an end, for there was nothing but Jalousy between the too Counterys, for war soon comenced &c –

* (1803) on January the 17th, my wife got her bed of our second daughter Hannah,[246] now we had 2 of each sort, this was a delicate little Child from its Birth, and was allways Small & tender, this year I do not remember any thing remarkable, I think about this time my wages was raised to 25 Shilling per week, & I had some Jobs by the piece, & then when I worked piece work a week I often got £2–6s or £2–8[s] a week. I now began to pay the House rent, & give my wife 20 Shillings a week but She was always Short of money, (this was my misfortune for if I could suply her with money, & never have ocation to reprove her, I could live with her peaceable enough) but we had often to differ on muney acounts, in Stead of mending the children clothes, She bought new ones, She did not like to mend, or to see them in mended cloths, (her Common saying was she did not like to be poor & seem so &c) about this time, I thought if I could get her to trade in a better way, we should do better, So I Bought sometimes loads of meal, & packs of flower, pots of Butter & Chees &c. and pottatoes, & Coals by the load, but that way would not do, for when they were done there was nothing towards the payment, all was Shut,[247] so this way would not do, for it was nearly the price of the articles of loss for She had money plenty to suply the family weekly, but She could not save a Shiling over a week – She was allways

245 Presumably Church Street: Benjamin did not go into the town centre to see the celebrations.
246 The baptism of Hannah took place at the Methodist Society: the register records that 'Anne Shaw Daughter of Eliz[th] & Benj[n] Shaw' was born on 18 January and baptized on 24 January 1803 (LRO: MPr/11/1).
247 used up or finished

contriving to borrow as She Called it, but nothing was paid back, I once kekt[248] my account against her a while, & when I got to £12 or 12 guineas, I gave over keeping my account &c –

– the political afairs of the year, of the greatest moment – governor wall executed for the murder of a Sergent, 9 years before in the Isle of Goree – february, Colonel dispard, & others Executed for Sedition, – war with france, & Holland, Comences again &c insurection in dublin, and the murder of lord Kilwarden – Execution of Counsilor Emmit in Dublin – St Lucia & Sumatra taken, by the English – Hanover taken by the french – the french army in St domingo capitolate with the Black natives to leave the Island – but afterward submit to the English Squadron of that Island, with their Ships of war & their Merchant-men &c.

* 1804 this year my masters Sleddons began to make machinery for their own factory, & intended to Carry on Both Cotton manufactering & machien making, &c, trade continued good, & they were getting money fast, but it was too soon for them to begin so Expensive an undertaking, however they being determined to try, they Set about it – but it is not wise to push on too rapidly, even in Prosperity, & to reach at more than one can compass – they got a room filled with mules, & preparations in another room &c – this year, (I think in the summer[249]) John Horrocks M.P. for this Burrough died, & his Brother Samuel was returned in his place. Sir Thomas Heskett, offered himself but it was settled, without a Poll, &c – this year my sister hannah was married the second time, to Henry Jackson, this was his 3rd wife &c,[250] –

* at the beginning of this year (1804 his late Majesty george 3rd was taken ill &c, – a french squadron in the east Indies, under admiral Liniou, was beaten off by the English east India Companys Ships &c – great Preparations in france to Envaid England, great armys Colected & trained, & called the army of England &c – Octobr a treaty agreed upon between france & genoa – decr, a treaty entered into between Sweeden & England &c, & december 2 Bonaparte Crouned at Paris by the Pope –

* 1805, this year, I had good work & wages, but my leg still continued very Bad, & on the whole it was worse, but I was Hard, & still stuck close to my work – this year I had another Child Born on the 18th of Septemr. & called her mary – this was the loveliest Child of all the others, healthy & good Humoured, & in all respects a lovly creature – but She died the year following, in July 23 1806, of the

---

248   kept
249   John Horrocks died on 1 March 1804.
250   Henry Jackson and Hannah Walker were married on 1 August 1804.

Meazles, we had all the helps we could get, & made use of every means but all in vain &c,[251] –

* lord Mellvil, was disgraced for misapplying the public money, – this year 1805, great Earthquakes in the South of Itily, when 20,000 persons perished – Admiral Calder Engagement with the french & Spanish fleets, he took 2 Ships & was afterwards tried & repremanded &c for not using greater exertion, &c October, admiral Nelsons engagement with the combined fleets of Spain & france, when he took 19 Ships of the line, & 1 French & 2 Spanish admerals, in which engagement he was killed, this was at trafalgar – the austrian army under General Mack, surrender to the french, they soon after enter Vienna, the English invade Hanover – Sir Sidney Smith fails in an atack upon the flottilla at Bologna &c, the Sweeds declare war againt france – the English & russians enter Naples – the Battle of austerlitz, in this engagement the Russians & austerns were beaten by the french, &c, this Victory was followed by the Peace of Presburg, between the french & austria &c –

* at the beginning of 1806, the funeral of lord Nelson, ocupied the Nation awhile &c, this year trade began to be wors, and our master turned many hand off, we was redused to a very few in number – our masters had begun to manufacture, Cotton, and was forced to take in a partner, this was M[r] Buxton a Corn dealer,[252] & he advanced a good deal of money, & trade going bad and not finding money came in as he expected, he turnt tirant as they that are the strongest in Purce mostly do they did not agree long &c, however I continued in the shop still – this year, my favourite Child died, in July, aged 44 weeks & 1 day of the Meazels (the first mary) –

* the Cape of good-hope taken by General Baird, & Sir Home Poppham – William Pitt died in January this year (1806) Fox is made Prime minester – the news of the death of Marques Cornwalles, in the east Indies arives in frbruary. (who died in Octob[r] 1805) the french takes Naples, the King & queen flee to Sicily – admiral duckworth Defeats a french squadron in the west Indies – the King of Prussia Shuts his Ports against the English – & an Embargo laid upon all Prussian Ship in our Ports &c the american States murmer at our Cruisers & great debates in the State Counsils – Joseph Bonaparte made King of Holland, in June the House of Commons pledges itself to abolish the Slave trade &c M[r] Windhams new training act Passed – war with Prussia &c

---

251 The baptism of Mary Shaw, daughter of Benjamin and Elizabeth Shaw of Preston, took place on 26 September 1805, at the Methodist Society (LRO: MPr/11/1). She was buried at Preston St John on 26 July 1806 (LRO: PR/1448).

252 Robert Buxton, son of Thomas Buxton, was a corn merchant. In 1818 he and his father had premises at 2 Lord Street (*Lancashire Directory* 1818, p. 18) and he lived at 43 Lord Street. By 1828 he was operating in his own right, from 1 Lord Street and the Peck Mill (Pigot's 1828 *Directory*, p. 438–9).

* 1807, trade Continued very bad, & work scarce, the machine making was very bad, and wages pulled down, but I had work at the old Shop, this Spring my wife was with child of Thomas, & She had a bad time of it, for she had such Pains in her Belly, like the Cramp that She used to Shout out like as if labour was coming on her, & I was obliged to help her up, for she could not help her Self or Stirr &c She got lighter on the 7 of may, (1807)[253] & we called him thomas, we had a great deal of trouble with him, for he was a cross child, & weak and much inclined to loosnes,[254] &c – in October this year, I became so lame that I could not work, was off for about 10 weeks, dureing this time the masters Parted – Buxton & William Sleddon,[255] remained at the old place, & frank went to a Shop that he took of T Crone,[256]

* when I got Better which was near Christmas, I went to work with frank, who was now becom poor again, for he had littl to call his own, but being know in the town he got work, & Cridit & Carried on by himself, work was Scarce and wages pulled down &c, – he rented a Shop under Mr Crone near the place whear he was, & had his laiths turned by Crones Engin, this winter Some of the factorys only worked between light and dark frank sleddon now seemed to get on a little, though the times was bad, I Continued to be very lame, yet I Stuck to my work untill July in the year (1808) then I was oblieged to give it up, for I could not walk to & from the Shop – I had saved a little money (about 26 Pound)[257] & it was useful, now, but when I could not work any longer nor likely to get better, I began to think how I might provide for my family, & as I was not Certain where I belonged to,[258] I was ancious to know that first –

* I had Served 3 years at dolphinholme, as an aprintice, under articles of

---

253　Thomas Shaw was baptized at the Methodist Society on 11 May 1807. The register states that his date of birth was 2 May, while Benjamin says 7 May. The figure is clear in Benjamin's text, but he could have miscopied from his own notes (LRO: MPr/11/1).

254　diarrhoea

255　William Sleddon was the brother of Frank Sleddon, and had been a junior partner in the unsuccessful attempt to develop a cotton spinning business.

256　Thomas *Crane* is meant here. Crane was a member of the Methodist Society at this period. He had an ironmongery business at 36 Market Place and a foundry and machine-making business in New Hall Lane, Fishwick (*Lancashire Directory* 1818, p. 22; Pigot's 1828 *Directory*, pp. 439–40).

257　This casual reference indicates the extent of Benjamin's extreme financial caution. He was able to save £26 despite his own lameness (and consequent lesser earning power), his wife's 'reckless' spending, and the growing numbers of children in his family. This achievement was required, at least in part, by his realization that if he were unable to work he would need a substantial reserve of savings, but it is also evident that thrift was fundamental to Benjamin's character. Betty was certainly not in sympathy with the attitudes which lay behind such thrift, despite the saving being intended for the benefit of the family. Benjamin, in turn, saw nothing commendable in her spending.

258　did not know in which township he had his legal settlement under the Poor Laws

agreement, only & not knowing whether that would give me a settlement or not, for the factory was in one township, & I lived in another,[259] , therefore I applyed to they Mayor, but getting a doubtful answer I enquired of different law men, & finding them differ in their opinions, I was advised to apply to preston for relief, so my wife got 5 Shilling or some trifle, & they removed us to Ellel, the town in which I lived when I was at dolphinholme,[260] we left 2 lads in preston with my sister, that was in work, & thought that they would keep themselves nearly,[261] & sleep at home, for we did not sell our house-hold goods we left Preston on the 5th of November, 1808 – the town[262] had no work house, So they aggreed to give us a petion,[263] till it Could be known whether we did belong to them or not, & we were to come-back to Preston & Settle, but as soon as we came to preston, the overseer of Preston would not Suffer us to stop in the town, So we were oblieged to go back to Ellel again,

* So they found us Boarding at a labourer house, & paid 20 Shillings per week for us, that would have done well for us at home, but it did nothing for us, for our Childrens Cloaths was soon wore off, & were Soon nearly naked &c, I Continued to be Still worse, & weaker, for now my health was much worse, & I thought I should not live long & had no medicine, & little beside what the family had &c – In this way we continued untill another overseer came, into office, for they only Served one year at that time, this man would have us come to preston, So he sent or got some of the heads of the town to write to Preston, requesting pirmition for us to come back, & got it,[264] So we being tired & nearly naked we

---

259   The question of Benjamin's settlement illustrates one of the anomalies in the settlement concept enshrined in the old Poor Law. The mill at Dolphinholme lay on the south bank of the River Wyre, in the township of Nether Wyresdale and parish of Garstang. The millworkers' cottages in the village of Dolphinholme were on the north bank, in the township of Ellel and parish of Cockerham. The law held that if a man completed a full term apprenticeship in a township or parish he gained a settlement in that place. Benjamin had actually *worked* in Nether Wyresdale, and had signed and completed his agreements there, even though he had *lived* in Ellel. To which township, therefore, did he and his family legally belong? Eventually Ellel accepted the responsibility, and thereafter the Shaws were held to be legally settled there.

260   The papers of the Preston overseers of the poor, and those of Ellel for this period, have not survived, but it may be assumed that a removal order was obtained by Preston.

261   Joseph and William were then fifteen and thirteen-and-a-half years old respectively and were working at the factory, so were able to hand over their wages to their aunt Hannah Jackson in return for their keep.

262   Ellel township

263   pension (allowance or poor relief)

264   When overseers changed, after a year in office, policies often changed as well. Ellel had no workhouse or township-owned cottage for accommodating the poor, and was therefore paying the rent and board of the family while they lodged with a labourer. The new overseer may have regarded this as a dangerously open-ended commitment, or may even have decided that Benjamin had more chance of employment in Preston – there was certainly little possibility of his finding work in Ellel. He therefore persuaded the Preston overseers to allow the Shaws back. The necessary permission would, however, only have been given after Ellel had accepted

gladly excepted the offer, this was in June, 1809, we had been here 30 weeks, & our children had very good health here, for it was a pleasant Situation, good air, & good water, with plenty of room for play, & other excercise, &c –

* by this time I was very weak, & not likely to get Better – at this time trade was bad, & a great deal of tradesmen failing, & – I continued to grow worce- slept little & helped my wife to wind twist, & the Children went to the factory, & our pention was a poor living for us, but time went on & Chainges all things, in the autumn of this year, the gentlemen of Preston, had taken measures to establish a dispensary in this town, by Subscription, & in winter it began to admit persons,[265] Sick & lame, in february, 1810, one of the Subscribers, which came Sometimes to see me, (Mr John Howard)[266] [asked[267]] if I would except of a Recomendation, to this new instetution, So I thought, I should get drugs cheaper &c, I thanked the gentleman for his kindness, my wife took the note to the place &, I happened to fall to the care of d^r Stclars, or St Clare,[268] this was at a lucky time, the physicians then visited the sick themselves, (but not so now) so he came to our house to see me, & ordered Something for me, &c – (he was a young man then, & not much known as a Physician, for he was only begining)

* I continued in this way 2 months, & was little if any better, one day when he came to me, he asked me if I would consent to have it taken off,[269] for he he [*sic*]

---

legal responsibility for future relief of the family, in the form of a settlement certificate. It is clear from the paragraph following that Benjamin was paid a 'pension' by Ellel township, to allow him and his family to remain in Preston.

265 The Preston Dispensary was established following a public meeting of gentlemen in October 1809. Donations were collected and annual subscriptions guaranteed, and in December the Dispensary opened in temporary accommodation at Everton Gardens, near the present bus station. It moved into new buildings in Fishergate in May 1811. Its aim was 'supplying the poor with medicine to their relief in case of sickness' (Wilkinson, pp. 25–39) and in this it was very successful. Whittle (p. 79) stated that 'the support it has experienced has enabled its conductors to distribute its benefits to an extent peculiarly gratifying to the humane and reflecting mind'. He goes on to explain the method of business: 'it relieves all objects of sickness and misfortune, provided they are recommended by a subscriber, and their case be such as come within the nature and object of the institution itself'.

266 The subscribers undertook to make regular visits to the poor who were being relieved by the Dispensary or who were thought to be eligible for treatment, and only a subscriber could recommend a name to the management committee. John Howard, who visited Benjamin, was one of the original subscribers. He was an attorney who had a law practice with his brother, Thomas, at 34 Fishergate: he lived at 35 Lune Street.

267 word missing in original text

268 Drs William St Clare senior and junior were leading figures in Preston society in the early years of the nineteenth century. The father had his practice at 56 Fishergate, and was originally in partnership with his son, William, the doctor who attended Benjamin. By 1818 William junior had a separate surgery at 1 Clark Yard. He was highly regarded for his medical, and particularly his surgical, skills, and Benjamin was indeed fortunate to have his personal interest and attention.

269 to have the leg amputated

Sade, it could not be cureed & it would be better to be cut off – So I considered about it, & was in the same mind that it was incurable, & takeing it off was the only chance there was for life, & was quite weary of living in this missery, so I concented, & a day was fixed &c the docters came, & it was taken of, this was on the 21 april 1810 there was 6 or Seven docters, & physicians, the opperation was 40 minits work, & I was put to bed,

* I never Slept for near a week, with the constant pain, & twiching, in the limb – the fever run high, (for their is allways a fever follows amputation, &) it was very hot wether – about the 7th day it was dressed the first time, & now I got a little Sleep, &c – I now began to mend, & in less than 3 weeks I went out of the house, &c – my health now returned, & in the June, I went to Black-pool, & stoped 5 weeks, in this place, I was ill for, I had nobody with me to help me, &c, my leg nuly taken off, & my right hand was become numb with my Crutch, so that I could Scarce use it, to do anything &c but my health was established greatly &c – my Stump was very Short, so that it was long before I could make any use of it, &, I partly dispaired of ever being able to work any more, however I had better health now than I had enjoyed for many years &c

* I now winded twist, all the day long, when we could get any,[270] & by this time our daughter Bella went to the factory[271] &c – I was now nearly Cut off from the world, was quite like a Prisoner &c, having nothing to do with any Scarsly, but my own family, my wife now Began to Bake oat cakes for the neighbours, for hire & I winded her twist, but this Bakeing is a very disagreeable Business in a house, & very ingurious to health[272] &c, She continued to Bake untill it had greatly hurt her constetution, & at last was forced to drop it, not being able to follow it any longer, in this way things went on with us, as poor as any family in the town, for the town kept droped our Pentions[273] frequently, & Bread was dear &c, –

* 1811, this Spring, my wife was big with Child, this made things worse with us, for there must be some provision made for the lying in &c, in may on the 27 of

---

270   Winding twist was a sedentary occupation which could be done at home, and was thus ideally suited to the physically disabled, housebound and those, such as mothers of newly-born children, who could not work outside the house. In this autobiography there are many references to winding in such circumstances: Benjamin's mother, Isabella, who was crippled with rheumatism, and his wife Betty are among those mentioned.

271   Bella, born in May 1799, was now eleven years old.

272   It is not entirely clear why Benjamin regarded baking oatcakes with such disfavour, but it may be conjectured that the heat of the fire, the dust from the oatmeal, the constant bending, and the cramped conditions resulting from baking and drying cakes in one room with a family of six, were at least partly to blame. To make any adequate income from such employment would have required constant work, resulting in physical exhaustion.

273   kept reducing the allowance from the poor rate

this month our Second Mary was born,[274] now we were Still poorer for our Bettys hands was fast with the young Child &c – however, we continued to make the best Shift[275] that we could, & time went on as fast as it did when we were in prosperity &c – & things are allways changing, & it is a Consolation to the poor to think, that time is on the wing, this causes them to hope for better times, & so keeps up their fainting Hearts &c,

* this year (1811), Provisions was dear, & trade bad, for the war Still Continued – March this spring, young Bonaparte was born &c – the Island of Java, in the East Indies, was taken from the french – the first Parliament under the Regency opened this year – great Comercial destress – the Slave trade supressed – war in spain Siege of Badajoz – Ciudad Rodrigo & Saragon – Storming of Salamanca – Siege of Borgoss &c –

* this year I dont remem any thing particular in the family, we continued all in tolerable health, and our afairs much the Same, my wife continued to Bake oat cake, & I winded twist, & we were very poor as usial, we used to wind (when we had work often untill 12 O'clock on the Saterday night) when other folks were in bed, or enjoying themselves and friends after the labour of the week, but there was no pleasure for us, this was indeed a trying time, & required much patience – it was trying indeed to us, but no to us allone, for there was great distress in all the manufacturing Districts, the last year the amirecans and us was upon bad terms, & this year they declared war against us, & now all trade with them was alltogether stopd, the people murmered, & met together, & Pittishoned but nothing was done for them. they therefore rose in Notenghamshire, & Lecestershire, & Broke the Stocking weaving frames – & in Yorkshire the Croping franes – in Lancashire the Steam Loomes and all the newly invented machienery,

* this year (1812) the ludites sprang up, & caused great fear, & this Summer, Percival the Prime Minister was Shot in the loby of the house of Commons, by John Belingham, who was hanged for it afterward – about this time the war raged in Spain, & france, germany, & Prussia, with all their allies under Bonaparte, declared war against Russia, & invaded that countery, with an army of (acording to some statments, of 600–000) men they Proceed through Poland, & after many Bloody Battles was fought, they reached Moscow, in Septem[r], this City was burnt down, & they returned into Polland, in their retreat, the french lost nearly all their army, by the frost, & fighting &c –

---

274   The baptism of the 'second Mary' was at the Methodist Society on 18 June 1811: Benjamin is described as a 'turner' in the baptism entry. This was the last child to be baptized as a Methodist, and it is likely that Benjamin's commitment to the movement was waning by this time (LRO: MPr/11/1).
275   make the best of things

* 1813 this year began with a dark prostect, Bread still rising, & labour falling, & great murmerings among the Poor, meal rose to 5 Pound per lead,[276] & other things in Proportion &c great preparations making for war, by England, against America &c, by france, & Russia & allies on the Continent &c this was indeed a hard time for us, we still Continued in tolerable health, but my wife though she stil continued to Bake, yet she complained heavely of growing weakness, & to make things worse, she was with Child, & this was an additional afliction, She got her Bed on the 18th of July 1813) of Agness, this was the last Child She had,[277] &c –

* great preparations was made this Spring for war, & in the Corse of the year, many Bloody Battles fought, among the many I will mention that of Dresden – Lipsic, & Hanua – the Confeatheration of the rhine was broken – Holland liberated, & Hanover &c, Sweeden made peace with England, &c the french lost ground in Spain, & all things went against the french, from the time of the burning of Moscow, the Princess of wales was tried, & aquitted by the House of Commons, who Justifyed her Honnour, & caracture, this was followed by the nations Simpathy &c, She had been charged with unfathfullness to the marriage engagement &c – towards the Clase of this year, the allied armies of, Russia, & Prussia – austria, & Sweeden, entered the Boundrys of france, after crossing the rhine, with an army of at least 500–000 men &c –

* 1814, Still trade continued to be greatly embarresed, & the Manufactering destricts full of complaints, & tradsmen failing &c, the american war continued, Several ingagements took place, Both by sea & land – Lord Wellington intirly cleared Spain of the french armies, & followed them into france this year – & the allies intered france from Saxony, & Switzerland, Generals Blucher, marches near to Paris, but was forced to retreat, when the Battles of Crone, & Loon was fought, but after the allies advance to Paris, & take it without a Battle – Bonaparte abdecates – Luis the 18th asends the throne – Bonaparte Sent to the Isle of Elba &c, a general Peace with all the Eurapion Powers, the Pope & the King of Spain, & Sirdinia restored & Holland, & Belgiam raised into a Kingdom – Peace likewise was contluded with america &c, and toward the end of this year, the Princess of wales leaves England, on her travels abroad – now we regoiced greatly, thinking we should have better times, But the repose of Europe was very Short, & we saw nothing like Peace –

* 1815 this year, I dont remember anything remarkable that took place in our family, Except our son William, who had 2 Chance Children fathered on him, when he was only 19 years old, we had a good deal of trouble on that account –

---

276   load
277   Agnes was baptized at Preston St John on 22 August 1813 (LRO: PR/1461).

Joseph our oldest son was married, 2 year since & had left us &c[278] – Williams first child by Martha Johnson, was born June 20th, 1815 & Sally Coyls Child was born October 20th the same year, he, afterwards married Sally Coyl, I think about 2 years afterward[279] –

* though Peace was made last year, with all Powers, yet trade did not go well, & people was ful of complaints, & greatly dissatisfyed, indeed we now found the Effects of the last destructive war, the Corn law prevented Bread from being cheap, & the emence National Debt, was then & allways will be found while it is recognized by the Nation, an unsuferable load to this Country, the general Peace of last year, was soon Broken, & all up in arms, for in the later end of february, Bonaparte began to prepare to leave Elba, & on the first of march landed in france – all europe was astonished – & a new Coalision was formed, on the 15th &c, Bonaparate advanced to Paris, without any opposittion, and entered the City, Luis the 18th fled away &c, Bonaparte forms a new Constetution, & adresses the Kings of Europe &c –

* great Preparations for war, & soon all Europe appears in arms – in June Bonaparate leaves Paris, to take the field near Brusels – on the 16th of June was fought the Battle of Quatre Bras, & Bonapart got the victory over prussians & on the 18th was fought the memorable Battle of Watterloo, the french wear roughted, & dreadfull Slaughter followed, Bonaparte soon after arived at Paris, But his fate was now sealed, after various consultations, he abdicates, & leaves Paris for Bologn, & soon after puts himself under the Protection of the English Squadron, and goes on Board the Beloraphan, & comes to England, but is soon Sent off to St Hellena – the allies soon after enter Paris, & Luis is restored again – & soon after the Holy allianc was set on foot &c – Bonaparte Sailed from off Plymouth, (for he was not Permitted to land in England) July the 4th, and about the 12th of Septemr landed at St Hellena, from whence he never returned &c – this year, the Corn Bill was brought into the house, & passed though there was great opossition to it, & So greatly were the people against that the millatery Serounded the House while it was Passed, to protect the members from the fury of the mob &c – General Ney, in france was arested, & tried, & Sentanced to be Shot, for Joining Bonaparte,

* towards the end of this year 1815, Thomas Hope, & Henry Park, machien makers, had took a Shop in the factory in Stanley Street.[280] & as I was well

---

278 Benjamin gives more detailed accounts of his children later in the work.
279 William Shaw married Sarah (Sally) Coyle at Preston in 1817.
280 Thomas Hope and Henry Park entered into a short-lived partnership in 1815. In the summer of 1817 they had notice to quit their premises in the Stanley Street machine shop. The partnership then fell apart: Park moved to Hebden Bridge, in Yorkshire, while Thomas Hope set up in business on his own, renting premises at 18 Everton Gardens (*Lancashire Directory*, 1818).

aquainted with both of them, they agreed to give me an envitation to come and work for them, & as the Shop was near, & they Promised to indulge me in any way, I concented to try what I could do, I therefore went on the 4th of december, & only wrought from 8 in the morning[281] for some time – the masters were very kind to me, & gave me work Suted to my State, & paid me after 20 shillings per week – I had not worked at my trade for more than 7 years, & 4 months – But I continued to work for them as long as they stoped in the town &c – 1816 in winter, I only wrought ¾ each day, but in the Spring, I got to work full time, though it was very hard work for me, but as the masters had been so kind to me, & they wanted work getting on, I Strove to obliege them,[282] this was a very remarkable year for wet, & cold weather &c, every sort of Vegitation partly failed, So that from the time of Harvest, there was scarce any wheat Sound, & Scarce a pudding made all year among the poor, & it was exceeding dear as high as £5 a load, or Pack, & every thing was bad, the weavers were forced to mix allum, & Vitriol with their Sowling,[283] to thicken it[284] &cr trade was a little better this Summer –

* about april, this year, lord Exmouth, made a treaty with the algeriens, that all the Prisoners should be released from Slavery, & from that time, all Prisoners taken should be only Prisoners of war, as in other Ports in Europe &c Should be exchainged as others &c, but while his lordship was on his way home, these Barbarians Set upon, & murdered a great number of English men, at Bona, a port in their dominions, on holy thursday at their devotion in the Church, this news reached England, near as soon as the admeral – the goverment determined to be revenged on them &c – accordingly, a Strong fleet was fitted out & Sent, under the commandment of the same admeral, lord Exmouth) he set sail from Plymouth, July 28th with a fleet of 24 Ships, & gun Boats & Bomb vessels Besides, & while he stoped at gibralter, was joined by 6 duch frigats &c, they arived before algiers on the 27h of August, and the same day after offering them Peace, by a flag of truce, to which they returned no answer, they Burnt all their ships in the Harbour, & nearly demolished all their Batteries, the next day 28 the admiral offered them Peace on the same terms which was Excepted, & articles signed, & the admiral returned home &c, –

281   The usual hour for starting work was 6 am.
282   The warm sentiments felt towards Hope and Park are clear: in no other instance does Benjamin give such unreserved praise in his account of an employer, and his wish to please them is as apparent as their exceptionally accommodating attitude to his physical disability. This was a rare example of mutual appreciation: Benjamin was a good worker and they were good employers, but a larger firm or the manager of a big concern would have had no need to be so kind.
283   'Sowling' was a paste made with flour and water, used by the weavers for sizing the warps.
284   The mixing of alum with flour was not confined to weavers: bulking out baking flour with large quantities of alum was one of the main, and most pernicious, forms of food adulteration throughout the nineteenth century.

* towards the end of this year, trade altered for the worce, & waiges was droped, & work in our trade Scarce &c, 1817) the Spring was this year a trying time, to the Poor for trade was Bad & Bread very dear, & very Bad, the worst that I ever remember in all my life, oweing to the wet & cold weather last year, Scarce any wheat could be got that was grown that year & nothing had a proper taste, as at other times &c, this Summer, my masters (Hope & Park) had got notice, to Shift out of the Shop that they had in the factory in Stanley Street, & they Shifted into Yorkshire,[285] to Hepton Brig &c, & Stoped to the last day, which was 23rd of Agust &c –

* our Son William was Married on the 11th of this month, to Sally Coyle, & on the 25 I went to work for John Welch[286] Roller maker, in the same building, this Shop was near to wheare I lived, or elce I should not engaged with him, for I did not like him before, or ever had cause to like him after, for I was Badly esed[287] all the time I was with him, Both by him & his men, but Still I stoped on account of it being near, and it was great advantige to me as I could but walk Slowly, & could not Stand wetting &c, in October, I shifted into the little Shop, which used to be Sleddons Smithy,[288] this was the Best Shop that I ever wrought in, for it was law[289] & cold in Summer, & warm in winter, But the worst master that I ever had &c, this winter, our Thomas was very Poorly long, we thought it had been the water on the Brain, but it did not prove so, he had some sort of fits &c, but got Better in the Spring, & got to work[290] &c –

* 1818, this Spring, trad revived a little, & work was more plentifull &c about this time a new whim appeared in this countery, called velosipeda or dandy Horse, this was a mechine for traveling on, but it was soon laid aside as useless, & about this time, the Coliedioscope, a tube to look into came into notice, but this was only a curiosity, & was soon lade aside, this summer we had a general Election, in Preston, the candidates were, Horrocks, Hornby, & Dr Crompton, from liverpool, the Polling continued 7 days, & then Crompton lade down, & Horrocks, & Hornby, were returned &c – this was on the 26 of June &c –

285 The evidence of trade directories suggests that only Henry Park went to Yorkshire: Thomas Hope remained in Preston.
286 John Welch or Welsh (the spelling varies between sources) was a roller maker with a shop in Stanley Street: Benjamin calls him 'the worst master that I ever had'. He changed premises in September 1818, though staying in Stanley Street, and in 1821 began to manufacture twist, but times were difficult and this line of business failed. In Pigot's 1828 *Directory* (p. 440) Welch is listed as a roller maker of Stanley Street.
287 used
288 In his rough notes (LRO: DDX/1554/3) Benjamin notes that the move was on 6 October.
289 'Law' is not traceable in dictionaries or glossaries of Lancashire speech, but the sense implies 'airy' or 'fresh'.
290 Thomas had been a sickly and unhealthy child (he was 'loose' for his first two years). In the spring of 1817 he was ten years old, and was thus of an age to go to work, but finding employment for him proved to be a difficult task.

* trade continued to mend this summer &c – my master welch, had been making a Steam Engin for his own use, & it Started on the 5th of Sept[r] this year, & we shifted in to a larger Shop on the 18th do – on the 12 Of Sept[r] we were Raised 2 Shillings per week – our new Shop had been an old foundry, a great wide place, and so cold that we were nearly Starced,[291] in winter, & Scarce could keep a candle or lamp in, when the wind Blew hard, &c – the floor was wet, & when it rained & the lodge[292] rose, we were flooded &c &c[293] – however we got plenty of work, & now the master got more hands, & did a great deal more Bissiness, & we got the Shop repaired by degrees, but the master was the most disagreeable man that I ever wrought for, in my life was miserable in part, & I was glad when the Sabboth came, &c –

* the Princess, Charlotte of Wales Died on the 5th of November last year, (1817) & the line of Succession being interupted, the Kings Brothers, Sought wives, to remedy the defeat, acordingly the duke of Cambridge, was married in 1818 april, to the Princess of Hesse Cassel – & in July the duke of Kent, was married to the Princess of Leiningen – & the duke of Clarence the same day, to the Princess Saxe Meininger – the Princess Elezabeth was united to the Prince of Hesse Hombourg &c – this year a meeting took place at Aix-la-Chappelle of all the allied Kings, where it was agreed that all the troops, that had been left in france, for the protection of the king should be dismised, & retire to their own Country, being no longer Necessary &c, – on the 17th of November, this year, the Queen Charlotte died, at Kew, aged 75 years – in this year there was much discontent in the Countery, & many meetings all over the Kingdom, & many were aprehended, & imprisoned &c – (1819) this Spring, the people was much inclined to rebellion, & training in arms was quite Common, the goverment Passed several restrictive acts &c, meetings Still continued, & Peticians Sent up from many towns &c, –

* this year we had trouble from a new quarter, & of a new description, our oldest daughter Bella was with child,[294] which gave us now Smale concern for her, as we feared, & it proved so, that she did not get married soon &c, – this Summer the famous meeting at Manchester took place, on the 16th of august, called by some Peterloo, this meeting was Broken up by the Millitary, when a great number was wounded, & several killed, &c – Hunt, & Healy, & Bamford, and

---

291   starved
292   mill reservoir or dam
293   The new steam mills had large reservoirs impounded by embankments. Their main purpose was to provide water for the numerous steam engines which drove machinery, but they also supplied water for other processes in the mill. Benjamin refers in several places to the use of steam engines, and notes how at new sites the lathes were turned manually until they could be connected to the engines.
294   Bella was born in May 1799, and so was twenty years old.

others, was aprehended, & sent to Prison &c, the goverment had determined to put a stop to all meetings if not called by the Magestrates &c, – soon after this, Sir Frances Berdett was aprehended, & inprisoned for writing a letter to his Constituants, &c – & Magor Cartwright was imprisoned, & Johnson, & many others, &c – July 31ˢᵗ our Bella fathered her child on William Roberts,[295] & on Sepʳ 18ᵗʰ went to dolphinholm, to ly inn, her Child was Born on the 9ᵗʰ of Novembʳ, 1819, returned hom on the 21ˢᵗ of do,[296] now we had as much trouble as if the Child had been our own, for he still amused her by marriage,[297] & was exed in the Church soon after,[298] but this was all Pollicy, in february, She filliated,[299] and now she got 2ˢ 6ᵈ per week,

* 1820, January 29ᵗʰ, George the 3 our King died, in the 60ᵗʰ year of his reign, & the 82 of his age, &c, & the duke of Kent about a week before his father, the King &c – George 4ᵗʰ, Proclamed King on the 31ˢᵗ of the same month in london – a general Election took place on conciquence of the death of the king, in february Horrocks, & Hornby, began to canvas the town of Preston,[300] the Election took place in march, we had 4 Candedats this time, namely Sameul Horrocks – Edward Hornby, & John Williams, & Henry Hunt,[301] &c – the Poling began on the 8 of march, – Henry Hunt left the town to go to his trial at York on the 12 &c – the other 3 Candedates stood untill the 22ⁿᵈ, on which day Horrocks, & Hornby, was declared duly Elected, & road according to Custom,[302] at 4 in the afternoon &c – Hunt, & others was tried at york, for the

295 She told the overseer that Roberts was the father.
296 The child was born at Dolphinholme in Ellel township. Bella was unmarried, and therefore retained her father's settlement, which was in Ellel because of Benjamin's apprenticeship there twenty-six years earlier. Although Bella had only once in her life been to Ellel it was to that township that she belonged. The baby had to be born in Ellel to ensure that Preston would not be troubled by claims for relief on the grounds of place of birth, but as soon as the child was born Bella returned to Preston: its baptism is recorded in the register of Preston St John: '26 December 1819 Benjamin, illegitimate son of Isabella Shaw, Church Street, Preston, winder (baptised at Trinity church)'. The address is incorrect: Bella was living with her parents in Dale Street (LRO: PR/1463).
297 He kept her happy or led her on with promises of marriage.
298 The banns (exings = askings) were read.
299 She went to the overseers to seek support for the child from its father. They would then have taken proceedings for maintenance, she having testified as to his identity.
300 The borough constituency of Preston was among the most democratic in the country until the Reform Act of 1832. As a result of a decision of the House of Commons in 1768 there was almost universal adult male suffrage. With such a large and politically powerful electorate it was necessary for candidates to seek votes actively and so, unusually for this period, canvassing was a standard feature of elections.
301 Henry Hunt, one of the leaders of the meeting which had been violently dispersed at Peterloo, was a hero of the Radicals. He stood at Preston because the large electorate had shown Radical inclinations and was not subject to the will of any vested interest. He was about to be tried for high treason for his actions at Peterloo.
302 It was traditional that the winning candidates in Preston elections rode through the town 'from barr to barr' – that is, between the gates at the outer ends of Church Street, Fishergate and

meeting at Manchester, on the 16th of augus, 1819, when they were found guilty, & were sentanced afterward at London, Hunt to be imprisoned in Ilchester Jail, 2½ years, & to find surety for his good behaver for 5 years, afterwards, Healy, & Bamford, and others, was sent to lincon Jail, for 1 year, & bound over to keep the Peace for 5 years – about this time Sir Charles Wolseley, & Harrison was Sentanced to imprisonfent [*sic*], each 18 months, & bound over &c,

* the autumn of last year, wore a gloomy aspect, & all seemed to be ready for revolt, but by the Prompt measures of goverment, things wears a better face at Presant, &c – in June this year, the Queen returned from her travels abroad, having been abstante 6 years – great rejoicing among the common People – Soon after her trial came on before the House of Lords, and continued long, many foreign wittneses were brought from Italy, &c – but nothing could be Proved against her, but indiscretion, the trial was at last Broken up, in the winter following, & great rejoicing & ilumenations followed in every part, &c – about this time, a Conspiricy was discovered in London, by the means of Spys, who joined the Party, & found money pretending friendship, & then went and informed on them, they were acordingly aprehended, & found guilty of Conspiring to assasinate the minesters, Sidmoth, & Castlreigh &c, they were tried, condemned, & hung, &c their Names were, Thistlewood – Brunt – Hynge & davinson &c

* this year, we had the misfortune to know that our second daughter Hannah was with child, by Samuel Whittle, & she was not quite 18 years old, this was a mater of greif, & trouble to us, &c, at the Beginning of winter, our mary began to work,³⁰³ we had Bella Child to keep, & all the trouble atending it, & now likely to have another, Parents trouble is not done when they have reared their Children &c –

* 1821, at the begining of this year, trade again Sickened (as it has done often, but never dies) & early in this year, wages was reduced 2 Shilings in the Pound, January 10th, I was droped & on the 16th our Hannah went to her town to ly inn,³⁰⁴ and got lodgins at Dolphinholme with Edward Fox, & on the 24th of February, got her bed of a daughter, & called her Betty after her mother, she came home on the 17th of march, the Child was a very little one, & Seemed not

---

Friargate, all the while being feted by the populace and distributing largesse in the form of celebratory drink.

303 Mary was born in September 1805, and so went to work when she was fifteen, unusually late in the circumstances of her family.

304 Hannah, like her sister Bella, had her legal settlement in the township of Ellel, and so her child was born there. 'Her town' indicates 'the town to which she belonged' even though like the rest of her siblings apart from Joseph, she was born in Preston and had only lived in Ellel for thirty weeks in 1808–9 when the family was temporarily removed there.

likely for life, but it continued to live untill the 8th of may and died,[305] we thought it had the hooping cough &c, it was never well from its birth &c – on the 28 february, my Masters Welchs wife died in Child bed, & left him with 5 Children, &c – in May this year, Bonaparte died, at St. Helena, where he had been 6 years &c, – George the 4th was crowned July 19th – the Queen applyed for admition to the Crownation, & being refused to enter, this seemed to have Burst her Heart, for she died august 7th, at night, the funeral Procession tok place on the 14th, to Harwich, from whence it Sailed for Saxony, She was intered at Brunswick &c –

* august 15, our Joseph Son, Benjamin, died, & Septr 3 Betty, & on the 7 Mary died, he buried 3 Children, in 3 week[306] &c June 16th, my father inlaw Edward Leeming, died, at new Preston, aged about 70 years, we Supose of a Short Sickness, this was indeed a great Blessing, Both to him, & his children, he was Poor, & his wives were all dead, (for he had 3) & he had only one son at Home, & he was young, and thoughtless &c – in october welch, my master, began manufactureing Cotton, (or rather twist,) trad still Continued to go worse, I had nowork [*sic*] for sometime, this month, (december), & this was a general complaint in the town, & Country, I continued to work with welch till after Christmas &c – then I was forced to leave, for there was little work, & he would neither let me have my Share of it, nor turn me off, till I asked, for my dis charge [*sic*], he had all ways Behaved Badly to me &c

* 1822, this year Began with a gloomy aspect, trad was down and no signs of amendment – I had no work from the 5th of January, untill the 21, I had been 6 week with half work &c – february 2nd I was discharged from John Welchs Shop,[307] & had no work untill the 26th this month, when I went to work with Frank Sleddon, my old master, &c, for if I had not been well known Both to him & foreman James Birkett,[308] I should not have got work now, trade being so bad, & work so much Sought after, &c – But I only got 19 Shillings per week, the least that I had got for 20 years, when I wrought at my trade &c, I had put up with many unpleasant things, while I was with welch, on the account that it was near home – I now began to feel what I had feared, namely the inconvenency of

305 No baptism entry has been traced. The registers of Preston St John record the burial on 10 May 1821 of Betty Shaw, aged 1, of Dale Street, Preston (LRO: PR/1475).

306 Details of Joseph's children are given by Benjamin later in the work.

307 Benjamin had been given a fortnight's notice on 3 February 1821, but this had not been put into effect. His rough notes record that he received 'indirect notice' of a month on 16 November 1821, was laid off between 22 and 31 December, put on half-time on 5 January for three weeks, and finally discharged on 2 February (LRO: DDX/1554/2).

308 James Birkett was a foreman with Frank Sleddon in 1822, but he had previously attempted to run his own business. In the *Lancashire Directory* of 1818 (p. 15) he is listed as a machine-maker, with premises at 16 Sill's Court, Church Street.

being far from the Shop[309] – I had now ¾ of a mile to go all sort of weather, & very bad road Some part of it, the worst that can be imagined, & quite exposed to the weather, &c – I went in the morning, & did not come home untill night, my wife or sambody brought my dinners, I had now 4 Shillings per week less than I had a little before, but I had a good master now, & the Shop men were very agreeabl, & in the Spring, I got a Shilling raised per week, & from this time trade mended a little –

* on may the 7th, a large & nearly new wind mill in the north road, was burnt down, & the same day Henry Jacksons, my Brother in law &, House was begun to bild, at the end of Newton Street, in the Park, – June 5, our Thomas went to work at M[r] Mondays Shop,[310] was to be a moulder for 6 years, but he only Stoped untill winter, & then he was dischargd on the 22, (June 1822) our oldest daughter Bellow was married, to willim Roberts &c, – about the end of June, Jacksons House was finished, my father had the over sight of it, while Building, & not traveling or walking much as he had been used to,[311] he now began to be lame & poorly, in July, he talked of geting a Crutch &c, in august, he was worse, & in September, was very Poorly &c, –

* on the 2nd this month, Preston Guild began, the trades walked in Procession, & on the 3rd, the ladies walked – 4th 5th 6th & 7[h] was the races, which had been put off from July – 9th a Baloon went of, M[r] Livingston went in it, & got out near Wholaw,[312] but the Baloon rose again, and went into yorkshire, near Selby &c, 10, 11, &, 12, there was Horatorys[313] in the Church, & the Theater at night, &c – on the 16th, this month my father entered into the dispensary, & continued in some time, – but got no better – in Octob[r] he began to Contlude he would not get Better, & asked me to sell his lath, So I got him a Chap,[314] he gave me some few tools, & his brother William, got his Cutting Engin &c, he now gave up his room which he had lived in 25 years,[315] & Shifted into the Park, to my sisters[316] –

309　Frank Sleddon was at this time running a machine shop in Back Lane behind Friargate. Benjamin's previous employment, with John Welch, had been close to Dale Street, and so despite the bad conditions and Benjamin's dislike of Welch he had put up with it. Sleddon, a much better master, was ¾ mile distant.

310　Thomas Munday was a machine-maker and iron-founder. In 1818, according to the *Directory*, he had a workshop in Bolton Street (almost certainly Bolton's *Court*). By 1828 he had moved to different premises, in Oak Street off Manchester Road. In January 1836 he was elected as a councillor for the St John's ward, and served on the Borough Council until 1844.

311　Joseph Shaw had been a travelling clockmender for many years. Dale Street, where he lived, was only a few hundred yards from Newton Street, and the lack of regular exercise is blamed for his physical deterioration – though he was now seventy-four years old.

312　Whalley

313　oratorios

314　a dealer in goods; chapman

315　This was the room in Dale Street, close to where Benjamin and his family lived: Benjamin's parents had moved there shortly after their arrival in Preston in 1795, and his mother had died there in 1798.

316　Hannah Jackson

* November 5th he was out, the last time, on the 8th much worse – 13, was the last time he was down stairse – in decemb^r he was weaker & worse &c, – on the 27 this month our Bellow got her bed of a daughter, & called her Ellin &c – all this winter, I allways went every night to See & sit with my father, though the road was very bad then, where dover streets is now, & there was no lamps &c, – in the night between the 6 & 7 this month, (decem^r) Sleddons new factory was Blown down, by a strong North west wind &c, – Septr.12, this year, (1822) the foundation of St Petter^s Church was laid[317] 1823, at the begining of this year trade was in a mending way, & my father continued to be Still worse, & was now very weak &c – still he continued to declare his confidence in god, & intimated that he should be saved, &c he continued to live untill february, & in the night between the 10th & 11th at 12. o'clock he died, quite sensable, & resigned to his fate, &c – he was buried on ash wedensday in the old church yard aged 74 years, & 25 days,[318] –

* in the last winter I was forced to make enquiry of my wife, what was the reason of so much seeming Poverty in the family, for I had continued to give her the same money that I had done for many years, & now all our children were got to work, & Bread was cheaper than it had ever been in our life time before, (I alowed her 20 Shilings a week), and all things else was cheap, – She told me that She was something in debt, & She was paying of that debt &c – no woman could have more liberty than she had, for I never enquired what she did with the money if I saw any simtoms of Provision being made for the family, I think if a man can get money, a woman ought to take care that it be well laid out, and the family Provided for in the best way that lies in her power, for if a man have Both to get money, & to trouble himself with the care of lying it out, what Better is he with a wife than he would be with a servant – or what woman would be content to have no share in the managment of the family – 20 Shillings was her allowance weekly, But I found my own Cloths, & every thing Such as Books, Pocket Money, &c – we had many words about being in debt, but it droped again, & I thought if she were Paying of it would be better than to be in debt, for I allways Detested being in debt &c –

* this was a troublesom time to me, for in february soon after my father was Buried, my Sister Hannah and me had to settle about my fathers good,[319] & she being so selfish & unfair (as I thougth) it caused us to differ greatly &c – on the 12 of January last, my father seeing he must die, told me & hannah how he

317 St Peter's church, in Fylde Road, served the growing suburbs around the canal basin and the Spittals Moss mills. The foundation stone of the church was laid during Guild Week in September 1822. The church is now the Arts Centre of Lancashire Polytechnic.
318 The 'old church yard' was the churchyard of St John's. The register records the burial of Joseph Shaw of Park Lane, Preston, aged 76, on 12 February 1823 (LRO: PR/1476).
319 goods

would have his goods parted, but as he was very Poorly, and it disturbd him much to talk to us, nothing was said but about the chief thing – my sister had got them all into her House, thinking to have them all or nearly all – & only those thing that I could remember just then, was mentioned, But my Sister told me that the things that was not mentioned, Should be devided which was all I wanted &c, –

* among the things my father mentioned was his choths [*sic*],[320] which I was to have, & to give what I thought fit to my son William, but when I came to receive them, She had kept all his Shirts, Brats,[321] Caps, hankerchiefs, Stockings, (but 2 Pair without feet), Singlets, Shoes, (1 wastcote & 1 coat that I knew &c) I was to have his traveling Box of tools – but out of that, She had taken, 2 Pair of Pliars – 1 hamer, 1 hand Vice, that I knew of &c, – he had a good Stock of tools, but she kept nearly all that was worth keeping – my father had said that I was to have his tools, but Hannah was to have a few that She thought would be useful to her, but did not name them, So She kept nearly all of them, though her husband was a warper,[322] and had no use for them, &c – the other things when we came to divide, th there [*sic*] was nothing to be seen, in stead of Bringing them forward, to divide fairly, they were all hid, & nothing to be seen, &c a few things that I knew and could remember, I mentioned, & some few was brought out, but the

[then follow two pages headed: 'turn Over this has been a Mistake &c', which were missed in the writing of the original work, and subsequently filled with the following additional memorandum. The original narrative is then resumed]

Note

my father was very Partial to my sister hannah she could not do wrong for him – But Henry[323] & him could not agree well at any time he used to live sometimes by him self & sometimes with Hannah &c – now when he lived by himself he Bought Potts and any thing that he wanted & got a good Stock of any thing usefull & when he went to Hannah to live he used to take his things with him well Soon they used to fall out with him & then he went home to his Room & then he had a fresh Stock to Buy for he could not thing [*sic*] of takeing his things from hannah &c – and in his last Sickness they would have Pretended that he had no money & that they kept him for his House hold goods and Henry Jackson sade so one day to our Betty but She knew Better & Sade to him well how is it for he had 42 Pounds a while since & he has not been Sick he must have money

320   clothes
321   aprons
322   A warper prepared the warp on the loom ready for the weaver.
323   Hannah's husband, Henry Jackson

this caused some disput Bettwen them & he detirmined to know how they Stood for all the neighbours sade that the House was his and many told Jackson so to his face so he would know how they stood

* my father to clear them from this Sent for 2 neighbours at my Sisters request to Clear her from the Charge of Cheating me of his house my father Sade before these wittness that he had only 26 Pound in money when he was taken ill and that after his Board was Paid to them and other exences[324] the remainder Should be left to my Sister Hannah he left her his watch also & she had a good Clock in the House and Scarce ever went out – he left her his large Bible & Birketts Notes on the new testament also though my sister could not read either of them for she scarce knew her letters &c But in everything his Partialaty was seen –

* She used to say she had to keep him mostly But while She lived with him when her first husband liven & untill She got married a seccond time she kept my father as poor as any Boddy whatever But when she left him to live by him-self then he began to save money Bedide [*sic*] doing much for her when he went to live with her at anytime he used to work for her mostly on the wet days when he saw that She wanted anything for he could make or repair any thing allmost & on the Saterday he went a marketting for her and all other Spare times he used to nurse & buy any thing for her that he thought there was a Bargin in &c – he likewis took some land several years and used to dig & weed & work it for them and in all respects he did for her as he would do for him self &c – when her Son William Jackson wanted a trade my father Choose his trade & gat him a place & it was sade that he gave his apprintice fee with him (and I partly Believe it for he had the ordering of all things about it &c) & when they Built their House my father Bargained for the land fixed the plan & ordered every thing almost about & overlooked the work & it is thought that this Brought on his last Sickness for he used to travle and now Stoping at home he could not travle any more &c

[the original narrative resumes at this point]

greates Part, She either denied, or said they were sold, while my father lived, or else my father had given them to her, or to some of her children &c, So very few things were divided at all, &c, – my father ordered that we were to join at his Bed so when that was Brought forward, there was nothing to divide but the Bare bed, & an old cover which had been in the family 30 years, & some parts of an old curtain, &c, I understood my father, by his word bed, all that belonged to his bed, Such as Sheets, Quilts, Balsters, Pillows, & cases, Blankets, & for my father had as many things about his Bed, as would have fit out 2 Beds, Say

324 expenses

nothing about Chaing, for he was old, & laid by himself, & used to say he had as many things on his bed as he could creep under, &c – however, She restricted his word BED, to the Bare Bed &c, this was to be divided, so it was, we cast lots for it, but we had a greed that whether ever got it, the other was to pay half of what it was vallued at, so we got the Bed, & had 16 Shilling to pay for it, which was its full worth, for it was a very Bad one, &c,

* on these accounts we differed & Both my sister, & Husband, ordered me out of their House & keep out many times, which I have observed to do ever since, &c – my fathe had 26 Pound in money, when he was taken ill in autumn, which was left to them, what there was to spare when all thing was settled, they charged 8 Shilings, Per week &c – he Sold his Lath, & some of his tools, & household good, & Brass, & Iron, & lead, & many things, which made many Pounds more, So that when all was settled, I reckenod [*sic*] that there was about 10 Pound left in money &c,

* this Spring trade went well, & we had Plenty of work, in march this year (1823, I got my wages raised from 20 Shilings to 23, do & all Machanick was raised, in general &c, But these times of revival in our Bussiness is a great evil to our trade in futer, for at such times all that can work any atall, can get work any where, this encourages many to travle to where they are not known, and pretend to be worksmen, if they can do any thing they get a place, and become old hand very soon, &c this also encourages apprintices, & such as are under agreements to run away &c – and when Bad times comes then those that have regularly served an apprinticeship are ill of to get work, for the new upstarts are so many & they will often work for less wages, &c, –

* about this time, I was resolved to know the Bottom of our family afairs, I had long waited thinking our debt would be Paid, & we should be better of, but I saw no amendment so on the 5 of april I turned tirant, and would part with no more money untill my wife gave me an account of the state of our afairs, She told me she had been paying of this year Back which made us so straitened, I deremined [*sic*] to know for once how we stood, & found that now she owed between 16 & 17 Pound She had 4 Scotch mens[325] Bills, & all the Cloths that she could spare was Paund, & She had taken my Coat, & wastcot unknown to me, & had robed my Box of money, I dont know what, but She owned to 40 Shillings, this was a sad discovery, after 8 years of Peace, & in a time when Provisions was cheaper than they had ever been since we had been married &c, – but this was her fault, She would allways be in debt, & would take no care to manage our concerns to advantage, &c I now began when it was to late, to be more strict to know how we stood, & to settle our accounts every month for some time after,

325   credit traders

* but now we had a trying time to come on, for our daughter Hannah began to be badly, She Come Home from her work on the 20 of march (1823 and never was able to go to work, or do any thing while she lived again (& she lived near 11 months after,) She had been poorly long before but still stuck to her work untill now &c, we got her medical asistance, but it did no good, for one thing She was very bad at taking medicine, so the doctor was forced to chainge her Medicine often, untill she would not take any thing &c –

* on the 30th of march, she was at the lovefeast[326] in Lune Street Chapple, this was the last time she was at the chapple She was a member of the methodist society,[327] &c – She had been very steady, & Pious some time, & knew the Power of religion on the soul, & she had need of all the comfort of devotion for her Sickness which was long & tedious, it was a consumption) required much patience, & fortitude to say at all times thy will be done, from the heart for nature is averce to suferings soon on in april her mother began to lie with her, & continued so to do until she died – on the 10th of april she was out of doors – 12 she was blistered, on the 20 She received the Blessed Saccrement, from M[r] Thompson[328] &c – may 2nd, Spit blood, whitsunday got up, from this time she thought she would not get better, June 8th the weather being fine she was down stairs, & in July was dresed 2 or 3 days, but this was the last time that she was drest

* this Summer our son thomas wrought in the Brick Croft, & the season being wet he was soon out of work, this Sumer, the great Factory in Fishwick Began to be built,[329] &c, October 21st, the foundation laid of St Pauls Church, in the Park &c,[330] – this year, our thomas on the 10th of Novem went to F Sleddons Shop to work, &c – & was to work at the laith, but was set to the Vice untill a place was vacent for him &c – our hannah still continued to grow weaker, & was toward the close of this year Scarce able to be stirred, & was so weak that she was not expected to live from day to day &c,

---

326 A Methodist feast at Communion time, when contributions were made by members towards their poor brethren: in token of the early Christian doctrine of selfless brotherly love.

327 The Lune Street chapel had been opened in 1817, and was the main chapel of the Preston Methodist circuit, formed in 1787 out of the Colne circuit. It replaced the old Methodist chapel which stood in Back Lane at the junction with Tenterfield Street.

328 George Thompson was the minister at the Lune Street Methodist chapel from 1820–3.

329 The 'great factory in Fishwick' was Bank Top Mill, begun in 1823 by Richard Riley and opened in 1826.

330 St Paul's church, now occupied by Red Rose Radio, was on Park Road (part of the present Ringway). It was opened in 1825, and is an excellent example of a 'Commissioners' Church', the entire cost having been met by the Commissioners for erecting new churches in growing residential areas and large towns. It was the nearest Anglican church to Dale Street, and from 1825 onwards members of Benjamin's family – and eventually Benjamin himself – were buried in St Paul's Churchyard.

* Still she was very Paitent, for one in her condition remarkably so, frequently talked of death as a desirable thing to her, &c, She had many Visitors, & delighted in Singing & Praying, untill She became so weak that she could not attend to anything, for any length of time together, yet some times at intervals of Pain, She would talk of the Saviour, & Heaven, with great delight &c, – we used every means in our Power to aleviate her condition, but what is it that we can do for the destrest with Pain, but to be kind & to encourage them to look to god, & to expect our reward in a Better world, & to be ready & willing to asist in every way Posible, to Comfort & wait with Patience on them, &c – this we did, to the oumost[331] of our Power, & to her full satisfaction, we are sure &c–

* 1824, January, Hannah still continued to worse, and weaker, we waked with her constantly, & did all we could for her, but it seemed that her end was fast aproaching, this month, her legs swelled, & She could not be turned in Bed, &c, often did we think she was dying, but she came round again, in february she became more miserable, for she could not be stired, and her skin came of where she lay, on her hips & thyes & ear &c, her weakness was exceeding great, & her eyes ofter [*sic*] failed, and she would enquire frequently how long we thought she should have to suffer yet, she said I have no fear of death, I wish to go to Jesus &c, She suffered much & as Patently as Posibly could be expected, & frequently Sade the will of the lord be done, &c,

* She continued to live untill february 25, and then died quite sensable, & Happy in the Lord – She was Buried in the old church yard, on the south east side, I got the Sexton to make her a very deep grave, as they some times shift them two soon, I thought she might rest undesturbed &c, She had been a slender & delicate child from her birth, & seemed not fit for any hardship, and from the time she had her child seemed to decline, She was 21 years, & 5 week old &c,[332]

* this spring & summer trade went Briskly & wages was good in our Business, but a great number got work in our Business that had never served any time to the trade, this is a great evil to our trade, for when trade is Bad the masters takes the advantage to put down wages, this summer, our Thomas left F Sleddon – he

---

331 outmost, i.e. utmost
332 The burial of Hannah Shaw, aged 21 of Dale Street, was at St John, Preston on 27 February 1824 (LRO: PR/ 1476). The old church yard was grossly overcrowded: as the town had grown rapidly the number of burials had increased sharply, and space was very scarce since the yard itself was not suitable for extension. Burial space was therefore made by removing bodies or remains not long after burial, and re-using the 'vacant' grave-space. Benjamin probably paid the sexton a small sum to dig an especially deep grave for Hannah, so that she could rest in peace for a little longer. The building of the new churches in the growing suburbs helped to relieve pressure on St John's churchyard, which was eventually closed in 1855 as a result of the 1852 Burials Act. This led to the opening of the new cemetery at Ribbleton, and the other town church burial yards were closed in the same year.

was to be aprintice and to have a lath but was put to the vice, as they sade until a lath was Vacuent but they did not offer to shift him, So he went & got work with Watts & Hodgson, a new shop in Bridge Street,[333] and got 8 Shillings per week, Sleddons only gave him 4^s &c – he began with them June 21st &c.

* this year, the Retail Brewerys began, (or as they call them here tom & Jery Shops much uneasiness in Ireland about now &c Septemr Lewis 18 King of franc died, & on the 26 Charles 10th entered Paris to succeed him &cr on the 29th Saddler of Liverpool, the famous aeronoat was killed, from his Balloon near Blackburn, he asended from Bolton, the weather being squaly &c, he was thrown out and hung by his feet or something, was dashed against a Chimney, and soon after fell from the Balloon, was taken to a public house & lived 17 hours &c, – the other man that was with him got out near whalley, & the Balloon rose and went into the sea near Flamborough head &c, – Septem^r 22nd a Riot took place in dubling at a Meeting of the Church Mishonary Society &c, – about this time the south american States was acknowledged free, & independant States, Both by England & the north american States &c, – October 23rd, I got raised a shilling a week wages, trade continued very good &c, – this month Funtleroy, a Banker was aprehended Charged with defrauding the Public of incredable Sums of money by Selling Stocks in trade without the knowledge of the properieters, Soon after he was tried & Condemned & afterward hanged &c

1825, January 2nd our bellow got her bed of a son & called him Thomas, trade in general good in this countery, but owing to some misunderstanding between the operative spiners and their employer, there were many out of work at glasgow. they had been out long before this time, & about now had agreed to go in without gaining the point turned out for &c – but about Hide, near Stockport many were now turning out it seems that the spiners had formed clubs, or what they call the union & the masters were determined to break them up, this caused the differance &c. – the Emegrants at the Cape of good Hope had undergone many hardships, through Poverty & want of Provision being made for their settlement, their case being known subscription was made Both in England, & in the East Indes for their relief, which they received a bout now thankfuly, but they complained hard of their governor at the Cape &c, at this time, and for some time back many Joink [*sic*] Stock Companys was Projected for diferand Purposed, the most of them fel away – some for cannals – Bridges – rail-ways – Banking companys – Mineing companys &c

* the first Steam Paquet to go to the east Indes, was launched at depford, and

---

333   William Hodgson was a spinner, of 22 Back Fylde Road, in 1818. Little is known about him, or his short-lived business venture with Watts – the partnership went bankrupt after only fifteen months. Bridge Street was usually called Bridge Lane: it was the upper end of the present Marsh Lane, between Friargate and the railway bridge.

was to sail in march &c, the acknowledging of Columbia & Mexeco free states by England, & the States of North america, has caused great murmering in the diferant States of Europe, &c – the greek still continue to Strive for their independancy, & it is sade there is some misunderstanding among the Turkish Chiefs &c – within little more then a year there is 20.000 more soldiers under pay, 15 000 this Spring is added & 5000 last spring, 5000 to go to Ireland & 5000 to the east Indies the 5000, to the east Indies, to be paid by that goverment, & the 15,000 by England – the Irish dissatesfied with their atturney general, & other officers of the Crown the weavers of Carlisle much discontented with their wages & the average of earnings

* may the 25 our thomas ingaged for 6 Months with watts, & Hodgson for 14 Shilling per week &c – for some time past trade carried on by Provincial Bank notes, very near no Bank of England Notes seen, & little gold or silver &c in the autumn of of [*sic*] this year, much fluctuating in trade, in the cotton districts, on account of some Stock Jobers in Cotton, intending to raise the Prices – but the Buyers determined not to trade with them, the concequenc was they Broke soon after &c, – November, about this time Alexander 1st of Russia Emper died, & was succeeded by his Brother Micael, 1st &c – about this time the Banks Began to fail, & trading companys followed fast, & the trade became very bad soon after, &c, a water company was formed in this town, to suply this town with fresh water more generally then it had been, but it has not got forward yet (1826) but still it is in agetation,[334] december 19th Frank Sleddon droped wages, for trad became very bad, & some hands was discharged &c, this year ended under a cloud &c –

1826 this year, comenced under unfavourable auspices, never was there so many Bank known to fail as had for 3 months back, & Still they continued to fail, & many old Established merchant companys, that nobody suspected & Strong companys in trade, in every part of the Countery, so that confidence began to fail, & things went from bad to worse, &c – in february, we were reduced in wages a seccond time, & a great number discharged, & this was a general

---

334   Preston had a piped water supply from 1729, when a reservoir was built on Avenham Syke with a pump to lift the water into the town, and thence into public pumps and pipes. The early eighteenth-century system functioned, increasingly unsatisfactorily, until the 1830s, by which time the population had increased fourfold. During the 1820s there were various projects to provide a more modern supply, and in 1831 the Preston Waterworks Company was formed. The intention, put into effect over twenty years, was to bring water from reservoirs in the Longridge area. Benjamin was particularly interested in the provision of a modern piped water supply, and makes several further references to the progress of the scheme. Like all working-class householders he must have regarded a domestic supply as perhaps the greatest of all the benefits of 'progress'. The availability of clean, accessible and (relatively) cheap water to replace polluted, expensive and often distant sources was one of the most important manifestations of progress in nineteenth-century urban living (see Oakes, pp. 6–13).

complaint in all the trading districts, & in all sorts of Business, cotton trade, & the silk – & woolling – Stockings – & cloths – gloves & Lace, but the weavers in Silks & Cotton suffered the most, thousands had no work, some half work, but very little for doing &c, this was general, for it did not afect us in England only But in Scotland, & Ireland &c. nothing that I ever could hear of but gun flints, the men employed in this work were more than full employed, this was for the East Indes, for the war was Still carried on against the Burmees &c, –

* februar, the Ribble navigation company gave a Premium of 100 Pound to M[r] Miller Survayer in Preston, for the Best Plan that was ofer to that Company, for altering & mending the river &c, in april a part of the plan was begun, that is shifting the rocks below the march[335] end[336] &c – great distress in all the counterys for the want of employ – Subscriptions made in many towns, his majesty has given 4000 Pound towards relieving the Poor at diferant Places &c – the Emperor of Russia was not Buried until the 20 of march – many Pettition sent up to Parliament to repeal the corn laws &c the list of Bankrupts was never so great as this Spring &c may 15 subscriptions opened in this town for the unimployed & destressed, and about 1300 pound was colected and a part given, but the Election coming on had stoped it &c –

* april 1, sleddons reduced wages the 3[d] time, and discharged many so that we are not the half number we wer 12 months since, 11 our thomas discharged from his emply having no more work, 30 the past week the weavers have risen in thousands & Broken the Steam & other Power looms, with in 10 or 12 miles of Blackburn, many thousand are destroyd, many lives has been lost, & many are wounded, & many gat into Prison[337] &c a Branch cannal has been cut from golgate to glazen dock, & so a comunication withe the sea, on the 16th of may the Sprightly was the first that came this way to this town from dutten with Slate, this

---

335   marsh

336   The decline of the small port of Preston in the eighteenth century had resulted in a plethora of projects to improve navigation on the Ribble. Some work was done by the Ribble Navigation Co. in 1806–11, but to little effect, and in 1823 the town authorities and some merchants provided stone quays along the bank by Marsh Lane. The deepening of the river and provision of groynes was the most pressing need, and in 1824–31 desultory removal of rocks and gravel shoals was undertaken. The 1826 competition was won by a plan which was 'more concerned with the reclamation of land than with the improvement of the navigation of the river' (Dakres, p. 14). The full-scale improvement of the river had to wait until the building of Preston Dock in the 1880s.

337   During 1826 serious rioting was widespread in Lancashire. The handloom weavers feared, rightly, a reduction in their wages and ultimately the loss of their livelihood as a result of the new factories which were springing up. Food prices were exceptionally high and supplies unreliable, as a result of bad harvests and drought, and unemployment was growing rapidly. The target of much of the violence was the new mills and their power looms, but there was a good deal of more general unrest. The 1826 General Election was also marked by rioting in Preston, and the military were twice called out to suppress the crowds.

spares unloading at Lytham, & Bringing up the river by lighters & saves much from wast by breaking &c,[338] – Machanics has wrought short time long sometimes 3 sometimes 4 days & less in the week, and trade continues to grow worse &c, –

* the Election took place June the 9th Stanley, Canvased the town in May early, & wood came in on the 15th May, & canvased the town also these got nearly the Promise of all – Cobbett came on the 15 & Stoped 3 days and went back to London & came the 2nd time, may 29th & Canvased a part of the town, the Pool[339] Comenced on June the 9th, the Parliament was desolved on the 30th of may, Captain Barrie, came on the day the Election took Place, many Parties went out to Canvas for him, this man was a tory, & Backed by the Corperation, & the manufacters &c, wood & Cobbett was Radicals, & Stanley a whig, &c –

the 3 first candidates had agreed to Pool the Catholics, without the oath of Supremancy,[340] &c But Barrie, insisted on the oath being taken, this made much confusion in the town &c, – this was a Strong contest, they continued to Pool to the end of the time allowed by law, for that purpose, when the Pool Stood Stanley 2944 – Wood 1874 – Barrie 1653 Cobbett 995 Stanley, & Wood, was declared to be duly elected, and on the 26 of June Road as is custom &c, – Cobbett left the town on the 27th trade continues to Slacken, July the 12, it is expected that the factorys will be put upon short time next week, & 1 is Stoped & has been many a month – the last weeks paper stated, that 200.000 were out of work within 20 miles of manchester, &c, & the long drought is expected to have materially inguered the Harvest, the hay harvest has compleatly failed, in all this Island, & we fear for the Corn, the Poor are in a Pitiful State, and what will be the end we cannot tell may god Bless us & Save us &c this Summer we have had 2 new chappels opend, 1 in Cannon St, & 1 in Pole St[341]

338   The original plan for the Lancaster Canal had involved a link southwards from Preston, across the Ribble by an aqueduct, to the Leeds & Liverpool Canal near Chorley, but the cost of the aqueduct was prohibitive, and a 'temporary' tramroad was built instead (it functioned for almost sixty years). The canal north of Preston was thus completely isolated, until the belated opening of a branch to Glasson Dock, at the mouth of the Lune, in 1827. This was of little value for coal traffic, since access required a coastal sea voyage, but it was well-used to bring slate from the southern Lake District to roof the growing town of Preston: *dutten* means Duddon (see Price, pp. 55 and 58–61).
339   poll
340   Preston, long before the Irish immigration of the 1840s, had a very large Catholic population. Its wide suffrage meant that there was at least the possibility that they could vote, subject to the swearing of the Oath of Supremacy. As Benjamin makes clear, some candidates were happy to ignore the requirement to swear the oath, in return for the support of the Catholic working men. Not until the Emancipation of 1829 was the question clearly resolved.
341   The Cannon Street chapel was opened on 9 July. It was the successor of the old Independent Chapel on the corner of Chapel Street and Fishergate. The Pole Street chapel, opened on

Having given some account of my relations, & my self, I will now give some relation of my wife, and her relations, but it is but little that I know, but what I know I will make known &c.

Edward Leeming, my wifes father, was a Native of Bowland, (or what one may call the hylands of Lancashire)[342] But of his relations, I only know that he had one sister, & of her I know nothing – it seems he had been born about the year 1750 (but he did not know his age himself) he served an apprintiship to the sea, (as we say) or to work in Ships, or sailing, with some merchants at lancaster (but I dont know who[343]) Sailing mostly to the west Indies &c, he followed this way of life after he was loose many years, &c – it seems he married about the year 1772, (But this is only conjecture) his first wife (for he had 3 wives) was Betty Robinson, daughter of thomas Robinson, (in or near lancaster)[344] By this woman he had 4 children the first Betty, (his only daughter, and my Beloved wife) was Born 1773, Novem^r 17th, thomas the 2rd, & 2 more their names I dont know,[345] but the 2 youngest died very young – his first wife died about the year 1781,[346] he still followed the seafairing Business – it seems he was guner of a Priveteer, Sent out from Lancaster in the american war, & had a clame to some Prize money, but he never got any &c –

* soon after he maried a mary Parker, of Lancaster, but I know nothing of this

---

9 April, was originally built by the Lady Huntingdon's Connexion, a group of strict and 'Calvinistic' Methodists, but in 1855 it was bought by the 'general Baptists', the body which had recently broken away from the Leeming Street Baptist congregation.

342 A search of all parish registers in the area between the M6, the river Ribble, the present border with North Yorkshire and the Westmorland border, has failed to produce evidence of a baptism for Edward. This may be because Benjamin uses the word 'Bowland' to refer to places well beyond the district to which the name currently applies. Edward Limming, who married Margaret Bland at Lancaster in 1744, or Edward Leeming, who married Margaret Charnley at Melling in 1747, could possibly have been his father.

343 The only surviving apprenticeship records from eighteenth-century Lancaster, the Lancaster Apprentices Register (LL: MS/160) has no trace of Edward Leeming being bound apprentice 1752–65. It is likely that if he *was* formally bound, it would have been as a parish (not a town) apprentice, and under the auspices of the overseers, rather than the Corporation or by private agreement.

344 The marriage of Edward Leeming of Lancaster and Elizabeth Robinson of Bolton-le-Sands, both single persons, took place on 19 January 1773 at Bolton-le-Sands. Thomas Robinson, Elizabeth's father, was one of the witnesses (LRO: PR/3315/1/8). The Marriage Licence Bond, issued on the previous day, states that Edward was a mariner, and that Thomas Robinson was a shoemaker of the township of Warton (LRO: ARR 11/1773 Leeming/Robinson).

345 The baptisms of the children of Edward and Betty Leeming were at Lancaster St Mary: Betty (14 November 1773); Thomas (19 May 1776); Edward (31 January 1779); William Robinson (28 January 1781) (LRO: PR/3262/1/3).

346 Elizabeth, wife of Edward Leeming of Lancaster, mariner, was buried at Lancaster St Mary on 20 July 1783. Their son Edward had been buried on 16 December 1779, but the burial of their son William has not been located – it was not at Lancaster St Mary (LRO: PR/3262/1/3).

woman, but that she was a very little woman, rather hump Backed, & by this woman he had 3 Sons – John – Christopher & Benjamin, (so called to Pleas my wife for we courted when he was born) this wife died at dolphinholme, about the year 1792,[347] he had shifted from lancaster, about 2 years before, & now wrought in the factory, & 3 Children &c (I think in the same year he married, Betty Buttler, then living at dolphinholme,[348] (and lived the next neighbour to him) She was a Native of Kockerham by this woman he had 3 Sons (She had 2 daughters by Chance before) Petter – Robert, & James (which are 1826 all living now in this town)[349] he shifted to lancaster soon and in 1793, & Bound John, & Christop apprintices to twine spiners, & he got work at the roop walk[350] &c,–

* he continued to live at lancaster untill the year 1802, soon in the spring he came to Preston, the 2 oldest sons were loos & out of their time[351] – But as the twine spining was not much carried on in Preston & the weaving was then good, they Both got to weaving, the other children wrought in the factory – he got work with F Sleddon, to turn the laith wheel before the Steam Engin was ready – Soon he got work in Horrocks factory, to overlook the drawing frames,[352] & continued in this work many years & other things about the yard &c,

* about the year 1819 his 3rd wife died, & he still kept on his house, his sons wear all married[353] but the youngest, & he was now about 17 years old, and was a rover[354] in the factory &c, – he was now become old, and was discharged from

347   Edward Leeming, labourer, and Molly Parker, spinster, were married at Lancaster St Mary on 26 April 1784 (LRO: PR/3262/1/20), and two of their children were baptized at the same church: John (17 October 1784) and Christopher (11 February 1787) (LRO: PR/3262/1/4). The family then moved to Dolphinholme, and the third son, Benjamin, was baptized at Over Wyresdale chapel on 12 May 1792 (LRO: PR/2955/1). Mary, wife of Edward Leeming, was buried at Lancaster St Mary on 14 October 1792 (LRO: PR/3262/1/4).
348   Edward Leeming, sailor, and Betty Butler, spinster, both of Cockerham, were married there on 21 January 1793 (LRO: PR/1376). His previous wife had been dead only three months.
349   The children of Edward and Betty (Butler) Leeming were baptized as follows: Robert, at Lancaster St Mary on 11 May 1794; Peter Butler at Lancaster St Mary on 8 December 1799; James, at Preston St John on 25 March 1804 (LRO: PR/3262/1/5 and PR/1445).
350   The rope walk: rope was made by twisting strands of fibre, and the enormous length of the finished ropes meant that the spinning had to be done by 'walking' in long narrow enclosures, called rope walks. Lancaster was a flourishing port in the eighteenth century, and this had stimulated a thriving local industry, producing rope and twine, sacking and hessian, canvas and sailcloth.
351   had served their apprenticeships
352   The drawing frames improved the uniformity of the sliver (the fibres which had been carded) and arranged them in a parallel order ready for spinning.
353   Betty Leeming, aged 62, of Elizabeth Street, New Preston, was buried at Preston St John on 4 January 1819 (LRO: PR/1475).
354   'Roving' was the first stage in the spinning process, a slight twisting of the fibres: it was done on a rover or roving machine (colloquially a Roving Billy), the operator of which was also called a rover.

his work, and his family being all off, he became poor (I think he had something out of the town[355]) he used to wind weavers bobins, and &c – in June, soon on, he was taken very ill, & on the 16th he died, & was buried in the old Church yard, aged as we supose about 70 years, & of age[356] he was a spare & slender man, about 5 feet 5 inch high, with a longish face – fresh looking – with red hair & beard & grey eyes, rather Bowleged – was not much of a Scoler – (seemed an easy man (rather fond on woman as it was reported &) fond of Bird breeding, Bird Catching, fishnig [sic] – Building Small ships, & Cages &c, – he had been in the methodist society, for the last 20 years of life –

Respecting my wifes mother I know Scarce any thin but her Name was Betty robinson, daughter of Thomas Robinson, near lancaster,[357] they were married about 1772, her father outlived her, he lived wath another daughter that was married to John young – my wifes mother had a sister older than herself, called agness, who married John young of wharmer,[358] a shoe maker,[359] she had a good round family all sons (for she never had a daughter) her father lived with them the later part of his life, my wife also lived with her after her mother died, she was then about 8 years old, She lived with her some years, bet [sic] the exact time I dont know, (I think this woman died about the year 1796 &c –

BETTY SHAW, wife of Benjamin Shaw, was born at Lancaster, November 17th 1773,[360] – was daughter of Edward, & Betty, Leeming, of that Place, She was the oldest child, & only daughter &c – her mother had 4 children, 3 sons younger than her, while her mother lived she was sent to the Charity School, (or as they call it there Blue School &c)[361] here she got the reading she had, which she

355 was in receipt of poor relief, granted by the overseer of the poor
356 Edward Leeming of Ann Street, New Preston, aged 76, was buried at Preston St John on 17 June 1821 (LRO: PR/1475).
357 The parish register of Warton, near Carnforth, records the baptism of Elizabeth, daughter of Thomas and Alice Robinson of Warton, on 19 June 1748 (LPRS vol. 73).
358 Quernmore, five miles south east of Lancaster
359 Agnes Robinson was considerably older than her sister Elizabeth. She was married to John Young, shoemaker, by licence at Warton on 28 June 1762. As her father, Thomas Robinson, was a shoemaker it is reasonable to suppose that John Young worked with him, or perhaps was his apprentice (LPRS vol. 37).
360 The register of Lancaster St Mary records the baptism of Betty, daughter of Edward Leeming, on 14 November 1773 – which implies a somewhat earlier date of birth – and so means that Benjamin's date of 17 November is incorrect (LRO: PR/3262/1/3).
361 The Girls Charity School or Bluecoat School, in High Street, Lancaster, opened in 1772. It took 34 poor girls (soon increased to 40) who were 'annually cloathed, furnished with Books, taught to read, write, sew and spin; and, that they may be useful Servants, are also instructed in the common necessary parts of Houshold-work'. According to some accounts, each girl was allowed a quarter of her earnings, payable at Christmas. Other sources suggest that such payments were made only to 'the most deserving and well-behaved'. No registers of admissions or other records of the school survive from before its re-foundation in the early nineteenth century (LL *Hymnsheet & accounts, May 1794*, Docton Collection No. 4330, in Girls Charity School File; also Clark, p. 50).

retained in a good degree[362] – her oldest Brother Thomas, afterwards went to Sea, & when he died is not known, She heard from him about the year 1791, he sent her some artificials,[363] from one of the west India islands, by a ship from lancaster But She never heard from him after, &c but to return her mother died when she was only about 8 years old,[364] leaving 4 Children, & her father following the seafareing life, the children was put in to the Poor house at lancaster,[365] She Stoped hear sometim, the 2 younges children died very young, & thomas some time after went to Sea, Betty had an Aunt, her mothers sister in wharmer, 3 or 4 miles of, this aunt took her home to her house, (her name was agness young wife of John young, shoe maker, here she lived some years, &c,

* her father soon married again, and had more children, she went home again, & hear she stoped some time, but as her father was not able to maintain his family without Parish relief, Betty was put out towns, or Parrish apprintice,[366] her lot fell to be with James Scirrah, who kept a Publick house on the green air, in Lancaster, (the Sign of the Joiners arms &c[367]) this man dealt in wood &c here she lived for some time, But it seems, as the master had several daughters, they

362   Elsewhere in the text Benjamin implies that Betty could also write, a skill which as a former Charity School pupil she would have been taught. His phrasing is somewhat ambiguous, and she did not sign the marriage register, but the balance of probability is that she was able to write.
363   Probably artificial pearls made from shell.
364   Actually eleven years old.
365   The town workhouse at Lancaster stood near the White Cross, at the junction of the present King Street and Penny Street. It was a small and inconvenient building, and in June 1787 (shortly after Betty and the other children were there) the Corporation, Churchwardens and Overseers of Lancaster agreed to build a new workhouse on a newly enclosed part of Lancaster Moor. The old building was closed in 1788 on the opening of its successor (Cross Fleury, p. 399, and LL: MS/4791).
366   Her father had applied for parish relief from the overseers of Lancaster, but very often a condition of such applications being approved was that children over the age of eight were put out as apprentices by the parish. In this way they would be self-supporting and the parish would not be paying for able-bodied children to stay at home. Betty was by this time in her mid-teens, and so well able to work. She was not a town apprentice (under the Corporation of Lancaster) but a parish apprentice bound by the Poor Law authorities. There are no surviving Poor Law or parish apprenticeship records from the eighteenth century, and so no documentary evidence of her various bindings can be found. The Lancaster Apprentices Registers (LL: MS/160 and 161) cover only the [male] town apprentices.
367   The Green Ayre in Lancaster was a tract of former saltmarsh alongside the River Lune, on the south bank below the slope on which the town was built. This open land was used for grazing until the late eighteenth century, when the growth of population and exhaustion of suitable building land within the town meant that housing and commercial development began to spread onto it. The process was accelerated when the railway line to Morecambe was built in 1847–8: the line and its Green Ayre station occupied a substantial area of the former marsh. Benjamin notes that Green Ayre, by the Lune, was a 'very pleasant place', an instance of his appreciation of environment.

could spare her, for they often sent her to wrae,[368] a smale vilage near Hornby, 10 miles from Lancaster, to help them at Busy times, these People were some relations to her master[369] &c – some time after, She was agreed for to go to A M[rs] dove[s] her husband was a sea captain, and mostly from home – they lived on the green are, a very Pleasant situation near the River lune here She lived some time –

* But disagreeing with her M[rs370] she took a French Lieve,[371] and went to her fathers, who had shifted some time Before to dolphinholme, in Ellel, 7 miles from Lancaster, & 6 from Garstang, east of the great road[372] &c – this was in february 1791 She got work in the factory, and lived with her father, She was now 17 year & 3 moth [sic] old, in the Sumer this year, I came to dolphinholme, & we soon becam Suters &c, She continued at dolphinholme, until Octob 1792, then another young woman & her came to Preston to live, she got work at the factory in moor lain, & lived sometime in the Shambles,[373] & then near the moss, she stoped in Preston untill July 1793 when she was sent out of the town, being with child, (for we still courted by letters, & I went over to Preston at Shrovetide, &c) She now went to Lancaster, her father was returned thither, here she lived untill she was married, which was on the 21 Sep[r] 1793 this was the first year of the last french war, which lasted 22 year

* She now came to my Place at dolphinholme, for I had more than 10 month to serve of my time,[374] she Brought me a Son on the 4th of november, (1793), we lived at this Place untill february 1795, she came soon after, at this time we went to Preston, and took a part of a house where we have lived ever since, (1826) I

---

368 Wray
369 James Scirrah (usually spelled Skirrow) described himself in his will as a yeoman, although he was also a publican and a timber merchant. He owned several properties in Lancaster, leaving in his will his dwelling houses and premises 'in Damside Street and in the Alley leading from Damside street to Sugar House Alley on the Green Area in Lancaster' and three houses in Back Lane or King Street (LRO: WRW(A) 1814 James Skirrow of Lancaster). The Skirrow family, as Benjamin suggests, had close connections with the Hornby and Roeburndale area, and historically the surname was unusually concentrated: almost all examples (apart from a few in Lancaster) occur in the parishes of Tatham, Melling, Hornby and Caton.
370 mistress
371 French leave: leave without permission, i.e. absconded
372 the Preston-Lancaster turnpike, the modern A6
373 The Shambles in Preston was the row of butchers' shops at the southern end of Lancaster Road, in the town centre close to the town hall and market place. It was built in 1715: 'butchers' shops occupied the basement part, and above – projecting, and supported by rude stone pillars – were dwelling places' (Hewitson, p. 346). By the late eighteenth century these had become notoriously poor slum housing, but the shops and dwellings survived until their demolition as part of extensive town centre improvements in 1883. The 'moss' referred to by Benjamin is Spittals Moss, at the north end of Friargate, close to the Moor Lane factory. Betty lived near here at the end of Kirkham Street.
374 left to serve of his apprenticeship

need not write every Particular here, as many of the thing are mentioned in the account I have given of my self, which see &c, – She has had 8 Children, as follows, 1 Joseph Born, November 4th 1793 2nd William Born July 29th – 1795 – 3, Isabella or Bellow May 7th, 1799 – 4 Hannah, Born January 17th – 1803 – 5 Mary, born Sept 18th 1805, died July 23rd 1806, aged 44 week & 1 day – Hannah died february 25, 1824, aged 21 years 5 weeks &c – 5 Thomas Born May 2nd, 1807 – 6, Mary the 2nd, Born May 27 – 1811 – 8 Agness Born July 18, 1813 &c–

* Discription, Betty Shaw is rather less tham [sic] many – Spare & thin, and weakly, Especially of late years, She used to be fleshy enough, But not fat – her hair when young was red, but now it is gone very dark – her Eyès Brown &c, She has had tolerable good health, but very frequently complaining &c – She was very unfortunate in the loss of her mother, when she was so young, she lost all that instruction so Necessary to a young woman, of care and and [sic] the managment of the small income that is frequently the portion of the Poor – She had been Brought up in Houses where care was not Practised, & She only a Stranger &c, She had not been Shown how to manage any thing to advantage, (or she had not learnt at least) so that she had everything to learn when she ought to have known it, &c)

* She was very remarkabl in some things, she seems to be nearly without Pride, quite careless about cloaths, this is Strainge, (I have my doubts whether I can gain credit for what I now say) but it has been a great misfortune to me, as well as to all her family, for Pride is as necessary as anything that Belongs to the female Characture, to Stirr them up to care & dilegence, to get & to save all that they can to appear respectable, & to be independant, & free from any obligation to any, (O that my wife had had a few grains of this usfull Pride,) but she was quite indifferant about Cloathing – furniture, Characture, &c, She was easy, and careless, and did not mind how things went so that she could have what she wanted, easily &c She kept company with the Poorest of the neibours, and learned many of their Bad Practises, She always traded in Shops, and was allways in debt, without endeavering to get out, (we have had more differance about this than a little,) for she was not fit to trade this way, for she did seldom keep account against them,[375] being Honest Herself, She did not suspect any Body &c,

* She scarce ever had any money by her, for she was allways behind hand, every where, She traded[376] and kept paying untill her money was done and then she Stoped, Sometimes when we had some differanc, or when the Crediters had to come for money, she would amuse me[377] with Pretending to be Paying off, but

375   kept a record of what she had borrowed
376   bought on credit
377   try to please me

this was all deception, for whille she was paying of at one place, She was chalking on at another, (from the time that we were weded to now we have never been clear of debt) & her allowance has been more than the most of womans from 1802, for 6 years I mostly gave her 21 Shilings per week, & found my own Cloaths, & Spending money, Beside paying the Rent, & for Phisic &c, I used to buy the Children Cloaths & her frequently &c, – often did buy her a load of Coals or a cheese found her money to Buy Meal, & flower, at the best hand, but all would not do &c, –

* She kept company with the very Poorest of her Neighbours, & they frequently deceived her, for if they came with a Pittiful Story, She would help them if she could, we suffered much this way – She always traded with Scotch men,[378] this is a ruinous concern, for the[379] Charge unreasonably, and Cheat frequently, in their reckonings, &c, Beside She hath frequently robed me of money – sometimes taken my cloths to Pawn, & once my watch, &c, and frequent told lyes to deceive me, But this was allways her way, for when She was young She never had any thing, Scarce any thing of her Back, She never had but one gown, all the time that before we were married I knew her, & that somebody gave her, & when She had had it a whille, She was out of Conceit with it,[380] & She gave it to her mother, (that is Step mother) to cut for the Children frocks, &c, and when she got any thing, Bedgowns, or hankerchiefs, or Stocking, or any article new, She gave the old ones away assoon as she got them or before, so that she never had any thing – so she had nothing to care for &c,

* when we courted, She had no Bonnet, & this was frequently urged as a reason for her not walking out, on the Sunday & I therefore Bought her one, Still she was something Short, this is her Plan, She will not have any thing, She knows that it is some trouble to have any thing – and She often says that her children shall not fall out about her things for She will not have any for them to differ about – when She was married, she had all to Borrow for the ocation, & So any Body may think, whether She will care for furniture, or Cloathing for others, But She has not every Bad Property, for She is Peasable, & good natuered, if one can Bear with her Particuler way, (every one has their way, and their faults, and it is not easy to say who hath the advantage, for every one thinks that if their wives, or Husbands, had any other fault, or way, they could do better, it would be more tolerable, or they could Bear it Better, &c) –

* my wife is Sober, Steady, & temperate, in eating, & drinking, & cloathing, is loving to her Children, (to a Blame[381] &c) is of a Simpathising, & feeling

378   pedlars or credit traders ('Scotch drapers')
379   they
380   no longer liked it
381   to a fault

temper, even to Straingers, (this has caused her frequently to be imposed on & she hath Suffered much on this account, &c) She hath Been faithful to the Marriage agreement, (for any thing that I know), this many would think the greates of a Blessing, though this is nothing more than the Bargin or Simple Justice, She is not a Common Liar, or Swearer, &c, – is Honest in owning her debts, & Paying when able &c – She is Paitent in general, and not easily Provoked, will easily forgive faults, if acknowledged, &c, – and She cannat easily deny any favour if asked in good Humour, & Pressed to Comply, this is one great fault, for as the Poet says – (that Mere good Nature is a fool[382]

* She has been frequently Imposed upon by Shop kepers, Scotch men, & other traders, that hath urged her to trade upon Credit, for if there was nothing to Pay now, it was like as if she thought there would never be any thing to Pay, &c & so got into difequiltes for want of fore sight, this is a fault in trading &c – She is now in tolerable good health, though weakly, But has many Simptams of old age upon her, more than many at her age, for she is only now 1826 53 years old, but She seems as though she would not live untill She was as old as many, but one cannot tell, She has Been in the Methodist Society 26 years, & has been tolerable Steady, She has 6 Children, & 11 grand children, living, with 5 grand children that is Buried, &c, I think that She is becom a little more carefull lately &c – She is very seceptable of feeling & is Happy or miserable as she is dealt with – very impatient of contradiction, /Reproof She cannot Brook – Milton

having giveng some account of my ancestor & Parents & my Self & wife & her Parents I will give some account of our Brothers, & sister, next & of my Brothers & Sisters first,

* My Sister Hannah was Born at dent, in the year 1774,[383] & Brought up in our family in that township, was learned[384] to knit stocking, & other knit work &c, & Sewing with what is common in the Cottages &c, She lived there untill the year 1791, when She went to dolphinholme with the family, when there, she went to the factory, & wrought at the winding frames, &c She shifted to Aconthwate green in the early Part of 1793, this is within a mile of milthrop,[385] the next year She with her Parents shifted into Milthrop, & in the year 1795, in may came to Preston, here she continued with her Parents until 1797, when she went to dolphinholme, again –

---

382   It has proved impossible to trace the origin of this quotation.
383   Hannah Shaw was baptized at Garsdale, her father's home township, on 27 November 1774 (CROK: WPR/60/1). She may therefore not have been born at Dent, as Benjamin suggests.
384   taught
385   Milnthorpe, Westmorland

* here she got aquarnted [*sic*] with Isaac Walker, a woolcomber,[386] and after some time was maried to him[387] – Soon after he Hired into the Lancashire Millitia, & went of to the Regement then in the north of England, & She came Home to Preston, in the later end of 1797, in the following Spring her Mother died, & she lived with her father a while, but about may 1798, She went to see her her [*sic*] Husband at Sunderland, & came back with child, she now lived with her father, & followed winding in the House, & Sewing &c, her child was born at the beginning of 1799, She called it Mary Walker,[388] She continued to live with her father &c, in the year 1800, in the Spring, Her Husband came Home Poorly, & soon after died, She still lived with her father until in 1803, her child died, about 3½ year old,[389]

* Soon after She was Married to Henry Jackson, a warper, he was a widower, with 2 children, & had been married twice before[390] &c, Sometime after she had a daughter, called Rachel, this Child died soon, the next was a son, Born in the end of 1806, called William, She has had 8 Children, 6 daughters, & 2 Sons – those that followed these I have named, were Sarah, & Bellaw – John – Hannah & Mary &c – the youngest was Born about 1820[391] – in 1822, She built a House in the Park, at the end of newten Street, She hath kept a Mangle some time

---

386   Dolphinholme produced worsted yarn, and so woolcombers were employed at the mill.
387   The marriage of Isaac Walker, woolcomber, and Hannah Shaw, spinster, took place on 23 October 1797 at St Helen's, Churchtown, Garstang. Both parties were described as 'of Garstang', and both made their mark. It is not clear why Hannah was apparently living in Garstang. However, the township of Nether Wyresdale (in which the mill at Dolphinholme and some of the cottages were situated) was in the parish of Garstang, and the explanation may therefore be that the couple lived on the south side of the Wyre at Dolphinholme (LRO: PR/2409).
388   Mary, daughter of Isaac and Hannah Walker, was born on 5 January 1800 and baptized at Preston St John on 1 June (LRO: PR/1445).
389   Mary, daughter of Hannah Walker, was buried at Preston St John on 16 May 1804 (LRO: PR/1445). Isaac Walker was not buried in Preston between January 1799 and December 1803; his place of burial has not been found.
390   Henry Jackson and Hannah Walker, both of Preston, were married at Preston St John on 1 August 1804: the witnesses were Benjamin Shaw [the author] and William Hodgkinson. Henry signed, but Hannah made her mark – as Benjamin notes in his account of their quarrel over their father's belongings, his sister was almost unlettered. The register, as was typical of many in Lancashire at this time, gives no indication of marital status (LRO: PR/1453).
391   The baptism entries of the children of Henry and Hannah Jackson reveal that they had Methodist leanings in the early years of their marriage: William (born 1 December and baptized 7 December 1806) and Sarah (born 17 April 1808 and baptized the same day) were baptized at the Methodist Society (LRO: mf 1/11). Isabella (born 22 February and baptized 27 February 1810) and John (born 4 December 1811 and baptized 26 January 1812) were baptized at the Grimshaw Street Congregational Chapel (LRO: mf 1/83). Hannah was baptized on 16 February 1817 and Mary on 5 May 1819, both at Holy Trinity, Preston (LRO: PR/1462). According to the IGI Rachel was *born* on 24 April 1805, but no baptism has been located for her.

there[392] – She hath 5 children Living, & 3 dead, her husband still follows warping, & is the Clark at the trinity Church,[393] & has been in that office ever sinc the Church opened, it was Consecrated in december 1815, &c – Hannah is a managing woman, but very Covetious & earnest to get money, She is rather inclined to be fat, of a middle Size, &c –

george shaw, son of Joseph &, Isabella Shaw, was Born at dent, in the year 1776,[394] was the 3rd child, & 2nd son, of the above &c, he lived with his Parents, & went to school, & learnt to Read & knit, as was the fashon of the time & Place &c – he had the natural Small Pox very Severaly, when about 6 years old, he was not expected to Survive, but he did recover, but was much Pitted with them &c – he lived at home all his life time – from the time he was 10 or 12 years old he was very fond of cocks & hens – chickins – dogs – Birds &c, this we did not like, & did all in our Power to hinder, but Still he was the same, he spent all he had in this way, indeed this was his Hobby alltogether,[395] &c – in the year 1791, he cam to dolphinholm with the family, & wrought in the Factory, but he did not long enjoy good health after, for the winter following he began to be ill, & continued to decline in health, & in the Summer of 1792,[396] he died, & was Buried at Cockerham, aged near 16 years, his complaint was a consumption, this was a very Sickly time hear &c

William Shaw, son of the above Parents, was Born at dent, in the year 1779,[397] he was the 2 son, & 4 child, he was an active child from his infantcy &c, was brought up at home, & in the usial way, he came with the family to dolphinholme in 1791, & became a spiner[398] in the factory, he lived at home, & stoped all the time his Parents did, which was untill 1793, in the Spring, when the war began with france, trade was very bad, and many was discharged & my fathers family with others, my father shifted to a place called Aconthwaite green, near Milthrop, Soon William was put apprintice, to Lenard Gibson, a Black Smith at the Endmoor, 5 miles South of Kendal, here he served a part of his time, but his master Shifted to Casterton[399] before his time was out, he

392   has taken in washing
393   Holy Trinity, Preston
394   George Shaw was baptized at Dent on 10 November 1776 (CROK: WPR/70/4), and was buried at Cockerham on 2 April 1793 (LRO: PR/1371).
395   It is not clear why the family was so anxious to prevent George from looking after and keeping animals and birds. Possibly they felt that this distracted his attention from his work, and hence from earning money, or perhaps they occupied space in the house and were dirty.
396   George actually died at Easter time.
397   William Shaw was baptized at Dent on 23 May 1779 (CROK: WPR/70/4).
398   spinner
399   The bundle of apprenticeship papers which survives among the Heversham parish records does not include one for William Shaw (CROK: WPR/8/Apprenticeship Papers).

served the list[400] Part of his time there – about the time when he was loose,[401] he married a woman of the name of Ann Hodgson,[402] at Casterton, & Soon Set up his trade, in Middleton, a village on the road between Kirby-lonsdale & Sedbergh,[403] here he lived a few years –

* he married about the begining 1800 about the year 1805, he shifted into Kirby-lonsdale, and followed his trade, and got Plenty of work, & was carful & industerous, But his wife Brought him Children fast,[404] &c – in the year 1807, many farmers about that Countery was going to America, & now he made up his mind to go thither, therefore early in the year 1808, he sold his furniture, & Stock in trade & gave up his house, & Shop, & after making araingments for his journey, & Voige, set of from Kirby, I think early on the 24 of february, 1808,

* they came to Preston on the 25, with his famely & goods, this was the last time that I saw him, I think he had 5 Small Children,[405] the next day they Proceed to Liverpool, to take ship ing [sic] for america – we had 3 or 4 letters from him, they got well there, and settled about 12, miles from new york, at a place called west farms, in the county of west Chester, & state of new york, he follows his trade, which is a good Business in that Countery &c, the last time I heard from him, he had Purchased about 50 acres of land, but did not say, whether he had Paid for it or not &c, he was very carefull[406] &c

400 last
401 had completed his apprenticeship
402 Her name was in fact Ann Robinson.
403 William Shaw of Casterton, blacksmith, and Ann Robinson of Casterton, spinster, were married by licence at Kirkby Lonsdale on 18 March 1800, in the presence of William Robinson and Miles Craston (CROK: WPR/19/6).
404 The older children of William and Ann Shaw were baptized at Kirkby Lonsdale: Joseph (born 16 April and baptized 31 May 1801); William (born 7 January and baptized 3 August 1806); and Benjamin (born 6 April and baptized 9 August 1807). The baptism of Thomas (c. 1804) has not been traced (CROK: WPR/19/3).
405 There were four: Joseph, William, Thomas and Benjamin.
406 The collection of Benjamin Shaw's papers and writings at the Lancashire Record Office includes several letters sent by William Shaw and his family between 1816 and the early 1840s. By March 1816 there were six children (Joseph, Thomas, William, Benjamin, Hannah and James Robinson); the family had built a house, and had half an acre of land with four cows and some geese. When William wrote to Benjamin in January 1831 he reported that Joseph was married with three children and had gone to live in 'upe Canaday' [Upper Canada – Ontario]. Thomas had married and had a child, Joseph, but his wife died of fever soon afterwards and he went to see his brother Joseph in Canada. He had written a letter from Utica, in upstate New York, but had never been heard of since – 'i lamente him Verey much'. Benjamin was married and living in New York, and Hannah and her husband lived at West Farms in Westchester County.
     The letter of 1831 asks after their father, Joseph Shaw, who had died in 1825: William had obviously not heard of his father's death. A letter written to Benjamin Shaw from New York by his nephew, Benjamin, in September 1842 [eighteen months after the death of the intended recipient] reports that William had died four years before (in 1838). Benjamin junior had also written previously, telling that his mother was 'a little Deranged in her mind' and giving details of the progress of the family (LRO: DDX/1554/22,24).

Joseph Shaw, the 4 Son, & 5 Child, of Joseph & Isabella Shaw, was born at dent, about the 1782,[407] & was brought up in his fathers family untill he died, this child when little was a remarkable bad talker, and on account of peaple takeing notice of him, & laughing at him, he became remarkablely Shy, & Shame faced this was the most particular child that I ever saw about his play things, he would teaze, and Ply his father, to make him Something to Play with frequently, and when he got any thing new, he would examine it with the greatest care, & attention, & if he found no fault with it, then he sade (it will do) but, if he found any fault in it (& he was a good judge) then he threw it on the floor, as though he would Break it to Pieces, & would not have it again at all &c,

* when we came to dolphinholme in 1791, he was employed in the factory, though he was a very little one,[408] &c, the first year he was in the mill he got catched, in the wheels (this was very common here) and one of his hands was sadly lamed, my father took him to the doctor at Lancaster, & I think 2 of his fingers was taken off, & his hand otherwise cut, & Bruised &c, this Scarce got well untill he took a fever, which raged there, at that time, & died in the Summer of the year 1792, of autumn he was Buried at Cockerham – this was a small child, of his age 10 yeare old

Peggy Shaw, the 6th child, & 2nd daughter, of the above, was born at dent &c, this was a Small & Blue looking child, when her mother lade inn of this child, the nurse that she had (Peggy Wilson was her name) gave us the Itch,[409] this went hard with the child, & it Scarce ever recovered from it &c, this child was born about the year 1785,[410] was very difequilt to sute with her meat, and was after poorly (a neighbour of ours used to call her Small hopes &c) frequently complaining, She was about 6 year old when her Parent came to dolphinholme, Soon after they left that Place and went to aconthwate, She Sickened & died in the year 1793, near 8 years old, & was Buried at Heasom[411] Church, the only one of our family that lies there &c –

Isabella (or as we called her) Bellaw Shaw, was the 3rd daughter & 7th child of Joseph & Isabbella Shaw, of dent, She was Born there about the year 1789,[412]

407　Joseph Shaw was baptized at Dent on 27 October 1782 (CROK: WPR/70/4), and was buried at Cockerham on 1 May 1792, three days after his younger sister Isabella (LRO: PR/1371). The description given by Benjamin perhaps suggests that Joseph was slightly retarded.

408　He was nine years old.

409　The 'itch' is scabies, a highly contagious skin disease producing extremely irritating scabs: it is caused by a minute parasitic worm.

410　Peggy (Margaret) Shaw was baptized on 9 April 1786 at Dent (CROK: WPR/70/4), and was buried at Heversham on 28 June 1793, shortly after her family had moved there from Dolphinholme (CROK: WPR/8/20).

411　Heversham, Westmorland

412　No trace has been found of a baptism entry for Isabella Shaw, but she was almost certainly

this was a very file[413] Strong Sharp & healthy Child, when her Parents came to dolphinholme she was about 2 years old, this was a lovly child, & greatly valued by the family, but this could not Sheild her from disease, for in the year 1792, in the autumn of that year, a time of great sickness & trouble, at that time & Place, she sickened & died, my fathe was ill long about this time &c, She was Buried at Cockerham near her 2 Brothers george & Joseph, on the north side near the middle Part &c, this Child was very remarkable for her having one eye Brown, & the other a light grey &c

I shall now give some few hints of my wife[s] Brothers (Sisters she had none except one that died very young at Lancaster about 1781 &c

Thomas Leeming – Son of Edward & Betty Leeming, was born at lancaster, about the year 1775,[414] he lived at home untill his mother died in 1781,[415] when he was 6 years old, after that he was put into the Poor house &c – when he was very young he went to the Sea, (but whether bound or not I dont know[416]) it seems that he followed it some time, but what came of him his relations never knew,[417] the last time that they heard from him was about the year 1792, he sent his Sister Betty some artificials from Jimaco,[418] in a Ship from lancaster, called the Sarah &c, this is all that I know of this man, &c –

John Leeming, Son of Edward & mary (who[s] maden name was parker) Leeming was Born at Lancaster, but the time I dont know, I supose about the year 1783,[419] this John when a Child, Seemed as though he had been ill used in his infantcy, he was a Sour looking child, Scarce ever laughed, & was not fond of Play, but Soletery, & Stayed, & Seemed as though he had bad health &c, though

---

born in 1789 at Dent. She was buried at Cockerham on 27 April 1792, dying of the same sickness (its identity unclear) which killed her brother Joseph three days later (LRO: PR/1371).

413 fine
414 Thomas Leeming was baptized at Lancaster St Mary on 19 May 1776 (LRO: PR/3262/1/3).
415 She actually died in 1783.
416 Bound as an apprentice: the lack of parish apprenticeship records from eighteenth-century Lancaster means that it is not possible to find any evidence about this. Neither Thomas nor any of his brothers entered into agreements as town apprentices, and no member of his family appears in the Lancaster Apprentices Register (LL: MS/161).
417 Lancaster had substantial trade with the West Indies, and the disappearance of young apprentices in this way was far from rare. The Boys Charity School registers record, for example, that in October 1795 a pupil aged about twelve 'went out to the West Indies and died soon after' (LL: MS/178).
418 Probably artificial pearls made of shell; from Jamaica.
419 John Leeming was baptized at Lancaster St Mary on 17 October 1784 (LRO: PR/3262/1/3). This paragraph, with its description of John's withdrawn nature, indicates that Benjamin was in little doubt that his brother-in-law had suffered physical abuse from his father and stepmother as a small child.

he was Constant at his work, &c – he worked at dolphinholm, where his father and mother went to live in the year 1790, he lived here and went to the factory untill the year 1793, when the french war began, then he went to Lancaster, with his Parents &c (in the year 1792, his mother died at dolphinholme &c and was Buried at lancaster,)

* Soon after this he was put apprintice to a twine spinner at Lancaster, & wrought at this Business untill he came with his father & Step mother to Preston, in the year 1802, now he learned to weave, for there was no work in the twine spinning[420] way &c some time after this his father shifted into new Preston, (lately Built) & Sometime after he married one Jeny Hunter, a weaver[421] &c, at that Place, this might be about the year 1806, by this wife he has had 7 children – Thomas – Mary – Peggy – Betty – Hannah – Christopher & another I dont remember [John[422]] &c[423] – 2 of these are dead (now 1826) his wife is living & they all follow weaving &c, this is a Poor Business, but he is Steady, & they live as well as most of the People that follow weaving &c –

Christopher Leeming, Brother to the above, & half brother to Betty Shaw, was born at Lancaster,[424] came to dolphinholme 1790, Stoped here untill 1793, went to lancaster, went apprintice to a twiespinner [sic], wrought at this trade untill he came to Preston in 1802, learned to be a weaver, & wrought at this trade for some time – went in to the lancashire militia, went to Ireland,[425] & returned

---

420   Spinning of rope and twine was an industry particularly associated with seaports, such as Lancaster, and although there was some ropemaking at Preston it was not sufficient to offer any employment to the Leeming boys.

421   The surname of John Leeming's wife was in fact Stewart. John Leeming, weaver, and Jane Stewart, spinster, both of Walton-le-Dale, were married there on 23 August 1807. The witnesses were Thomas Hunter and John Tomlinson: the surname of the first witness suggests that Jane's family had connections with a family called Hunter, which may explain Benjamin's confusion (LRO: PR/2948/1/10).

422   Added subsequently by the author.

423   Margaret and Elizabeth, daughters of John and Jenny Leeming, were baptized at Preston St John on 10 February 1815. Subsequent children were Hannah [baptized as Ann] (16 August 1816); Christopher (28 October 1818); and John (13 July 1825). In each entry John Leeming is described as a weaver; in 1825 the family lived at Green Street, New Preston (LRO: PR/1461, 1462, 1463, 1465). Baptism entries for Mary and Thomas have not been found. The 1841 census shows the family at Green Street East: Mary was twelve years old, so born c. 1829, suggesting that the first Mary (referred to by Benjamin in 1826) had died young. In 1841 John was a handloom cotton weaver, while Hannah, John and Mary, still living at home, were power loom weavers.

424   Christopher Leeming was baptized at Lancaster St Mary on 11 February 1787 (LRO: PR/3262/1/4).

425   During the Napoleonic Wars there was a serious and continuing fear that the French would invade Ireland, which was relatively under-garrisoned and had a disaffected population, as a prelude to an attack on Britain. This view was reinforced by the active participation of French forces in the large-scale, but ultimately unsuccessful, Irish risings of 1798. English militia

after the general Peace in 1815 – it might be 1817, before he came back he had married, & left his wife in linconshire, when he came from Ireland, he Stoped a few days in Preston, then went to his wife, the weather was wet & he got cold on the road, which brought on a fever of which he died, in 6 days after he got to his wife, &c &c &c –[426]

Benjamin Leeming, son of Edward & mary Leeming [3rd Son[427]], was born at dolphinholme, in the year 1792,[428] in the same year his mother died, & was Buried at Lancaster, the same year his father married Betty Buttler, of Cockerham, the next year his father Shifted to lancaster, & lived there untill the year 1802, when he came to Preston, he went to the factory when he was big-enough, & continued untill he Learned to weave, with his Brother, (I Supose) at new Preston for they all lived there, he from his Child-hood had never known the Happyness of a Mother, but was Brought up by a Step mother –

* he hired into the Lancashire Militia, & was in Ireland with the same, untill after the Peace with france &c, Perhaps about the year 1817, when he came Back home &c, But he did not like work, so was very Poor, (for this Seems to be a family complaint they are nearly all alikue) Sauntering away their time, Constantly in some difequilty, & to get out has many Sceems, frequently hath he cheated, & robed his father & family, &c, after some time he married[429] [he had a Bastard child before &c[430]], – & has had many Children Constantly Poor, & Still full of Comical Shifts,[431] &c, he now lives at new Preston with his family &c (1826.

Petter leeming, Son of Edward & Betty Leeming, (his 3rd wifes first son, he was Born at lancaster in the year 1793, I think,[432] this Petter was brought up at

---

regiments were therefore sent to Ireland to reinforce existing troops and to help to garrison the island against the French (and against further threats of rebellion by the Irish).

426   Since the information given here is so vague, no attempt has been made to trace the burial of Christopher Leeming. He presumably died in Lincolnshire.
427   Added subsequently by the author.
428   Benjamin Leeming was baptized at Over Wyresdale chapel on 12 May 1792 (LRO: PR/2955/1).
429   Benjamin Leeming and Ann Williamson, both of Preston, were married there on 18 June 1818 (LRO: PR/1456). Their children were William (baptized at Preston St John 17 October 1818); Edward (7 March 1820); Peter (7 July 1822) and Ann (22 June 1834). In 1822 the family were living in Leeming Street, but by 1834 had moved to nearby Thomas Street (LRO: PR/1463, 1464, 1468). They still lived there when the 1841 census was taken. It lists additional children for whom no baptism has been traced – Richard (born *c*. 1831), Mary (*c*. 1832) and Betty (born January 1841). Benjamin was a handloom cotton weaver and Peter a fur cutter. Edward and Richard (only ten years old) were cotton piecers.
430   Added subsequently by the author.
431   ludicrous or ridiculous changes or actions
432   Peter Butler Leeming was baptized at Lancaster St Mary on 8 December 1799, and there is no evidence to suggest that this was other than an infant baptism. Peter was thus six years younger than Benjamin thought (LRO: PR/3262/1/5).

home, & had all the advantige of a mother, (which is no little thing) he was Brought up at Lancaster untill he was about 9 year old, when he came into Preston with his family, & wrought in the factory a while, but nearly all the family was in the weaving Branch, of Business, he soon learned to weave also, he married (Perhaps about the year 1820, or sooner) I do not know her maden name, Peggy is her Christian name[433] (this woman is sade to have been a trader in the small way &c) she was a wever & a Pretty good match for him, for they never had a child yet, or likely to have, yet they are as Poor as any Body,[434] (they have very few household goods &c, he followed weaving untill about 2 year since, but now he is Spinning, he lives in willow Street,[435] (and was Sold up[436] not long since) he is fond of Birds, dogs, hens – fishing &c – is well fathered & well matched &c &c (1826)

Robert Leeming, 2ʳᵈ Son of Edward Leeming, (by Betty his 3ʳᵈ wife) was born at Lancaster about 1796,[437] Lived at lancaster untill 1802, when his father came to Preston, he learned to weave soon with his Brothers, in his fathers Shop, (for his father had a Shop & 5 or 6 looms which he rented of Horrockss) he was in the Lancashire Millitia, & was in Ireland when his Brothers was there, & came back with them in (1817) i think (he Brought Back with him an Irish wife,[438] (and as he had all Ireland to chouse out of you may think She is no ordinary Person &c) and I give him Credit for his Choice, for they are not fit to enjoy the liberty of others &c, this woman has 2 or 3 Children & is a limb of the divil as we say, She frequently Beats him &c &c it is said (& I Partly Believe it) that this Robert married a woman in Ireland, Before this wife & left her in that Countery (this was lucky for her &c)

---

433   Peter Leeming and Margaret Stanley, both of Preston, were married at Preston St John on 1 February 1818, in the presence of Richard Wilson and Lawrence Tomlinson (LRO: PR/1456).

434   This is incorrect. The 1841 census records Peter and Margaret Leeming, of Willow Street, with their large family. Betty (aged 20, which by the notation used in the 1841 census means born between 1820 and 1823) was born before Benjamin wrote his account. The other children were James (born *c.* 1827), John (*c.* 1831), Jane (*c.* 1836), Thomas (*c.* 1838) and Margaret (*c.* 1839). Peter, his wife Margaret, and Betty were cotton weavers.

435   Willow Street was off Oak Street, behind Manchester Road on the southern edge of the town centre, in an area of closely packed small houses and workshops.

436   bankrupt: had to sell his goods to pay debts

437   Robert Leeming was baptized at Lancaster St Mary on 11 May 1794, and so was older than his brother Peter (Benjamin apparently thought he was the younger of the two) (LRO: PR/3262/1/4).

438   The destruction of most Irish parish registers in 1922 means that research into genealogical problems in Ireland is often impossible. No marriage has been traced, and the maiden name of Robert Leeming's wife is not known, but the evidence of baptism entries for their children shows that she was called Margaret. The following children were baptized at Preston St John: Edward (12 May 1816); Peter (19 November 1817) and Mary Ann (28 March 1822) (LRO: PR/1463 and 1464).

James Leeming, son of Edward d°, was the youngest Child of his Parents,[439] this James went to the factory young, and did not learn the weaving Business, his mother died when he was a bout 14 or 15 years old, soon after his father gave up the weaving Shop to his son John, & took a room, this James was the only Child at home, his father & him lived together, untill his father Died, June 16th 1821, after this James Boarded himself out & wrought in the factory, about this time got to a Roving Billy,[440] this made him more money &c – a bout – 1825 he had a Child fathered on him, but he is not married yet &c[441] – this is the most respectable man of any of the younger Brothers,[442] &c &c 1826 – this Child died in august 1826 &c

Having given some account of my ancestors my Parents & their Brothers & Sisters & of my wife & her Parents & her Brothers I shall say something of our Children & then contlude this Short & very imperfect Piece &c &c

Joseph Shaw, Son of Benjamin & Betty Shaw, was Born November 4th 1793, at dolphinholme, in Ellel, 3 miles from golgate, this was the first year of the french war, which lasted with a short interval in (1802) 22 years &c &c he shifted to Preston in february 1795, being 1¼ year old, in the year 1798, he had an impost,[443] or something like it, (that is a Blood Vessel) when he threw up a large quantaty of clotted Blood, (I think near a Quart) we did not expect him to live, (I thought every Boddy that Passed my window was coming to tell me of his death, 2 or 3 days &c) however he got Better of it, & has not had anything of the Sort Since &c, he went to the factory to work young, was mostly in the Card room &c, when we were removed to our town in 1808,[444] he & his Brother William was left with his aunt Hannah Jackson, untill they came back in 1809,

* Soon after this he went aprintice to Mr Horrockses & C° &c, where he had mostly wrought, to be a Carder, & Served his time with them at the yard, (or their works at the Bottom of Church Street)[445] in the year 1813, on december 27

---

439   James Leeming was baptized at Preston St John on 25 March 1804 (LRO: PR/1447).
440   'Roving Billy' was the colloquial name for the machine which twisted the carded and drawn fibres, the sliver, and made it into an attenuated strand which was ready for spinning yarn.
441   It is possible that this was the James Leeming who married Elizabeth Hesketh at Preston St John on 23 May 1836.
442   James Leeming is described as 'respectable' in the same sentence in which his bastard child is noted: this reflects Benjamin's priorities, in which a high standard of financial and domestic orderliness carried far more weight than sexual propriety.
443   abscess
444   The thirty-week stay in Ellel township forced on the family in 1808 after Benjamin had applied for poor relief.
445   The 'works at the bottom of Church Street' was the so-called Yellow Factory, immediately adjacent to Dale Street where the family lived. The 'yard' was the alternative colloquial name for this factory, and it was often known as 'Horrocks Yard'. The 'Yard Works' was the later collective name for Horrocks's four adjoining factories in this area.

he Married Nanny or Ann Walker, daughter of William & Ellin Walker, of this town,[446] by her he has had 6 Children, the oldest died about 2 years old in the meazles, & in the year 1821, 3 of his Children died in about 3 weeks time[447] – he followed the carding Business untill the year 1824, when trade was good, he got to work in the Machine way, he first went to tom Parrishes, Shop[448] (this was a throstle Spindle & fly Shop &c) & some time after to the Spittles Moss Shop, under Horrockses, concern &c – But trade going bad in the later end of the year 1825, he was discharged & is now tenting a Steam Engin in Bridge Street – 1826 – he has only 2 Children living Jain, & Hannah, Jain was born June 16th 1822, the other to be called Hannah[449] Born July 13, 1826, he now lives near the moss[450] – his wife has Bad eyes this is a loss &c July 17 1826

William Shaw, 2rd Son of Benj[m] & Betty Shaw, Born July 29th 1795, in Preston, in the dale Street N[o] 1, and was brought up there with his Parents, he was Sent to the factory young, & wrought in the yard at Horrocks in the Card room, – in 1808, when his family went to Ellel he & his Brother Jo went to live with his Aunt Hannah in the same Street, & was there untill his Parents returned in June 1809 – he was now 14 years old, & I would gladly have got him a trade, but the trade was Bad & we could not get him to any trade, so we agreed to get him to learn to weave, so we aggreed with Edward Sallisbury, to learn him to weave[451] – he was to serve 12 months, the Master to have the half of his Earnings, & he was to Pay half of looming – winding, candles[452] &c,

---

446   There is no trace of an entry for this marriage in the registers of Preston St John (the only Anglican church in the town licensed for the celebration of marriage) or at the two Catholic churches, St Mary and St Wilfrid. Neither was the marriage conducted at Walton-le-Dale or in any of the Catholic chapels in the vicinity of Preston. Nonconformist churches did not conduct marriage ceremonies at this date.

447   The earlier children of Joseph and Ann Shaw were all baptized at Preston St John: Benjamin (29 May 1814); Mary (1 December 1816); Benjamin (22 April 1818); Elizabeth (5 November 1820); Jane (21 July 1822); Hannah (30 July 1826) – she was born as the last pages of the first volume of Benjamin's autobiography were being written, and her death on 13 April 1830 is recorded in the second volume (LRO: PR/1462, 1464 and 1465). In all the register entries Joseph is described as a carder, and the family's abode is stated to be Dale Street. There were other children born after 1826, whose births are recorded in the second volume of Benjamin's work.
      The burial of the first child, Benjamin (aged 2), was on 24 May 1816 at Preston St. John. The three children who died within three weeks were also buried there: Benjamin (aged 3) on 17 August 1821, Betty (aged 1) on 4 September 1821, and Mary (aged 5) on 9 September 1821 (LRO: PR/ 1475).

448   Thomas Parrish was connected with the business of John Par(r)ish, engineer and millwright of Church Street (*Lancashire Directory* 1818, p.47) and of Bell Street (Pigot's 1828 *Directory*, p.439) but little else is known of him.

449   The child had not been baptized when Benjamin wrote this part of his account.

450   Spittals Moss, at the north end of Friargate

451   In 1818 Edward Salisbury, a weaving master, was living very close to Benjamin, at 10 Dale Street, and it is probable that he was there in 1810 when William Shaw was apprenticed to him.

452   The master agreed to pay half of these costs, normally the responsibility of the apprentice and his family.

* on this aggrement he entered May 21st – 1810, & Served according to this engagement, untill November 13, the same year, & then his master durst keep him no longer, for at this time the weavers was Subscribing to get an act of Parliament to force all that learnt to weave to serve 7 years to the trade, & they threatened to send Law to any that would not turn their learners off, & not take any for a less time than 7 years[453] &c &c – Soon after he went to new Preston to learn his Bisiness out &c – he continued to weave at this Place many years – about this time weaving was very good, they could ged 20 Shilling per week or more,

* in the year 1814, he courted a young woman at new Preston, & on the 18 of october 1814, She fathered a Child on him &c – the Child was not born untill June 20 – 1815, – in may this year Sally Coyle fathered a Child on him, a month before Mattys Johnsons Child was born, &c Sallys Child was born Octor 20, 1815,[454] – he Paid a while & Some time after was put in to the House of Correction for debt,[455] for his child,[456] he continued this way untill he married Sally Coyle on the 11 of august 1817,[457] Soon after Matty Johnson died, & the Child was Brought up by her Parents &c &c he followed weaving many years, & lived at new Preston,[458] But weaving is gone very Bad of late years, & now is so Bad a man Cannon get Scarce a living without a family &c, – he has now 5 Children, & the wife is near her time of another now, (July 1826)[459] – he is now in Horrocks factory, overlooking the drawing frames, & has been more than a year, this is a little Better wages but at this time all trades is bad &c &c See Page 8th 2nd vol.[460]

453   The weavers were attempting to restrict access to their trade, so that only those who had served a full-term apprenticeship as a weaver could be employed. As William was supposed to be learning to weave in only one year, after which time he would have been eligible for employment, his case was one of many which went against the demands of the experienced weavers. Salisbury therefore felt obliged to terminate the agreement.
454   The first of these children was born on 20 June and baptized on 6 August 1815 at Preston St John (the entry reads 'Joseph A Bastard Son of Martha Johnson, Preston'). The second of William's illegitimate children in 1815 was born on 20 October, as Benjamin notes, and was baptized on 22 October ('Bridget A Bastard Dr of Sarah Coyle, Preston') (LRO: PR/1461).
455   In the Quarter Sessions records there is no trace of any papers which relate to this case. The Preston overseers' records have been lost or destroyed.
456   He had not paid the maintenance for the child.
457   William Shaw and Sarah Coyle were married at Preston St John on 11 August 1817 in the presence of John Hodgkinson and Lawrence Tomlinson. Both parties signed with their mark (LRO: PR/1459).
458   The baptism entries for his children 1818–24 all describe him as a weaver of Ann Street, New Preston (LRO: PR/1462–5).
459   The children of William and Sarah (Sally) Shaw born within wedlock were baptized at Preston St John: Thomas (5 June 1818); Joseph (29 March 1820); Benjamin (8 May 1822); Nancy (23 July 1824) (LRO: PR/1462, 1463, 1464, 1465). A daughter, Betty, was born in about 1826 but no record of her baptism has been located.
460   Page reference inserted by Benjamin Shaw: William's early death is noted on that page.

Bellow Shaw, was Born May 7th 1799, in dale Street Preston & Brought up with her Parents – was the first daughter of Benj[n] & Betty Shaw, &c this was a fine Strong & healthy child, & good Humoured when a Child &c She went to the factory young, & wrought in the Card room[461] &c, and when she was too big for the Card room, she went to the winding frames, She allways wrought at Horrocks yard, & was near her work[462] &c in the year 1819, She had the misfortune to have a child (which she fathered on William Roberts (who afterwards married her) (July 31 –) which was Born November 9th – [Benjamin Roberts is his name &c[463]] She went to her town, Sep[t] 18th and got lodgings with Edward Fox, at dolphinholme, in Ellel, &c, She continued to live with her Parents, who brought up the child, untill She was Married, which was on the 22rd of June 1822,[464] & her daughter Ellen was born december 27 – 1822[465] – , She has since had a Child which was Born on January 2rd 1825, called Thomas Roberts[466] – She is now in the family way &c (July 1826) her husband is a turner in the Machien Shop & has been out of work about 4 months, trade is so bad at Presant &c &c

Hannah Shaw, the 4th Child, & 2rd daughter, of Benjamin & Betty Shaw, was Born January 17th – 1803, in dale street, Preston, in Lancashire &c this Child was a little one when she was born, & through the bad Management of her navle, by the woman Presant, this Child was recovered with great difequilty, & was thrown down[467] so that she scarce ever recovered,[468] (if at all) She was a Small and Puny Child allways, yet when she got a few years old, She had good health but was all ways Small & delicate &c, She never went to the factory untill she went to the winding frames, when she was perhaps 14 years old, She was employed in the House with her mother[469] &c, –

461   The room in which the carding engines were used to disentangle the threads before spinning.
462   lived near her work
463   Benjamin, illegitimate son of Isabella Shaw, was baptized on 26 December 1819 at Preston St John; his mother is described as a winder (LRO: PR/1463).
464   There is no trace of this marriage in any Preston church registers (Anglican or Catholic), or in adjacent churches of either denomination. Nonconformist churches did not conduct marriage ceremonies at this date.
465   Ellen, daughter of William and Bella Roberts of Church Street, was baptized at Preston St John on 10 January 1823 (LRO: PR/1465). Her father is described as 'mechanic'.
466   Thomas, son of William and Bella Roberts of Nile Street, was baptized at Preston St John on 26 January 1825 (LRO: PR/1465). Nile Street was a short street leading off the north side of Church Street near Derby Street: in the entry for the baptism of their previous child William and Bella are described as 'of Church Street', and it may be that Nile Street was already their address, Church Street being used as a district name.
467   Probably implying 'became sick or ill', rather than its literal meaning.
468   The midwife who attended the birth mismanaged the umbilical cord in some way, and the child was born with great difficulty.
469   Probably winding twist.

* in the year 1820, She was courted by a young man, (a neighbour) of the name of Samuel Whittle, & Became with child by him &c, – 1821 January 16th, She went to Ellel to lie in, & got lodgins at dolphinholme (She was only 18 years old at this time, &c) & on february 24 – 1821, got the bed of a little daughter, &c[470] – in March She came home – the child was a very little small thing, & seemed not likely to live long, it had something like a gathering[471] in her head, & soon after took the Ching cough,[472] & died in the night between the 8th & 9th of may 1821, aged 10 weeks 3 days -, Hannah never recovered from this perfectly after, though she went to her work for a while, Still She went weaker, & was plagued with a Cough,

* Still she wrought untill the 20th of March, 1823, from this time She became quite weak, we got her Medical asistance, but it did little or no good, & Soon she began to think She should not get better, & She was hardly to be Preveiled upon to take her medicine, &c – (march 30, She went to the Methodis Chapple in Lune Street, to the Lovefeast, (for she had been in the Society Some time before, &c) this was the last time She was there, &c Soon in april She was so weak that her mother Began to sleep with her, & did so untill she died &c, april 12, She was out of the House, was Blisterd[473] &c, on the 20th She received the Sacrement, from Mr Thompson, &c Soon after She began to Spit Blood, & Cough much &c June 8th She was downstairs, & in July was dressed 2 or 3 days &c, but was never dressed again, (though she lived untill february), She still continued to go worse, & weaker, untill she died – before Christmas She was so weak, that we thought she might die any day, yet she continued to live untill february 25, 1824, when she died aged 21 years 5 weeks 4 days, in Sure & Certain Hope of Eternal life through our lord Jesus Christ, She had the Methodist Singers, & was buried at the old church yard, the south east side in a deep grave febr. 27 1824 &c &c

* Note, Hannah Shaw Began to be Religious about 2 years before her death, & soon after entered into the Methodist Society, She soon obtained an asurance of the favour of God, this was the Suport of her mind in the time of her long, & Painful Sickness, She often Spoke of the goodnes of God to her Soul, & her asurance of his love to her, &c, this is the only thing that can suport the Soul in dying Circumstances, with becoming Resignation, & Holy Patience – her love of

---

470 No baptism has been traced for this child (who was called Betty after her grandmother) in the registers of Preston, Cockerham or Over Wyresdale, the three possible locations. She was buried at Preston St John on 10 May 1821 (LRO: PR/1475).
471 very large swelling
472 whooping cough
473 Blistered: blood was drawn from her by blistering. A cut would be made in the flesh and a hot cup placed over it. As it cooled the suction drew out blood and, it was fondly supposed, impurities and infections from the body.

this world was Subdued, & had no fear of death – nay She earnestly wished for death, but was resigned to his will, to die or to suffer, saying frequently thy will be done not mine, &c, this confidence she had to the last minute of her life, it was her greates Pleasure to be talking of Heaven, & god, & Saved Souls &c, – as long as she was able to attend to any thing, She delighted in Singing, & Prayer, & reading the Scriptures, Particularly the 14 Chapter of John[474] &c – this was a favourite Virse of hers,

Arise my Soul arise, Shake off thy guilty fears,
The bleeding Sacrifice in my behalf appears,
Before thy throne my surety stands, my name is written on his hands

She was Small & Slender, with Something like a Consumptive appearance about her, She had full Breasts – Square Shoulders – a longish neck – dark hair & Eyes, Blueish teeth, was rather deaf, this was a misfortune to her, as it is to any Person who hath the misfortune to be so, She had a Strong & Chear[475] Voice, was fond of Singing &c &c &c

the first Mary Shaw, 3 daughter & 5 child of Benjamin & Betty Shaw, of Preston, was born September the 18th, 1805, this was a lovely Child, the best tempered, & the Pleasantest of any of our children by far, But her good Qualitys was not long enjoyed by us, for while we were walkin out, early in July with her in the fields, she was taken ill, and her mother was forced to make haste Home with her, before the time we intended to return, &c &c this Proved to be the Meazles, & in about 15 days after She died, on the 23 of July, 1806, aged 44 weeks & 1 day,[476] we had the docter to her, & all was done that could be done, Except a Blister, which was Put on her breast, & as soon as it was put on she went into a Convultion fit, & her mother would not led it continue on, for she thought it was the Blister that did it, &c & – & we could not Prevail with her to Suffer it to remain any longer on &c

Thomas Shaw, 3 Son & 6 Child, of Benjamin & Betty Shaw of Preston was born May 2rd, 1807, this was a troublesom Child from his Birth, Cross, & Peevish, was mostly troubled with a loosness, which continued while he was under 2 years, & this kept him weak & Poorly, with a Bad Stomach, & every way full of trouble &c, he was Sent to the School when young, & when he was abou [*sic*] 9 years,

---

474   The 14th chapter of St John begins 'Let not your heart be troubled: ye believe in God, believe also in me. In my Father's house are many mansions . . . I go to prepare a place for you, And if I go and prepare a place for you, I will come again, and receive you unto myself; that where I am, there ye may be also'.

475   clear

476   Mary Shaw, daughter of Benjamin Shawe [*sic*] was buried at Preston St John on 26 July 1806 (LRO: PR/1448).

was sent to the factory &c, Still he continued to be full of trouble to us, for he came home nearly every day, with his fingers or hands or cloaths torn &c, when he was about 11 years old he had a something like the water on the Brain, & we did not expect him to live for sume time, fut [*sic*] he got better, & since that time has had no simptoms of it, &c –

1818, this Summer he wrought at Voxes factory,[477] & in the autumn he winded a while at Henry Pearsons,[478] for the weavers – after he went to Horrocks yard, & continued to work there mostly untill the begining of 1822, trade was very bad now, & I had a great deal of trouble to find him a place, to learn a trade he would not work any longer in the factory, he was not fixed in his choice as to a trade, but no body would engage any aprintices at this time, &c however we got him a Place at last, with Thomas monday,[479] & he went on the 5th of June, 1822, was to be a Moulder for 6 years, he wrought here about 8 months, & then some differance happened with the masters son & him, his master gave him a month notice, to leave his Place which he did at the month end, (for he was not bound) the next summer 1823 he wrought in the Brick Croft, for Swainson[480] &c, untill the time they gave over work, from this time untill November he had no work, on the 10th of November [1823], he went to F Sleddons Shop, &c, he was to work at the laith, but there was no lath at Presant at liberty, So he was set to the Vice to file, &c &c, here he continued a good while, with only 4 Shillings per week, &c, and was not set to a laith acording to agreement, So he left, and trade was now Better,

* he got work with Watts, & Hodgson, in Bridge Street, A Shop lately Begun, here he got 8[s] per week, &c, he Began work June 21, 1824, about the end of this year, he was raised to 10 Shillings, & in the Spring to 12[s], & in May on the 25, 1825, he engaged to serve 6 months with them for 14 Shillings per week, & at the

---

477   John Vose was a cotton manufacturer, who was in partnership with James Bleasdale. Vose & Bleasdale's cotton mills were in Stanley Street, opposite the road leading to New Preston (i.e. New Hall Lane). John Vose also had premises in Back High Street, in the town centre, where he had a sizing business.

478   Henry Pearson was a weaver who worked for Horrocks and had a workshop in the yard of Horrocks's factory (hence the progression from Pearson's to Horrocks's works).

479   Thomas Munday ran an iron-foundry in Oak Street, and also had a machine-making business at the same premises. He, like many of those working in this trade, was a Nonconformist (Pigot's 1828 *Directory*, pp. 439–40).

480   John Swainson was proprietor of the Willow Street cotton mills at the corner of Leeming Street and Willow Street, and also ran a machine shop in Willow Street. Both were close to Dale Street and thus especially suitable for Thomas Shaw. In 1826 Swainson went into the partnership of Swainson, Birley & Turton, and opened new cotton mills at Fishwick. John Swainson was one of the Trinity Church Committee, the management committee which organized and oversaw the construction of Holy Trinity Church in 1815, and helped to raise funds for the work (LRO: PR/2307). He was elected to the Borough Council for Fishwick ward in January 1836, and served until 1841.

end of that time to have Piece work, &c – but at the End of that time trade was much worse, and he was glad to have the same wages with out Piecework, about Christmas Machanic[s] wages was reduced, trade still continuing Bad, the Banks Breaking, &c, in the Spring of 1826, great rioting about Blackburn, & Breaking the Power looms, many hundreds was broke in april, about febry or march, he was reduced a Second time, and on the 11th of april there was no more work at his Shop for him, untill June 30th, and how long it will continue we cannot tell, he is at work now July 20th, 1826, was discharged august 1[st481]

2rd Mary Shaw, the 4th daughter, & 7th Child, of Benjamin & Betty Shaw, of Preston, was Born at N[o]1 dale Street, May 27th – 1811, this was a fine fat Child, & Healthy, & good Humoured &c, She was brought op rather hardly, for Bread was dear, & her father was of work many years when She was born & and her mother was forced to wind, & Bake, &c, and She had not so much time to tent[482] her as she had formerly &c, however the Child was mostly in good health, & when She was about 9 years old, She was sent to the Card room, here she continued to work untill She was about 13 years old, then she went to the winding frames, (which is become all the work nearly for young woman here at Presant, &c) She is still in good health, & inclined to be fat, She is rather deaf, whether this is caused by the noise of the factory I cannot tell, but it is a Serious loss for any person, &c &c –

Agness Shaw, 5th daughter, & 8th Child, of Benjamin & Betty Shaw of Preston, Born July 18 1813, She was born with a Vail on her head & She was but a little Child, but very lively, & Mostly healthy, She was Brought up at home with her Parents, A[483] went to School when little, She is Still Small but active & Strong, She went to horrocks Card room, in the yard when young, & continued untill She was about 12 years old, then went to the winding frames at Horrocks yard, untill the year 1826, when at the general Election, She with 2 or 3 more shouted Cobbett, when Barrie[s] Parttie was Canvesing their room,[484] & for that trifleing

---

481   These three notes were added as Benjamin continued writing, so that the account was as up-to-date as possible.

482   tend, look after

483   This is used as an initial, i.e. Agnes.

484   The wide suffrage enjoyed by Preston meant that the candidates in the 1826 General Election had to carry their messages into the mills and factories, to woo the working-class voters. This is why Captain Barrie went to Horrocks's. The 1826 election in Preston was of special interest: there were four candidates for two seats, and each had a different party label. Captain Barrie was an arch-Tory, and was opposed by the Hon. E.G. Stanley (Whig), John Wood (Liberal) and the celebrated polemicist and writer, William Cobbett (Radical). It is not clear if Agnes was simply making an outrageous show by shouting the name of the Radical candidate in front of the Tory, or whether she had genuine political beliefs: Benjamin's description of her suggests that she was likely to have enjoyed the sensation her actions must have caused. They would have been contrary to the regulations of the factory but, as the Horrocks family was strongly Tory, they would have been intolerable on political grounds as well.

offence, She was discharged, this was in June 1826, She was at home a few weeks, and in July got to Reel at the factory in Leeming Street where She now is,[485] (July 21 1826 &c &c) She has Been mostly healthy, & is Sharp & Strong, but Slender or Spare & Small, but rather Pert & saucy &c &c She is sharp at learning anything, takes learning well, & is a good worker, &c in many things she resembles her sister Hannah, & is not unlike her in her outward appearance, dardk hare [*sic*], & dark eyes, Slender, & &c – fond of dancing & in everything very like her as every I saw –[486]

1826 this has been a year of much trouble & great Privations at the end of last year (1825) trade failed & wages was pulled down on account of the Banks failing this year comenced with further Batements[487] in february we were droped in wages the Seccond time – the Banks continued to Stop & Break & trade almost at a Stand many thousands out of employ & others but Partially employed april 1st Sleddon droped wages the 3rd time – on the 11th tom Shaw, our son who wrought with watts & Hodgson was discharged they had no more work – this Spring the new wood Bridge over Ribble at Brockholes was in forwardness & was opened in the summer[488] – this Spring lady Huntindons Chapple in Pole Street was opened – the work-house had been much enlarged was finished this Spring – in april the hand loom weavers about Blackburn rose & Broke many thousands of looms in the factorys and Shops that wrought by Steam or water called Power looms &c – many were taken up & Put in Prison & at the asises were tried Some got off some transported many imprisoned &c

* in april Stanley canvased this town for the ensewin general Election & wood from Liverpool & Cobbett from Kensington came in may – this Spring the new Court house at the south east end of the House of Correction Began to be Built[489] – June the new corn mill with 5 Sailes near the north road was set to work – this month the general Election Comenced on the 9th the Candidates were Stanley & wood Cobbett & Capn Barrie they continued to the 26 to pool when wood & Stanley was returned & rode the Same day July this month the factorys were many of them Stoped at Burnley 20 factorys in & about that place were stoped & wages were lowered 10 per cent – this month the lin factory in

485 Vose and Bleasdale's factory (see above).
486 The main body of the original text ended at this point. Benjamin then updated his account by adding further paragraphs at intervals during the second half of 1826 and into 1827 before concluding with a detailed description of Betty's last illness and death.
487 stoppages
488 The wooden toll bridge which was the predecessor of the present main A59 road bridge close to the *Tickled Trout*. Because of its toll, it was generally known until recent times as the Halfpenny Bridge.
489 The new Court House was built on the edge of the town at the eastern end of Church Street, almost opposite Dale Street where Benjamin lived. It was completed in 1829.

friars lane[490] was burnt down – this summer the king gave 2000 pound to the destresed unemployed in & about Blackburn & many were relieved by Subscriptions in every town –

* august 1 Sleddon Signed over all his efects & on the 22 was mad Bankrupt & Soon after his land was Sold & all the machinery at Hole Bottom was brought to Preston & the leas & fixters sold – September 1st the ports was opened for all sorts of grain But wheat the Price had risen from 31s to 51s the load of & wages droped 30 or 50 per Cent – Sleddons droped wages again this was the 5th time within 9 months – Septemr St Pauls Church concecrated – it was finished in the Spring, on the 17 opened by R Wilson Vicker – 19 Began to Bury in the yard – October 7th the new Court House reared[491] this month Holaday Savage & grundy Signed over – & Watts & Hodgson Broke – 30 Sleddons Houses[492] – 32 in No was sold & the factory offered to Sale but not Sold – Novemr the Parliement met to endemnyfy the ministers for opening the Ports in September & Broke up decem 14 but before they ajourned they agreed to Sent help to Portingale – 5000 men was sent off emiadiately to check the Spaniards december 23 frank Sleddons factory Burnt down Set on fire by the gas – valued at 14000 a month before &c

* 1826 This year we as a family had our Share of trouble for I have been droped wages, 4 times & for some time had only $4\frac{1}{2}$ days – then 5 do – tom[493] was turned of in april and has had only 3 weeks work since (January 1827) & agness was discharged in June from Horrockes for Shouting Cobbet at the Election – & our Betty my wife has been very Poorly Since august & under the docters care & still continues to be very Porely & weak – 13 July this year our Joseph had a child Born & called Hannah – augus 23 our Bellow miscarried – october 7 our son thomas got married to ann Richardson who had lived servant in this town some years her Parents lives at Newton near Kerkam in the fild[494] they were married at Kerkam a fortnight before we knew[495] – Novr 9 our william had a Child born called Betty do 18 our thomas Child was Born & called Jain &c or Jane – Christioned at Preston Sunday 15th January[496] &c this year was remarkable for a

---

490   This was a small linen factory which had been opened in 1799 in the converted ruins of the old Franciscan friary, at the north end of Friargate.
491   topped out
492   Frank Sleddon owned thirty-two houses in New Preston, most of which were let to his employees.
493   Benjamin's son, Thomas
494   Newton (with Scales) near Kirkham in the Fylde.
495   The Kirkham parish registers record the marriage on 7 October 1826 of Thomas Shaw and Nanny Richardson, both single persons of Newton. Both parties signed their names, and the bride used the form 'Nanny' rather than Ann (LRO: PR/2064).
496   Jane, daughter of Thomas Shaw, mechanic of Dale Street, and Ann his wife, was baptized at Preston St John on 14 January 1827 (not 15 January as stated by Benjamin) (LRO: PR/1466).

drought in the Summer which Burnt up the ground so that there was very little hay & the oats & Barley & Beans was very Scarce &c, But the Hop Harvest was aboundant & wine on the Continant was an excelant crop &c –

PS this summer the Independant Chapple at bottom of Cannon Street was finished and opened about June or July –

1827 this year Comenced with a gloomy aspect trade was Bad & work Scarce my wife had been ill from July 1826 & Still continued to grow weaker all the Spring yet she continued to do a little in the house but She gave up washing & anything that required Strength or Stiring, february 28 our thomas got work with Frank Sleddon – he had been out of employ 11 months & we had to keep him & 3 weeks at Christmas his wife & Child came to our house & in the begining of march[497] she came to live at our house & we kept them until april 28 for 9 Shilling per week then they got a few thing & we found them a few more & and they went to house near the 3 tons north road,[498] & he continues to work with Sleddon now (1828 janury) my wife Still continued to grow worse & one thing was given up after another of her work untill she could do nothing – aplil [*sic*] 15th our Joseph was turned off at Paileys, & was some months off work he got to know his Settlement he was aprintice to a carder at M[r] Horrockes, but the town disputed his clame till he proved by his indenter,[499] his settlement &c June the 29th he got work at Chorley, tenting a Steam Engin his wife & goods went on the 20th of august,[500]

* august 8th our Betty (wife) being afrunted at my grumbling at being disturbed with her, left my bed & went into the other Room, & we never Slept together after &c, august 12 William Roberts went to Manchester to work, & Bellow & Children & goods went Octob[r] 12 – Bellow got her bed of her 4 Living Child Betty[501] September 11 – my wife still continued to be wors & weaker notwithstanding all the means we could use & in October, 13 She Spit a great deal of blood, which so afected me that I fainted & fell from my chair the first time that I

497 The rough notes record 'march 2nd ann came to us' (LRO: DDX/1554/2).
498 The *Three Tuns* public house in North Road.
499 Joseph Shaw had lost his job at Paley & Riley's factory, and was therefore destitute. He applied for poor relief to the Preston overseer, but his right to relief from Preston was disputed by the town. His original settlement, like that of his sisters, was in Ellel, where Benjamin had served his apprenticeship and gained a settlement. Preston presumably tried to claim that this still applied. Joseph had, however, served an apprenticeship himself, as a carder at Horrocks's factory, and so was eventually able to prove that he had thereby gained a settlement in Preston.
500 The new job was short-lived: according to the rough notes made by Benjamin, Joseph was 'turnd of' at Chorley on 12 January 1828 (LRO: DDX/1554/2).
501 Elizabeth, daughter of William and Isabella Roberts, was baptized at Preston St John on 30 September 1827 (LRO: PR/1466). Benjamin's rough notes record that 'Betsy Roberts died at manchester aged 44 wee [*sic*] & 2 days' on 17 July 1828 (LRO: DDX/1554/2). Benjamin specifically uses the word 'living' because Bella had a miscarriage in 1826.

ever fainted in my life &c 18 Sep this month our Mary was turned off work at Horrocks & as our Betty was so weak & poorly She has been at home ever since – Betty Still continues to get up every day but is so weak that she can scarsly Stand & all this winter we have had to keep the fire in day & night She has been 18 months ill & how long She may continue I cannot tell &c

– Politics february 5th the Duke of York died Parliament met 14 – about this time Lord Liverpool being Primer had a Stroke which disabled him from that time for business 23 april this Spring was cold as winter & a great deal of Snow fell april 12 Mr Caning was apointed Prime minister & soon seven cabinet ministers resigned & July 6 a treaty was signed at London to mediate between the turks & the greeks their Subjects who had long been at war they proposed to mediate between them but the turks on the 30 of august declared that they would not hearken to any proposals or alow them to medle – the Allied Powers that Signed the treaty was the French – Russians & English &c – October 20 the Egigtion & turkish fleets at Naverin was destroyed by the allied powers in the Harbour in the Morea in greece – august 8 the Prime minister Canning died but before the Parliament broke up they agreed to let all the grain in the warehouses out of Bond this was in favour of the poor for it Brougth down the Price of grain a good deal frower[502] Super Fine was in may 44 to 48 per Pack & meal 41 to 42 – & it Settled to 40 to 42 & oat meal from 27 to 28 before the end of the year in Sept Lord goderidge was Prime minister but he Resigned about december and now there is a new ministery forming but nobody knows who is to be minister &c – this year 5 Protestants Bishops & 1 Cathlic have died –

* this year in October the new Court house in Preston was opened &c this year thow trade has been better than the last yet wages has been law & still many are out of work – I this year have lost 2 Pound 6 Shillings in lent money[503] besides other losses in Sickness & extra Expences, & wages 4^s per week lawer than they were in 1825 & likely to continue yet I have cause to be thankful for work at any rate &c and that so many of our family have had good health &c – PS this year Captain parry undertook to go to the north Pole but it did not succeed – and Captain Franklins expedition to the north west to find a passage to the Pacific ocian by Sea like wise failed &c but it is expected to be undertook again &c &c –

Some account of the last sickness & death of Betty Shaw

Betty Shaw began to be ill & unable to do her work in July 1826 & from that time continued to waste in Substance & Strength untill her death – She

---

502   flour
503   Unpaid debts: it is not clear to whom Benjamin had lent money, but it is likely that it was to his children, who were in acute financial straits.

continued to do some little & was able to go out a little untill about may 1827 her complaint (a consumption) continued to gain upon her & about July 1827 She was so weak as to use a Stick to come up stairs yet she continued to come downstairs untill about the begining of Nove[r] our mary was turned off work in Sep[r] and so she was employed in the house to wait upon her mother – Octor[504] Betty Spit a great deal of blood as she had done before the begining of November we Shifted up stairs & She was never down any more yet she continued to get up every day a little untill She only got up while they made the bed &c & – this was the latter end of January – She now wanted more room in bed & mary Slept in another bed &c –

* february 4 her legs swelled very much – but she was not allarmed but rejoiced & sade she as not afraid to die She Sade She was happy in her mind & had many a Comfortable hour when She could not Sleep in reading her testament & hymn book & praying &c feb[y] 6 She told me how she wished to have her things dealt among her children – to Jos[h] her wheel[505] to William her Testament – to Bellow two Smallbooks & a tea canister to Thomas her Hymn book & a bed quilt which he had – to mary a large tea tray & to agnes a Clock & her Cloaths was to be dealt between mary & Agness only[506] Sally Shaw Wills wife was to have her Stays & me to have 2 hankerchiefs – She told me of her debts at least some of them & on the 10[507] most of her Children being presant it being Sunday She wished to be raised in bed & Sade as many of them was presant & as time was uncertain with her She wished to say some thing to them she seemed greatly efected & So did the most of them & She sade I shall not be long with you I could wish you all to Study to live peacably with your familys & to be Honest in all your dealings to be Sober & industerous & to use econemy & care this will be a great comfort to you & your famylies & when you come to die you will not repent of this conduct – but above all get reliegion this is what can suport us in health & in Sickness without this we cannot die happy & life is uncertain[508] &c

* february 14 to 18 very drowsy & weak Sickly & a little loose & took but a littl – 20 her legs swelled more She sade thank god for every fresh Simptom I shall not be long here She had a bad night 21 a aather[509] better 22rd a bad night they came into my Room about 1 O,clock I thought She was dying She was so short of

504 October
505 Probably her spinning wheel.
506 except that
507 10 February
508 As this is a fine statement of Benjamin's own views on life and its management, it may reasonably be supposed that he has freely interpreted Betty's actual words.
509 rather

Breath – 23 before I went to my wort She Sade farewell if I See thee no more – I thought She would be dead before I returned but She was much the same at night She was wery badly & nearly lost her Speech 24 She could only whisper but was quite sensable she continued all day to breath Shorter & seemed to be more restless untill 6 O,clock in the evening while me & her Brother John was praying for god to releace her from her misery She resigned up her breath in peace with god & all mankind She died febr[y] 24 – 1828 aged 54 years 14 weeks & 1 day had been maried 34 years 22 week 2 days &c She was buried in St Pauls Church yard about 15 yards off the South east corner in a Southeast direction in a deep grave about 10 feet deep[510] – She was about 5 foot 5 inch high rathe Slender & weakly – when young her hair was red & when She died nearly Brack[511] her complection fare &c She was born at Lancaster but has lived in the House where she died 33 years at N[o] 1 dale Street bottom of Church Street Preston[512] &c

for more of her life see mine at Page 21 to 31
See page 69 See Note betwee 25 & 26[513]

[there then follow 3½ pages comprising an index of persons only, listed in alphabetical order of christian name with short notes as to their relationship with the author: subjects and places are not indexed]

[below the last line of the index is a note in tiny writing: wrote and bound by the author Benj[n] Shaw 1826 august 20th 1826 Preston in lancashire, *which indicates the date when the original text was completed. The notes for 1826 and 1827 and the description of the last illness and death of Betty Shaw are later additions]*

Finis   April 20 1828

on Betty Shaw wife of Benj[n]. Shaw

The time is past that I should her condemn,
Child of caprice, and to her will the slave,
She had her virtues let me think of them,
Her faults be Buried with her in the Grave

---

510   The St John's register records the burial of Betty Shaw of Dale Street, aged 54, on 26 February 1828 at St Paul's (LRO: St Paul's Burial Register Transcript).
511   black
512   The rough notes give the date of the funeral and then record that 'funeral morning & debt Paid cost £13 6[s] 6[d]' (LRO: DDX/1554/2).
513   Page numbering in original manuscript.

on Betty Shaw

My wife, can I forget thee? while the ray
Of busy memory brightens o'er the past;
While feeling rools, or life's pulsation play,
My wife! can I forget thee? to the last,
No, nor Shall thy memory from my Heart,
But with my life's last fluttering Sob depart

As those we love decay, we die in part,
String after string is siver'd from the heart,
Till loosen'd life, at last, but breathing clay,
Without one pang is glad to fall away,
Unhappy he, who latest feels the blow,
Whose eyes have wept o'er every friend lade law,
Dragg'd ling'ring on from partial death to death,
Till, dying, all he can resign is Breath

this was her favourite verse

Who suffer with our master here
We shall before his face appear
    And by his side sit down
To patient faith the prize is sure
And all who to the end endure
The Cross shall wear the Crown

Benjamin Shaw[s] Buck 1828

A Short Account of Benjamin Shaw
and his Family continued
written by himself
Partly for his own use &
Partly for his Children
after his time &c &c

Volume the 2nd

Begun – for, 1828 – & following years

Preston, february 15th 1829
N[o] 1 Dale Street,
&c &c

January 1828 this year began with dark Prostects as to trade & prosperity – Lord Goderich had resigned the office of Primier & the duke of Wellington was put in his Place the Ministry was new moddeled & they met (the Parliament) on the 29th & praposed many things but did little but quarrel &c this month was a gloomy time with me for my wife continued to be worse & had long been confinded to her Room but now to her Bed & there was no prospect for life &c – Bread was Cheap at the begining of this year about 50 Shillings the Quarter for wheat & 26[s] for Oats – February this month my wife died on the – 24 quite worn down by sickness untill she was unable to move hersef & was little more than Skin & bone her complaint was a consumption & she had been sick 20 month or more &c – She had long enjoyed that Religeon that Set her above the fear of Death or the love of life, resigned to the will of god and died in Sure & certain Hope of Salvation through Jesus Christ &c

* March – I now began to feel the cares of family affairs to to [sic] press hard upon me for I had two daughters one 14 the other 16 to take care of and they were at an age the [sic] is as unmanagable as at any time of life[1] for if they had been younger they would have been fore[2] submisive or older the would have had more sence & managment but they had all to learn &c and they learn slowly mary the older kept the House & agness went to work[3] –

1   Problem teenagers are not a new phenomenon.
2   more
3   The proportion of political news and current affairs in Preston and beyond increases rapidly

April, this month the Test & Corperation Act was Passed the only one of any Concequence that passed this sessions (that was an act to allow the Protestant decenters to fill any office without Receiving the Sacrement in the Church &c) this month the Russians Declared war against the Turks & Don Miguel was proclamed King of Portingale though he was the Second Son of King John his father & his Brother Pedro was living in the States of Brazeel, he was for the old form of Goverment & his Brother Pedro was for a Reformed Goverment &c – May – this month the Russians Invaded Turky & the war continued with various success many towns & citys taken & nearly destroyed but as the year advanced the turks was more formedable & drove the [*sic*] back more north but great preparation are making for this campain (1829) on both sides the Russians have Blocked up the dardenelles & Basphorus to cut of Suplys &c –

this month our ministry was broken into again 4 of them was discharged Husskinson & dudley, grant & Lamb &c – July 1st Clare Election Began in Irland and O,Conell was Elected, he was a Roman Catholic & the head of the Catholic association but it was two late for him to take his place in Parliement that Sessions but he is now in London (february 1829) & and the eyes of all Europe is fixed on his reception whether our Protestant goverment will suffer a Catholic to enter or not &c July the 15 it Began to Rain & Continued to Rain for 6 week nearly altogethe[4] the concequence was the grain Harvest was much spoild & from that time Began to rise in Price & was bad in quality &c & this was the case in all Europ & america so that by October it was to 72s10d the empearial Quarter & (in January 1829 old wheat was at 92s the quarter & other grain in Proportion &c)

September this month the french sent a fleet to free the morea (the southern division of greece) from the Turks & Egeyptions &c – & having acomplished their design they are now returning (febry 1829) this month the Irish asembled in diferant Parts of the Country in great numbers partly armed &c and Showing Simptoms of Rebellion & – about this time the young Queen of Portingale landed at Falmouth & was received as a queen though she was only 10 years old &c (She is the daughter of don Pedro Emper of Brazil) – about this time a new Instetution Began in this town called the Society for Promoting Knowledge & by January 1829 700 members & more had entered –

* November this month I was off my work a month poorly & I had 2 gathering[5] 1 on the top of my thigh the other on my Bottom & the remainder of the winter I have been poorly &c and in this last year I have lost 42 Days work &c this has

---

from this point, and Benjamin generally gives a great deal less detail about domestic affairs and family news.

4   15 July is St Swithin's Day.

5   very large swelling: in these instances, possibly carbuncles

been a troublesom year to me having no wife to care for the concerns of the House nor any Company or any to care for me &c –

1829 this year Comenced as usual with a gloomy aspect trade in a Sickly state and likely to continue so or worce as the goverment has determined to Stop the smale promisery notes great chainges in trade is expected & that wages & prices of goods will greatly fall the notes is to be stoped by april 5th &c february the parliement met on the 5th and the Kings speech has alarmed many as it appears the goverment intends to emancipate the Catholics But first to put down the asocciation Irland &c

this year the Minster in the City of York was Burnt down february 1st by a Maniac of the name of Jonathan Martin who was Sentanced to impresonment for life &c febru^y 10th Pope Leo 12th died at Room – 12th the Catholick association in Ireland was desolved in order to Emancipated [*sic*] the Roman Catholicks &c april 5th the Small Notes or the 1 & 2 pound promisery Notes were Stoped payment 10^h do the Catholick Bill passed the lords 13th Signed by his Majesty 23rd put in force May 1st great complaint in trade and Rioting in many towns 6 men killed at Rochdale & many wounded – the turks & Russians at war this summer the Russians Succesfull took Adrenople this Campain in august 20th & a peace was made soon after Septer 14th & the Russians retired to their own Countery – no publick Business done in the parliement this sitting but the Emancipation of the Catholicks though the countery was greatly oppresed &c – this year the House of Recovery on the Moor was built & reared October 10^{th6} – the School at Spittle Moss opened in Sep^r – and that in Pole Street Reared in Sep^r –

* Soon on in this year (1829) it was known that our Mary was with Child & that her chap (Bob Smith) was in the House of Correction for an asault & at the Sessecions[7] he was sent to Lancaster 6 months[8] this was a bad job for me for she began to use all kinds of fraud upon me to suply his wants in Prison – She kept the Money that ought to have been paid[9] & contracted Debts in my name &

6 The new House of Recovery was built in 1829–33 to replace the former inadequate building in the town centre. It was situated at Deepdale, on land formerly part of Preston Moor, and it formed the basis of the later Preston Royal Infirmary.

7 Quarter Sessions

8 Robert Smith, aged nineteen, was committed to Lancaster Castle at the Sessions held in Preston on 14 January 1829. He, Robert Nightingale and John Eddington, also nineteen, were found guilty of riot and assault against John Wilson, Mark Birkenhead and Robert Scott on 21 December the previous year. Perhaps this was some pre-Christmas rowdiness by the youths involved, although no detailed account is given in the court papers. The shortness of the sentences indicates that it was a relatively minor affair (LRO: QSB/1/203/Jan 1829, QSO/1/198 and QJI/1/203).

9 Money set aside by Benjamin to pay bills.

Cheated every way &c he came out in July – June 20th Mary went to Galgate to lie inn but come back with Cirtificace July 6[10] – 14th Bob came out of Lancaster 23rd Exed[11] in the Church – She got her Bed Sep[r] 3rd at 3 in the afternoon call him William – they were Married October 24[th12] lived with us untill Jenuary 23 – 1830 when they took a room but parted Soon after – April 3 Thomas Shaw[s] Child (John) born[13] – 13 Joseph Shaw[s] Child (Hannah) died – May 27 William his Son Born[14] – July this year I got wet in a thunder Storm & got wet was of work in concequence 3 weeks & – work was Scarce & Bread Dear & great murmering & Discontent in the countery Many Peticions sent up to Parliement but nothing done for the Poor &c[15]

1830 the year Commenced as usial with a gloomy Aspect trade down & bread dear & parliefen [sic] met February 4th – in January Many County Meeting were Hold to get up Peticions praying Parliement for many things particularly for to take the Exice of ale & Porter &c) Soon on in this year our Mary & Bob Smith parted & She came home – both her & her sister Agness did badly for me by runing into Debt and Pawning their Clothes & my Bed Cloths & Book or any thing that they Make Money off &c this year I lost 7 or 8 Pound in Money by them & lost very many thing alltogether[16] –

* Nothing was done in the Parlement this Sitting but the Beer Act (that is they took the Excise off) & opened the trade to any that would take out a licence to Sell beer Porter tobacco &c this was the only thing of note in the Sessions which took place on the 10th of October &c – his Majesty George 4th died this Summer

10 Mary Shaw was not married, and therefore retained Benjamin's settlement at Ellel, as her sisters Bella and Hannah had done. Although thirty-six years had elapsed since Benjamin had completed his apprenticeship at Dolphinholme, he had been unable to do anything which would qualify him for legal settlement in Preston. However, in Mary's case the overseers of Ellel issued her with a settlement certificate, acknowledging their responsibility, and then sent her home to have her baby in Preston. In this way Preston was excluded from any responsibility, while it was at least possible for the baby to be born in its mother's and grandfather's house.
11 the banns were put up
12 The Preston St John registers record the marriage of Robert Smith and Mary Shaw, both single persons, on 24 October 1829. Both parties signed by making their mark (LRO: PR/1459).
13 John, son of Thomas and Ann Shaw of Marsh Lane, was baptized on 12 July 1829 at Preston St John (LRO: PR/1467).
14 Neither a burial entry for Hannah Shaw nor a baptism entry for her brother William has been found.
15 While listing the births and deaths of his grandchildren in 1829 Benjamin omitted Sarah, daughter of William and Sarah [Sally] Shaw, who was baptized at Preston St John on 15 March 1829. Her father was described as 'carder', and they lived at Thomas Street, New Preston (LRO: PR/1477).
16 Benjamin was now living with Mary, Agnes and Mary's child, William, and was their main means of support. Mary and Robert Smith had parted very shortly after their marriage, but were eventually reconciled. They continued to live with Benjamin until December 1834. Agnes, meanwhile, had gone to live in Manchester.

June 26 & William the 4th was proclamed the same day in London – in Preston on the 30th 1830 – George 4th was Interred July 15th – at the Begining of this year the Birmingham Union for the purpos of forwarding reform & Soon after that in London for do in June the french sent an Expedition against Algiear they landed 14th took the City & the Dey July 5th with a great deal of Money Some say 5 Million & about this time Prince Lepold Son in Law to george 4th gave up all pretence to become the King of Greece – about which much was sade at the time &c

* the Parliement was desolved July 23 & the Members hastend to their Respective places to be Elected again – for Preston we had 3 Candedates W Stanley – John Wood & Henry Hunt – the pole began 30th & August 1st – 2nd – 3rd when Stanley & Wood was Returned – Stanley Pold 7959 wood 6713 Hunt 3715 &c in this Election there was no drinking but on Stanleys Side[17] – no Ribbons no frags[18] or Musick – 10 Pole Booth was Erected near the Corn Exchange the town was divided into 10 Distrects and every man poled in his own Booth acording to his district July 27–28 29 the french Revolution Broke out in Paris which ended in the expultion of Charles 10th from france – he came to England soon after; then to Scotland and took up his Risidence in the Ancent Pallace called Holyrood house they called to the throne Loues Phillip Duke of Orleins &c – Septemr 26 27 28 the Belgeons Revolted from the dutch first at Brusels then at Antwarp and succeeded in their design – no other powers interfearing with them &c –

* great discontent in many Places this Autumn in Switserland in germany in Poland the Beere Act came into force October 10th and great No ingaged in Selling but how it will answer time only can tell it is 4d per quart at the new Shops & 6d at the old where they have fire & house room &c – October 26th the New King & new Parliement met But in Novemr16 on the Question of Civil List the Ministery was in the Minorety and was therefore oblieged to resign, So ended Wellingtons Ministry &c the same day the King appointed Earl Grey Premier & he called a new Miniestry 25 in all – all Whigs &c – they Promised fair and the Countery gave them Credit for much but not much was done – Much discontent Raged among the labourers in the South – in Kent at first – then in many other Counties in the south & some in the north – the peasontry went about at nights destroying the threshing Machiens & Burning Hay & Corn Stacks & making farmers promise to raise wages & Parsons give up their tithes &c –

* the Ministry have determined to raise 10 thousand more Souldiers to keep the

17 Plying the electors with drink was a venerable tradition of Preston elections but, as Benjamin suggests, it was falling into some disfavour.
18 flags

countery in subjection but it is thought it cannat be kept long down &c – this year Bread and all sorts of Provisions have been dear and many out of work – wages in many trade have been pulled down many turn outs among the Manufactering part & much Complaining & Suffering &c Sept[r] 15th the Rail Road between Manchester & Liverpool was opened when William Huskinson M.P for Liverpool was killed with a Steam coach runing over him & the Coaches at sometimes run at the rate of 30 Miles in an hour & Moving Slowly can carry 90 ton of goods &c –

* with us at preston we had 2 Elections 1 in Summer at the general Election & 1 in December M[r] Stanley having taken office in the Ministry was obliege to give up his place of Member for Preston the Election began 14th Stanley having Canvased the town by proxy four times before – M[r] Henry Hunt[s] friends oposed him Polling began 15 the first day Hunt Polled 1204 Stanley 791 Majorety for Hunt 413 – polling lasted 7 days Hunt was 338 a head but Stanley declared he would Scrutenize the Election in Preston for 30 days preparations was made on both sides for that purpose but M[r] Stanley gave it up on the 2(*illegible*)[th] on the 24th Hunt was returned by the Mayor duely Elected but did not ride untill the 27 he had the grandest procession that has been in Preston for Many years &c 5 Bands of Musick 31 flags & Baners &c the Procession was 10 minutes in Passing or more[19] in this Month (December 1830) the French Ministers of the late King (Charles 10th) was tried for conspiracy against the Peoples Rights & was Sentanced to Impresonment for life the Pope of Room lately died at Room – by the title of Pious 8th he had been on Since March 1828

* this year I (B Shaw) have had much trouble with my daughters Mary & Agness, – Mary Married last year (1829) but in January this year 1830 they quarreled & parted & She has been with me & her lad all the year, & has behaved Badly, putting me to much expences & trouble &c Agness went to Manchester April 22,[20] & came over at Whitsunday having left most of her cloths in the Pawn Shop, in this town though she was not out of work & while she had the manigment of the house I have her Money to keep us Both & She had her own wages Clear[21] She has had 7 or 8 gowns in a little more than 2 years –

---

19 Henry Hunt, as the hero of Peterloo and the most prominent Lancashire Radical, was immensely popular with the ordinary people. Their triumph in electing him to Parliament was reflected in the scale of popular celebration.

20 Although Agnes had been working in cotton mills, she had also apparently been in service in Preston before leaving for Manchester. In his rough notes Benjamin records that she left home for the first time on 9 January 1829, and 'went to ann Hesket' and on 30 January 'went to Jen Taylor' (LRO: DDX/1554/2).

21 The sense is confused here: the implication is that Benjamin had used *his* money to support them both, and that she had kept her own wages for extravagant expenditure on frocks. The word 'given' is probably missing before 'her Money'.

– this year I have had tolerable health but I have gone smaller & weaker,[22] or we say aged our trade as far as respects that has been tolerabl good & with some a little advance of waiges but not in general in december this 1830 I got my thumb crushed in the Laith where I work & have been off work 3 weeks but it is Mending but far from fit to go to work with as yet (January 2nd 1831) –

* October 17th this year, our William Shaw[23] Died rather suddenly he had been ill long but not so but he went to his work[24] – he was ill the last winter and in this Spring was in the Dispensary long but got no better he coughed much & was horse & Short of breath & weak but he was much better when warm than cold & his Room where he wrought was warm he continued to go to work untill the last week of his life for he had 7 Children most of them small & was poor & afraid of loosing his work he continued as long as he could for the last day he was oblieged to be carried home he died at 2 O.clock on the 17th & was Burried the 19th at St Paul's Church near his Mother[25] &c Note he wrought in Card Room 5 years

William Shaw was about 5 foot 10 inch high & had he been in good Circumstances might have been a Stout man (But he was poor) & had to live upon a little &c – he was dark complectioned – Rathe Crock-kneed – was a plain man simple & honest well meaning man – he enjoyed but little of this world's good, wrought hard – lived poor & died without much atention from docters or others – he has left 7 Children – he was 35 years & 3 month old &c

* 1831) the later part of 1830 & the Begining of 1831 was a troublesome time many fires particularly in the South – the labourers went about the countery and others that were out of work Burning threshing machiens & Hay stacks & Corn & farming Stock &c it was said that there has been 2000 fires of late – 3 churches 1 at Blackburn & 1 at Luisham in Kent, & another at Birmingham – wages was low & work Scarce & Bread & all kinds of Vituals dear &c – the goverment Sent out a Spetial Commition into the Disturbed destrects & many were transported for life a few hanged Some impresoned &c January O conel & others in Irland was tried for conspiring against goverment,s [sic] orders But were aquitted – great Preparation for war Beating up for recruits examining the pentioners &c february – Richard Carlile was tried for Ceditious pamplets & Sentanced to 2 years imprisonment & fined £200 – William Cobbet for Something in the Regester but got of this month wheat was 73 Shillings per quarter oots 26 & every thing dear Butter 1^{s}2^d per lb –

22 Benjamin was beginning to decline into old age, worn out by a hard life, by troublesome children, and by the long illness of Betty. He very clearly missed her company and presence. In December 1830 he was fifty-eight years old.
23 His son William.
24 not so badly that he could not work
25 The St John's register records the burial of William Shaw, aged 35, of Thomas Street, New Preston, on 19 October 1830 at St Paul's (LRO: St Paul's Burial Register Transcript).

* february 3 Parliement met great number of Pettisins sent up for reform of Parliament this month the Duty taken off Printed callico good & Sea Born Coals this countery felt the good efects of the first & in london & other Places who were supplyed with coals from a distance by Sea the Second &c – great uneasiness on the Contenant insurections in Polland Italy Spain & other Places – the Russian army enters Polland to Settle them &c march 1 the reform Bill Came into the Commons House &c – Pope gregory the 15th chosen news of the Liberater Bolliver of South america S[26] Death about this time – 22 the Reform Bill read a second time – great contentions in Holland & Belgeam & preparation the Polles & Russians at open war – April the reform Bill Passed the Commons but was [rejected by the lords & on][27] the 22 the Parliement was Desolved &c

* John Wood & Henry Hunt & Cornel Evens came into Preston 25 as candedates on the 29 wood & Hunt was Elected & Rode without opposition June 15 {*or 14*}[28] the new Parliement met great uneasiness in South Wales among the miners at tidvill & other places – this month the militia was trained in this town without arms &c the Cholera-Morbus raged with violence in russia & Polland Saxony &c this was little if any inferior to the Plague thousands died in 4 or 6 hours Sickness & was Buried imediatly &c – august the 8th King William 4th & Queen Adelade was Crowned – Sep[r] 22rd the reform Bill Passed the House of Commons – October 7th was rejected in the House of Lords – Riot in Bristol 26 27 & 29 when 400 or 500 was killed the Bishop Pallace & 3 Prisons with about 80 houses Burnt down several warehouses – November 5th – a sort of riot at Preston & Several were impresond & condemed to various length of confindment in Prison &c

1831 – Octobe this month the Cholera Began in this Country first at north Shields & from there to newcastle & all over the country in this & following year &c at Notingham this month there was a great riot & some were afterward hung others banished – Family concerns this year at the beginin I was lame of my thumb a good while but it got well in 3 o 4 months provisions was dear at the begining of this year but in august the Harvest being good Bread & other Provisions fell in Price &c our trad was very Brisk we had Plenty of work – May 12th Joseph Shaw s Child Born[29] – 22 Sally Shaw went to manchester but came to Preston the Same summer[30] – July 12 Cousin[31] William Jackson was married

---

26   i.e. 'the Liberater Bolliver of South america's Death'
27   Deleted in the original text.
28   Unclear in original.
29   The child was a boy, Thomas: he died in November, but no baptism entry has been found (see below).
30   Sally was Benjamin's daughter-in-law, the widow of William Shaw: she remained in Preston, and is recorded in the 1841 census at Bread Street, when she worked as a handloom cotton weaver. Her family at home in 1841 were: Bridget (cotton carder); Thomas and Joseph (cotton spinners); Nancy (power loom operative); Elizabeth (cotton piecer) and Sarah. There was also a child, William aged three, who was possibly the illegitimate son of Bridget.
31   Nephew (son of Henry and Hannah Jackson): William Jackson and Ann Bradshaw were married at Preston St John on 12 July 1831 (LRO: PR/1459).

October 30 Joseph Child Died[32] – thomas Shaws child Benjamin Born december 9[th33] Bellow Roberts do[34] 12[35] – this Summer the Factory in Sedgwick Street was built &c – the war between the russians & Polles was Caried with various success but in the last end of summer the Polls was crushed with number & put down many sent into excile &c –

– 1832 this year comenced with discontent & murmering as usial But provisions was cheaper than formerly & trade pretty brisk, yet many out of employment & very poor in January this year there was a great riot in Bristol, & a special Commision was sent to try them that were taken 6 condemd to die, but only 3 was Hung, many banished, some imprisond &c – the parliement met soon & began with the reform Bill which miscarried last year & this was the only Bill of moment that was passed the whole year except the Desection Bill to decect unclamed persons in Prisons, Hospitals & poor Houses &c the reform Bill was Passed in June for England, & in august for Scotland, & Ireland – Parliement Broke up august 16th the last of the old sistom – in November the Commishoners were sent into the election towns to examin the Clamants & give cirtifacats & in december the Election took place – in preston we had 5 Candedatee [sic] T Stanley & Peter Hesketh of Rosal Hall was Ellected – Hunt – Forbes & Charles Chrompton lost

* this Spring the Cholera morbus spread through the Country in the great towns made sad destruction &c in Paris it made sad work & in America &c But it ceased all together in the autumn in this countery, we were greatly favoured in Preston, for though many cases were reported, yet some doubt whether the real asiatic cholera was ever known hear &c, this spring the factory in North road (Paul Caterals) gated[36] &c, the Butteris[37] round the House of Corection was finished[38] & the new Lock up in Haynham Street was finished[39] – this Summer

---

32   The burial of Thomas Shaw, infant, of Bowram Street, was at Preston St Peter on 1 November 1831 (LRO: PR/1477).

33   Benjamin, son of Thomas and Mary [sic] Shaw of Friargate, was baptized 12 February 1832 at Preston St John (LRO: PR/1467). This is undoubtedly the correct entry, with the name of the mother wrongly given as Mary instead of Ann. Thomas is described as 'mechanic'.

34   ditto (born)

35   The child was not baptized for almost a year. Hannah, daughter of William and Isabella Roberts of Hulme, mechanic, was baptized at the Collegiate Church in Manchester [Manchester Cathedral] on 18 November 1832 (LRO: Manchester BTs 1832, mf 5/87).

36   opened

37   buttresses

38   The House of Correction in Preston was opened in 1789, and replaced the former building which had been converted from the ruins of the Franciscan friary in 1618. The new House of Correction was enlarged in 1817, and in 1832 it was reinforced and fortified by the construction of four 'martello towers': it is these which Benjamin calls *butteris*. They were built in response to the riots of 1831, in which a crowd had threatened to attack the prison, and were demolished in the 1860s and 1870s (Hewitson, pp. 281–3). Benjamin lived almost opposite the House of

the methodist chapple in chadwicks orchard was opened[40] – the water works from Longridge was begun – this spring the land round the House of recovery was plough,d &c, august the King of Belgium married the king france's daughter, the despute between Holland & belgium continued & in November Antwarp was stormed & taken by the french – July Portingale was invaided by don Pedra Brother to the king & he fortified Oporta & caried on a war all the year out

* Joseph Shaw Burried his child William in November[41] – this year was a very good Harvest with Plenty &c – april 1 mary Smiths Child Betty was Born[42] – great oposition to tiths in Irland &c

* 1833 this year I had tolerable health and full employ in the later end of sumer there was an advance of wages in our trade (Machanics) some got rais'd several times – great shifting about &c & there was a general rise of 1ˢ per week this year Bread was good and cheap particularly wheat & oats – onions &c &c – nothing remarkable in our family happend this year – bellow had a child died at manchester in november[43] – in the cource of summer great uneasines among tradsmen & many turn-outs in various Branches – Sayers – Brick-layers, dyers, Masons – Smiths, plasters, painters, Hatters wool-combers & others with machanics &c – the Catholic Church, Call St Ignatius was begun on whit-

---

Correction, and so could see the building work in progress. In 1870 its ownership was transferred from the County Justices to central government and it became Preston Gaol, which it remains to the present day.

39 The 'new Lock up in Haynham Street' was the new police station in Avenham Street, completed in 1832. Its predecessor, a small and inadequate building in Turk's Head Yard, had been badly damaged during the riots of 1831, when the mob had smashed windows and pulled down parts of the walls in order to liberate the prisoners housed in the cells. The new building, on the east side of Avenham Street, was stronger and more secure. The town's police force, however, still comprised only six men (Hewitson, p. 283).

40 The Orchard Chapel was opened by secessionists from the main Methodist movement who had separated in Leeds in 1829.

41 William Shaw, aged 3, of Bowram Street, was buried at Preston St Peter on 27 November 1832 (LRO: PR/1477).

42 Elizabeth, daughter of Robert and Mary Smith, Dale Street, spinner, was baptized at Preston St John on 1 April 1832. The child was baptized on the day of her birth because she was not expected to live (she had a badly-deformed back) although in fact she survived for four years (LRO: PR/1477).

43 By the middle of 1833 Benjamin appears to have been losing interest in his family, and the numerous births and deaths of grandchildren no longer held much significance for him. It is not clear which child died in November 1833. William and Bella Roberts had moved to Manchester two years earlier, and Benjamin seems to have had little communication from them except an occasional begging letter. One of these, written in January 1840, survives in the collection of his papers at the Lancashire Record Office (LRO: DDX/1554/23). However, in 1836 Bella did come to help Benjamin with nursing Agnes.

monday[44] – the governors House in the front of the house of Corection was built – And a large factory in friars lane for lin,[45] belonging to furnus & Inksman was Built – pipes for the water works was put down from the House of Corection gates to ribleton &c[46] –

* the parliement met in february –, the first thing they did was the Irish Coercion Bill to prevent them meeting or piticioning parliement – a good of oppositon to it but it pass'd – great opposition in irland to tiths an in Summer an act was pass'd to free the farmers from it & england was to pay 1 milion for them of orears and the land owners to pay in futer &c – the Slave act was pas'd like wis the planters to be paid from goverment 20 million for their loss of Slaves – the Slaves to be free in 12 years, but many alerations in their favour for the presant all children 7 years or under to be free if their parents could keep them – their time for labour restricted &c – peace this sumer between Holland & Belgium contluded – war between Egypt & the turks the Egyptians took a good deal of Syria and would have over run the whole but the turks called in the russians which Stopt them &c & – war in portingale Between the two brothers Don pedra took lisbon in july and Don miguel retired &c, this year the king of spain died fardinand the 7th this year the East india & Bank of England Charters were renued for 21 years the trade thrown open to china and the East indies for all merchants &c –

* the factory Short time bill passed, not to employ children under 11 years the nex year all under 18, to work only 8 hours each day &c august 8 a part of the Custom House in dublin burnt down – our marys Husband was out of work the greater part of the year he only has work'd about 8 weeks, was sick 9 weeks, this autum was wet weather nearly constantly no frost or Snow this winter, very wet

* 1834 this year commenced with brisk trade & cheap provisions & enlargment of trade Bellow Roberts paid us a visit this month (January) &c – february 1st – 2 lettars from agness informing us she was in the family way She went to manchester where she had been for some years, this year all of my three daughters were with Child &c June 22 Mary & agnes Both got their bed the same day – both lads but agnes Child died soon[47] – bellow got her bed July 2nd[48] and in

---

44   The foundation stone of St. Ignatius's church was laid on 27 May 1833, and the church was opened in 1836. It is in St Ignatius Square off Meadow Street, close to the Park and the area which Benjamin knew well.

45   linen

46   The Preston Waterworks Co., established in 1831, was authorized to build a reservoir at Gamull Lane, between Preston and Longridge, to supply the town. Pipes were laid to the town along the Longridge road through Ribbleton in 1833–4 (Oakes, p. 12).

47   No record has yet been found for the baptism or the burial of this child in the registers of Manchester Cathedral or other central area parish churches. The name of the child is therefore still unknown. There is no information at all as to where in Manchester Agnes was living. Mary's

November thomas wife got her bed of twins 1 was dead born[49] &c – August 3 I fell down stairs backward and hurt my ankle much was of work 3 months &c[50] –

* the winter between 1833 & 34 was mild No frost nor Snow all winter – this spring the House Tax was repealed which was 1ˢ6ᵈ in the pound on Houses £10 rent &c April insurections in france – paris – Lions &c Darth of provisions in the east indes – a riot in oldham & many great meetings – new trades unions formed but the goverment took measures to put them down compleetly – in may the new Catholic Church Called St Ignacious was begun – & the Rail-way bill to wiggon passed[51] and pipes was laid in the Streets for water from Longridge – a Commision of enquiry was appointed for information respecting the Irish Church &c wheat Sold at from 36ˢ to 44ˢ the quarter & meal 26 to 28 the load – this autumn the Cholera prevailed in many towns many died &c – warm weather &c – the trade unions broke up Compleetly – November the whig ministry desolved – & Peel & Wellington ministry apointed A great many fires in many towns and farming stock destroyed by fire for mischief

* Bob Smith & mary left me december 13ᵗʰ & the 30ᵗʰ both Houses of parliement was burnt down &c Tea made a free trade – till now the east India Company Monopolized this trade Solely to themselves war in Spain don Carless Striving to obtain the Crown &c – this year 2 new factorys began near water lane ends marsh[52] &c the Catholic church was reared in Summer & continued in finishing – august 1ˢᵗ this year the Slaves in the west Indes was put on their aprintiship to be free in 12 years & at the Cap of good Hope November 1ˢᵗ &c all Children under 6 years free now if their parents could mentoin them &c

---

son was called John – he is referred to by Benjamin in his account of 1836 – but a record of his baptism has not been found.

48   No entry has been found for the baptism of this child in the Manchester parish records: it was possibly called William, since a letter written by William and Bella Roberts in 1840 refers to a son of that name (LRO: DDX/1554/23).

49   Joseph William, son of Thomas and Nanny Shaw, mechanic of Friargate, was baptized at Preston St John on 22 February 1835 (LRO: PR/1468). The 1841 census lists Thomas Shaw, mechanic, and Ann, his wife, at Saul Street, Preston. Their children at home were Jane (cotton operative, aged 14); John, aged 12; Benjamin, aged 10; Joseph, aged 7; and William, aged 3.

50   The 1841 census (Park Place, Preston) indicates that Joseph and Ann also had a child born in 1834, a daughter Sarah: she is not mentioned by Benjamin. Neither was their daughter, Mary, who was born in 1828 and is listed in the census return. Joseph and Ann, who had lost six children in infancy, had three children living in 1841 – Jane, Mary and Sarah.

51   The Preston & Wigan Railway Act was passed on 22 April 1831. The directors were unable to raise sufficient money to complete the line, and on 22 May 1834 the Preston & Wigan Railway was amalgamated with the older Wigan Branch Railway (which had built the Wigan – Newton-le-Willows line) to form the North Union Railway. It is this amalgamation, rather than the authorizing Act, to which Benjamin refers. The railway was opened on 21 October 1838 (Holt, p. 201).

52   The Victoria and Wellfield mills are probably referred to here.

* 1835 this year began with plenty of work and provisions cheap, plans for improvement &c the Rail-way to wiggan was let in january & they began in the Spring – at the north end the wire Rail way was projected and an act was got this Spring but not begun this year[53] 5 new factory was either began or Carried on 1 water land end – greenbank, gallas-hill – Broom-field – grimshow Street &c[54] – in the corse of the year a rail-road to longridge projected & preparations made[55] – 2 new churches begun 1 Christ Church in bow-lane 2 at ashton brow[56] St Ignatious Church was finishing but not open'd this year a factory in fishwich near Ryleys begun & preparations for one, & a warehouse & gashouse in Horrocks's yard making the walks on the more further finished[57] & Some of the ground let for pottates & –

great alterations in the Countery for enlarging the manufactoreing Concerns – & great demand for mesheenery wages was raised in all businesses an plenty of employment for all sorts of hands – a great deal of complaints from the Agreculterers grain Sold so Cheap & meat was low But the last end of the year things got up in price &c – the king of france was shot at in July with what was call'd an infernal macheen 24 gun barrels discharged at once many was kill'd and wounded but not the King three men was gulantined for it in february 1836 – Hally's Comit apered in august, its return is 75 yeare it was not much seen the weather was unfavourable – this sessions of Parliement the Corperation reform Bill was the main thing done which was put in force at the end of the year and comenced at the begining 1836.[58] 36 Counsil men & 12 aldermen in Preston & 6

53   The Preston & Wyre Railway Act, authorizing the line from Preston across the Fylde to what would soon be Fleetwood, was passed on 3 July 1835. The line was opened on 25 June 1840 (Holt, pp. 203–4).
54   Preston was experiencing a second wave of steam factory building in the mid-1830s, and most of the locations listed were on the outskirts of the town. The Greenbank, Broomfield and Moor Brook ['gallas-hill'] mills were at the northern end of North Road/Moor Lane; and the 'water lane end' mill was the Tulketh Factory in Fylde Road. Grimshaw Street mill was just behind Dale Street.
55   The Preston & Longridge Railway was promoted in order to carry stone from the quarries on Longridge Fell for building work in the town and for dock construction at Liverpool. It was authorized on 14 July 1836 and opened on 1 May 1840. A passenger service of two trains each way, on Wednesdays and Saturdays only, was provided (Holt, p.203).
56   The two churches referred to are Christ Church, Bow Lane, and St Andrew's, Ashton-on-Ribble. Both were in growing suburbs. Christ Church was consecrated on 11 October 1836, and has now been demolished apart from the west front and entrance porch, which have been incorporated within extensions to County Hall. St Andrew's was opened in 1836.
57   In 1834 Preston Moor, the great expanse of open grazing land north of the town, was enclosed by the Corporation. Part of the land was developed, but much was retained and landscaped as parkland, Moor Park. The 'Ladies Walk' on the south side and the Serpentine Road on the north were laid out in 1835–6, and it is these to which Benjamin refers. Part of the land, not yet landscaped, was let out as allotments on a temporary basis.
58   The Municipal Corporations Act of 1835 required the election of a new and democratic Corporation in Preston as in many other boroughs. The new body came into being at the start of

wards – &c this gave general Satisfaction about this time great preparations for Rail-ways in all parts of England & Scotland & some abroad &c Spain Still at war this year about 9 or 10 thousand volenteer'd & went to Spain to help the queen but they did little good don Carles still kept his ground & A great Nº of Convents Brook up in portingale & Spain &c

* as to my self I have had good health the greatest of all Blesings but feel the growing efects of age and infirmity[59] &c I was not raised wages at the general rise and some others that was old mist &c age is not so active & are overlook'd &c – the water works from longridge took a wide spread in the town this year &c – toward the end of this year my daughter Agnes was discharg'd from her work at Horrockes yard as I found afterward for being with child – this was a Sorry Concern for me & cost her, her life &c –

* 1836 this year Began & Continued a troublesom year to me, for agnes was without work & ill, & soon on in January, our mary's child John had the Inflamation in his Bowels & agness went to help mary & the weather was Cold & wet She got cold & was thrown down[60] thoug the lad Recovered She Continued ill until She got her bed on the 18th of february, of a daughter calld Betty[61] But She never recoverd only so far as to Stirr about for a few weeks very feebly indeed &c

1836 at the end of march our mary's Betty fell ill, & languish'd in great pain untill the 24 of Aprill, then died, aged 4 years & 3 weeks – this was a pitiful Child, Born with an excresance on the Small of her back, which prevented her from walking, was forced to Sit Still, & was a vast of trouble to her mother – She was patient & Content[d] too for all that, &c[62] – Agnes was now much worse, & no Signs of recovery, we apply'd to Dr Harrison.[63] Soon in may, he Sade She must reconcile herself, for there was no hope – She would not see the month out,

---

1836, and in mid-January there were further elections to replace the twelve councillors who had been elevated to the aldermanic bench.

59   Benjamin was sixty-three in December 1835.

60   came down with sickness (rather than had a fall)

61   The baptism entry for this child includes some confusing information. She was baptized at Preston St John on 6 March 1836. The names of her parents are given as Benjamin and Agnes Shawe [*sic*] of Dale Street, mechanic. The minister was apparently under the impression that Benjamin and his daughter were husband and wife. Agnes was weak and ill, and probably did not attend the baptism, so it may be supposed that Benjamin himself took his granddaughter to church and was mistakenly thought to be the father (LRO: PR/1468). At least Betty thereby avoided the stigma of having her illegitimacy noted in her baptism entry. The accuracy of baptism registers may in consequence be called into question.

62   Elizabeth Smith of Hopwood Street, aged 4, was buried at Preston St Paul on 26 April 1836 (LRO: St Paul's Burial Register Transcript).

63   Dr James Harrison was the doctor to the Preston workhouse; his private surgery was at 35 Church Street.

trade went well, & every boddy was in work, I could not get a nurse for her [agnes],[64] & mary had a family, to do for, at last I got a nurse from the work house, but the woman could not do to be disturbd at night, She only stopd a forthnight, then went back ill, She rcaved[65] a littl & came out, of the house, But died before Agnes &c, our Bellow & a little lass[66] then came from Manchester, She Stop'd 6 week, then went home – Agnes lingered on weaker every day untill August the 19th, 1836. She was Buried the 21st, at St Pauls Church,[67] &c –

* this was trying time to me, I wrought all day & at night went about the town for some thing for her, till late oft, then got up 2 or 3 times at night – her Child was ill, was nurs'd out,[68] it was wain'd[69] at 5 weeks old, & I had much to do to get any boddy to keep it it was so troublsom at night – Soon after agnes died I was forced to change its nurse, & Soon after it Lay a forthnight in fits, yet it recoverd & got a little Better, But is a Small pittifull ill doing thing Still[70] –

* trade went well all this year & the Spiners thinking they ought to Share in the times agreed to turn out – their plan was to turn out of one factory at once, But the masters So this Scheam agreed to Stop all their works at once & they accordingly lock'd their doors Novem[r] 5th & it was february before the[y] gated again[71] &c this was an impoverishing time to the town in general, as all as well as spiners suffer'd & when they did begin it was partially with new hands, mostly at first &c However the old hands was forced to go in, as they could agree with their employers, for little more than they had before &c –

* the Parliement met in february, But during the Sessions they did nothing of any moment – great murmering in the manufactureing towns about the poor Laws &c the Railway to wiggon went on rapedly, the foundations of the brig at

---

64   Added subsequently by the author.
65   recovered: Benjamin means that the nurse recovered.
66   Benjamin could not remember the name of this granddaughter: she was probably Hannah, born in 1831.
67   The St Paul's register records the burial of Agnes Shaw of Dale Street, aged 23, on 21 August 1836 (LRO: St Paul's Burial Register Transcript).
68   sent to a wetnurse
69   weaned
70   The child, Betty, was alive shortly before January 1840, when her aunt and uncle, Bella and William Roberts, wrote to Benjamin from Manchester, 'let us know how Betty his coming on' (LRO: DDX/1554/23). When the census was taken in April 1841, Benjamin was living alone. However, the census records that in the household of Joseph and Ann Shaw, in Park Place, was a six-year-old child, Betty Shaw: this was probably Agnes's daughter, their niece.
71   The 660 spinners of Preston were locked-out between 5 November 1836 and 5 February 1837. They demanded more pay – a 'Share in the times' – but were forced back three months later on the employers' terms. A further 7,840 operatives were laid off as a consequence, and the cost of the dispute (to the employers) was said to be £108,000 (Hewitson, p. 175).

Ribble was laid,[72] &c the Railway to wire mouth begun,[73] but not much done – Christ's Church Built & in the autumn the Church near the House of Corection was begun[74] – the factory in Grimshaw St gated – Horrocks yard factory in forwardness &c water works spread much &c[75] –

72   The bridge referred to is the Ribble Viaduct, carrying the main railway line over the river south of Preston station. It was completed in October 1838 and still exists, although much widened by the addition of parallel structures.

73   Wyre Mouth, i.e. Fleetwood

74   St Mary's church in St. Mary's Street, off New Hall Lane. It was begun on 2 May 1836 and opened on 13 June 1838.

75   This is the last entry in the book. Benjamin had, in previous volumes of writing, made a neat conclusion and had written such words as 'Finis' or a note of completion. The implication of this abrupt ending is that he intended to continue with an account of 1837 but, perhaps because of increasing mental weariness, or physical infirmity, he did not do so. The rough notes include a very few entries for 1839–40, but it is clear that he did not keep a systematic record after the beginning of 1837.

APPENDIX 1
Family Trees

THE DIRECT ANCESTRY OF BENJAMIN SHAW AND BETTY LEEMING

BENJAMIN SHAW b 1772 d 1841	JOSEPH SHAW b 1748 d 1823	BENJAMIN SHAW b 1708 d 1794	RICHARD SHAW b *c.*1670 d 1744
			MARGARET HODGSON
		HANNAH HANDLEY b 1713 d 1797	WILLIAM HANDLEY
			ISABEL BOUSFIELD
	ISABEL(LA) NODDLE b 1752 d 1798	GEORGE NODDLE b 1715 d 1769	JAMES NODDLE
		MARGARET ELISHAW b *c.* 1715 d 1793	
m 1793 Lancaster	EDWARD LEEMING b *c.* 1745 d 1821		
BETTY LEEMING b 1773 d 1828	BETTY ROBINSON b 1748 d 1783		
		THOMAS ROBINSON	
		ALICE	

Family Tree 1: THE FAMILY OF RICHARD SHAW
(Great grandfather of Benjamin Shaw)

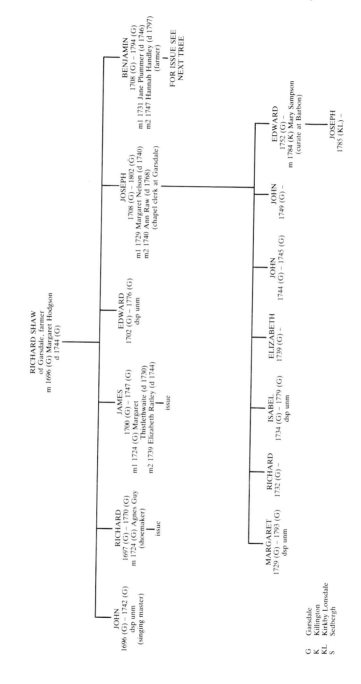

G Garsdale
K Killington
KL Kirkby Lonsdale
S Sedbergh

Family Tree 2: THE FAMILY OF BENJAMIN SHAW
(grandfather of Benjamin Shaw)

BENJAMIN SHAW
1708 (G) – 1794 (G)
m1 1731 (G) Jane Plummer (d 1746)
m2 1747 (G) Hannah Handley (d 1797)

WILLIAM
1748 (G) – 1834 (P)
m1 1772 (G) Mary Winn (d 1794?)
m2 1798 (Sb) Easther Richmond

JOSEPH
1748 (G) – 1823 (P)
m 1771 (D) Isabel Noddle

FOR ISSUE SEE NEXT
TREE

BENJAMIN
1744 (G) –
married and went
to Kendal

issue

JOSEPH
1737 (G) dii

BENJAMIN
1741 (G) dii

JOHN
1735 (G) –
m1 1759 (G) Elizabeth Parkin
m2 1772 (G) Eleanor Edmondson
m3 1780 (KS) Isabel Turner
m4 1788 (R) Dorothy Haygarth

MARGARET
1733 (G) –
married and went
to Co. Durham

RICHARD
1732 (G) –
married and went
to Kendal

issue

MARGARET
1784 (KS) dii

MARGARET
1791 (KS) –

MARY
1794 (KS) –

BENJAMIN
1773 (G) – 1792 (G)

JOHN
1774 (G) – 1788 (C?)

HANNAH
1778 (G) –

JOSEPH
1780 (G) –

THOMAS
1782 (G) –

WILLIAM
1784 (G) –
married and went
to North Shields

MOLLY
1787 (G) –
m 1808 (WD)
Anthony Greaves
and had issue

BETTY
1798 (Sb) –

PEGGY
1804 (WD) dii

PEGGY
1806 (WD?) –

child
c. 1796 by his
niece Mally Winn

JOHN
1799 (Sb) –

MARY
1754 (G) – 1842 (G)
m 1786 (G) John Davis

EDWARD
1752 (G) – 1836 (G)
dsp unm

ISABEL
1750 (G) – 1821 (G)
m 1774 (G) John Watson

AGNES
1775 (G) –
m 1795 (G) John Holme
and had issue

JACOB
1787 (G) – 1804 (P)

BENJAMIN
1790 (G) –

C   Colne
D   Dent
G   Garsdale
KS   Kirkby Stephen
P   Preston
R   Ravenstonedale
Sb   Samlesbury
WD   Walton-le-Dale

Family Tree 3:   THE FAMILY OF JOSEPH SHAW
(father of Benjamin Shaw)

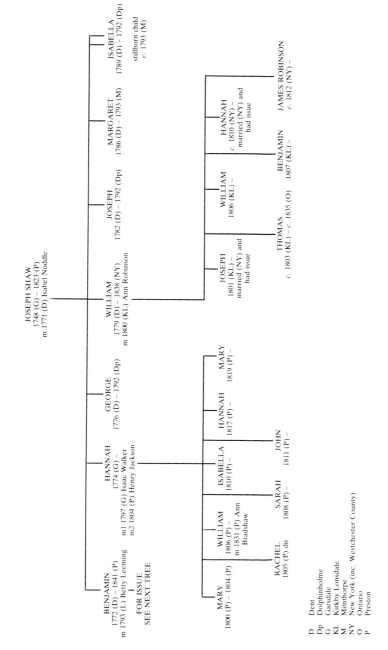

JOSEPH SHAW
1748 (G) – 1823 (P)
m 1771 (D) Isabel Noddle

BENJAMIN
1772 (G) – 1841 (P)
m 1793 (L) Betty Leeming

FOR ISSUE
SEE NEXT TREE

HANNAH
1774 (G) –
m1 1797 (G) Isaac Walker
m2 1804 (P) Henry Jackson

GEORGE
1776 (D) – 1792 (Dp)

WILLIAM
1779 (D) – 1838 (NY)
m 1800 (KL) Ann Robinson

JOSEPH
1782 (D) – 1792 (Dp)

MARGARET
1786 (D) – 1793 (M)

ISABELLA
1789 (D) – 1792 (Dp)

stillborn child
c. 1793 (M)

MARY
1800 (P) – 1804 (P)

WILLIAM
1806 (P) –
m 1831 (P) Ann
Bradshaw

RACHEL
1805 (P) dii

SARAH
1808 (P) –

ISABELLA
1810 (P) –

HANNAH
1817 (P) –

MARY
1819 (P) –

JOHN
1811 (P) –

JOSEPH
1801 (KL) –
married (NY) and
had issue

WILLIAM
1806 (KL) –

HANNAH
c. 1810 (NY) –
married (NY) and
had issue

THOMAS
c. 1803 (KL) – c. 1835 (O)

BENJAMIN
1807 (KL) –

JAMES ROBINSON
c. 1812 (NY) –

D   Dent
Dp   Dolphinholme
G   Garsdale
KL   Kirkby Lonsdale
M   Milnthorpe
NY   New York (inc. Westchester County)
O   Ontario
P   Preston

Family Tree 4:   THE FAMILY OF BENJAMIN SHAW

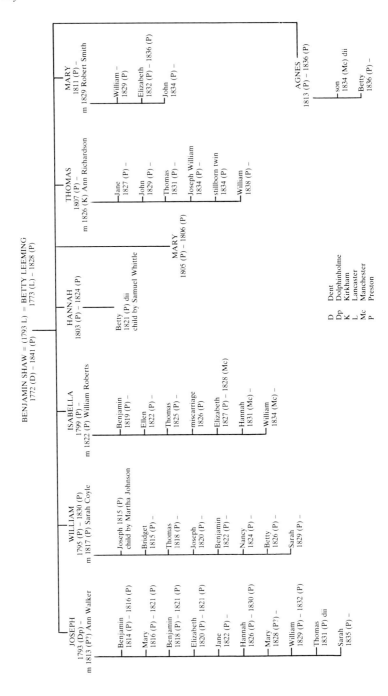

Family Tree 5(a): THE FAMILY OF ISABEL NODDLE (mother of Benjamin Shaw)

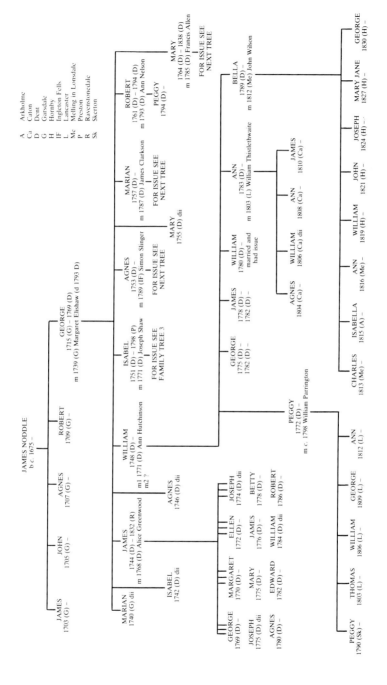

A   Arkholme
Ca   Caton
D   Dent
G   Garsdale
H   Hornby
IF   Ingleton Fells
L   Lancaster
Mc   Melling in Lonsdale
P   Preston
R   Ravenstonedale
Sk   Skerton

Family Tree 5(b):   THE FAMILY OF ISABEL NODDLE (mother of Benjamin Shaw)

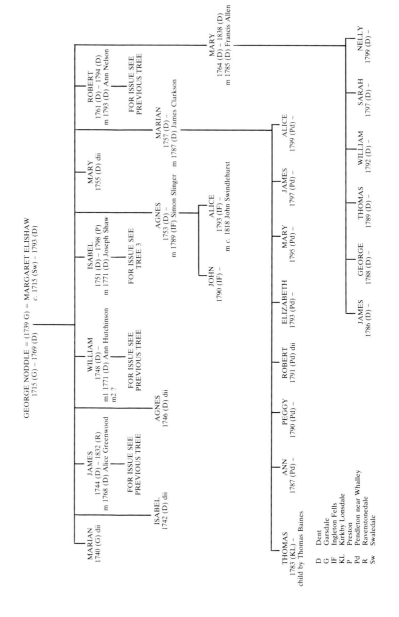

GEORGE NODDLE = (1739 G) = MARGARET ELISHAW
1715 (G) – 1769 (D)   c. 1715 (Sw) – 1793 (D)

MARIAN
1740 (G) dii

JAMES
1744 (D) – 1832 (R)
m 1768 (D) Alice Greenwood
FOR ISSUE SEE
PREVIOUS TREE

ISABEL
1742 (D) dii

AGNES
1746 (D) dii

WILLIAM
1748 (D) –
m1 1771 (D) Ann Hutchinson
m2 ?
FOR ISSUE SEE
PREVIOUS TREE

ISABEL
1751 (D) – 1798 (P)
m 1771 (D) Joseph Shaw
FOR ISSUE SEE
TREE 3

MARY
1755 (D) dii

ROBERT
1761 (D) – 1794 (D)
m 1793 (D) Ann Nelson
FOR ISSUE SEE
PREVIOUS TREE

MARY
1764 (D) – 1838 (D)
m 1785 (D) Francis Allen

AGNES
1753 (D) –
m 1789 (IF) Simon Slinger   m 1787 (D) James Clarkson

MARIAN
1757 (D) –

JOHN
1790 (IF) –

ALICE
1793 (IF) –
m c. 1818 John Swindlehurst

THOMAS
1783 (KL) –
child by Thomas Baines

ANN
1787 (Pd) –

PEGGY
1790 (Pd) –

ROBERT
1791 (Pd) dii

ELIZABETH
1793 (Pd) –

MARY
1795 (Pd) –

JAMES
1797 (Pd) –

ALICE
1799 (Pd) –

JAMES
1786 (D) –

GEORGE
1788 (D) –

THOMAS
1789 (D) –

WILLIAM
1792 (D) –

SARAH
1797 (D) –

NELLY
1799 (D) –

D   Dent
G   Garsdale
IF   Ingleton Fells
KL   Kirkby Lonsdale
P   Preston
Pd   Pendleton near Whalley
R   Ravenstonedale
Sw   Swaledale

Family Tree 6: THE FAMILY OF BETTY LEEMING (wife of Benjamin Shaw)

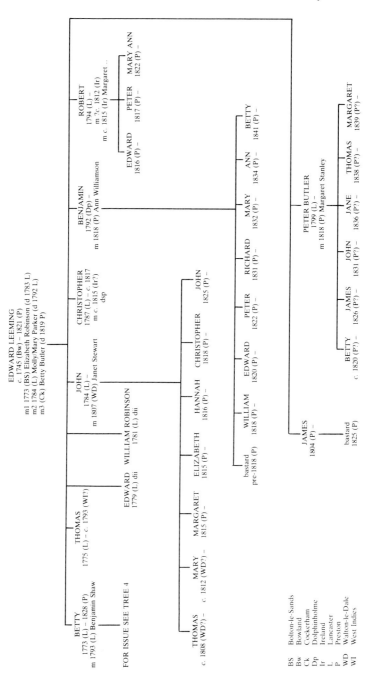

EDWARD LEEMING
c. 1745 (Bw) – 1821 (P)
m1 1773 (BS) Elizabeth Robinson (d 1783 L)
m2 1784 (L) Molly/Mary Parker (d 1792 L)
m3 (Ck) Betty Butler (d 1819 P)

BS   Bolton-le-Sands
Bw   Bowland
Ck   Cockerham
Dp   Dolphinholme
Ir   Ireland
L   Lancaster
P   Preston
WD   Walton-le-Dale
WI   West Indies

APPENDIX 2
Maps

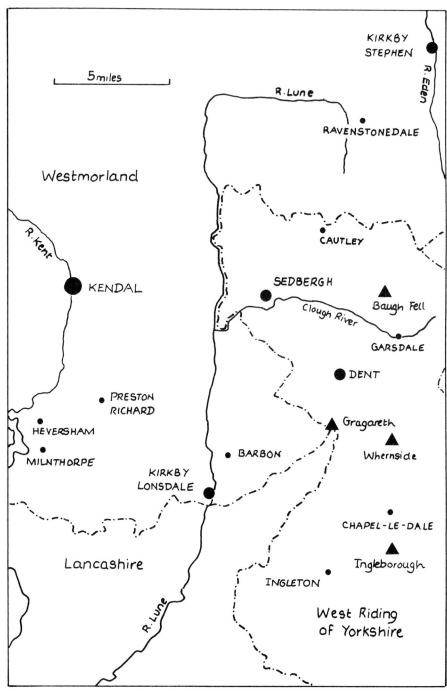

Map 1: the upper Lune Valley and the Sedbergh district

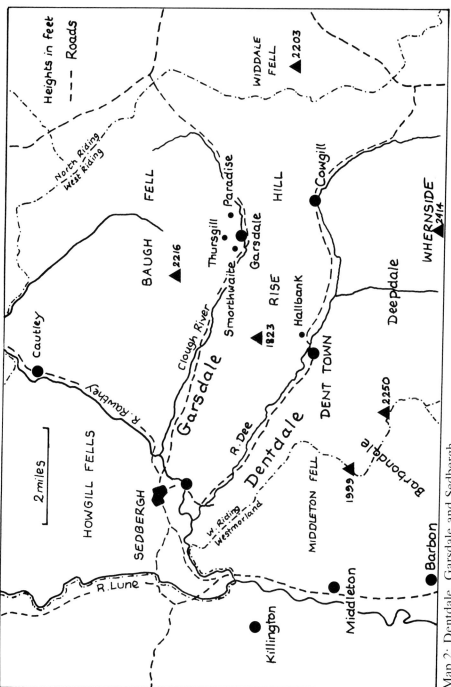

Map 2: Dentdale, Garsdale and Sedbergh

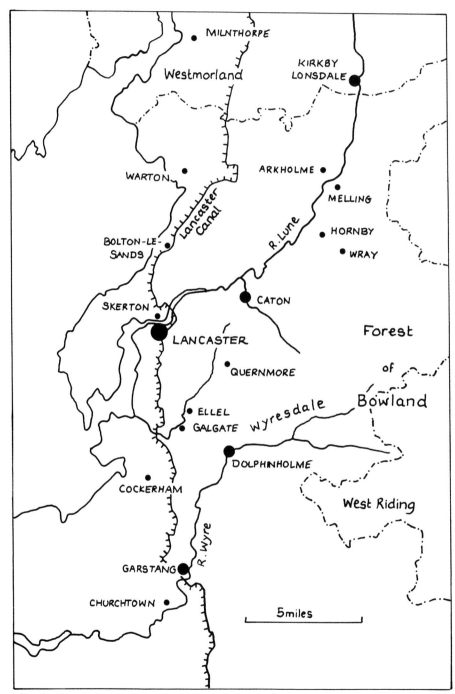

Map 3: North Lancashire

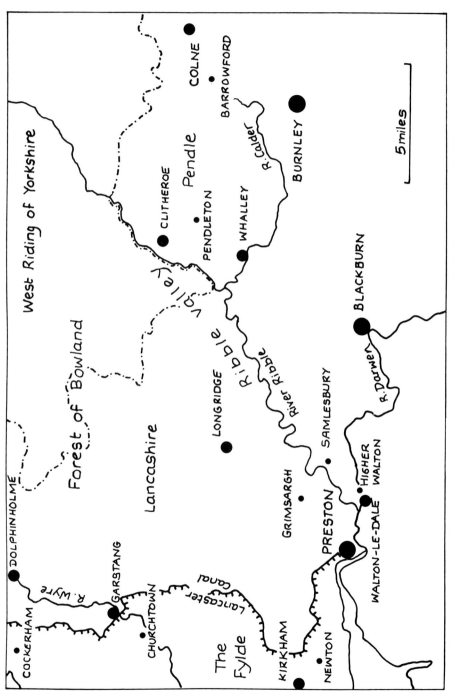

Map 4: Preston and the Ribble Valley

Map 5: Preston in 1824 (from Baines's *History, Directory and Gazetteer of the County of Lancaster*). Dale Street is at the eastern end of Church Street, at its junction with Stanley Street. Spittals Moss is at the northern edge of the map, in the vicinity of Maudland Road.

INDEX OF NAMES

People whom Benjamin describes in detail are listed in capital letters, e.g. LEEMING, BENJAMIN. Married women are indexed under their married names but cross-referenced under their maiden names, e.g. Bousfield, Isabel *see* Shaw, Isabel. Where different individuals have the same name, *either* their relationship with Benjamin Shaw [BS] or with Betty Shaw [BL] is given in parentheses, e.g. SHAW, WILLIAM [son of BS], *or* a maiden name is given in italics and parentheses, e.g. Shaw, Jane (*Plummer*). Where necessary a birth date is added for additional clarity. Persons named in the political/current affairs sections of the text are not indexed unless they are connected with Lancashire or with local events. Benjamin Shaw himself is indexed with subheadings relating only to major aspects of his life.

135

INDEX OF PLACES

In this index all references to streets, districts and buildings within Preston are listed under the overall heading *Preston – localities:*. For other places they are listed under the general headings.

INDEX OF SUBJECTS

consumption (TB) xi, xvii, xxxvii, 27, 65–66, 80, 91, 97–100
convalescence 50
deafness lx, 92, 94
deformed back 111n, 115
diarrhoea 47, 55n, 92
eyesight 88
fevers xv, 7, 27, 50, 81n, 82, 85
frostbite xvi, 34
lameness xvi, 15, 17, 21, 28, 34–36, 37, 42, 44–45, 47–50, 60, 113
measles lxiv, 46, 88, 92
rheumatism xxxiv, 12, 25, 50n
scabies 82
smallpox lxiii, 18–19, 23, 80
stillbirths/miscarriages 7, 12n, 96, 97n
whooping cough 59, 91
homesickness xxvii, xxxi, 21, 26
horse-dealing 11
house-building 9, 60, 63, 79
household:
    finances xlii, xlv–xlvi, xlvii–lii, lx–lxii, lxvii, lxviii–lxix, 12, 14, 20–21, 30–31, 34, 41–42, 44–45, 47, 49–50, 61, 62–64, 76–78, 80, 97–98, 105, 107
    goods xvi, xxxviii, xlvi, xlviii, lxii, lxx, 9, 29, 31–32, 34, 43, 48, 62–63, 81, 86, 97, 99, 105
    management xvii, xx, xxv, xxxix, xliii, xlv–xlix, l, lxix, 3, 12, 17, 21, 25, 34, 41–42, 44, 47, 61, 63–64, 76–78, 87, 97, 102, 107
    size xvii, xxxviii–xli, lxii, 8, 24, 34, 37, 44, 104–105
housekeeping xlvi, xlviii, lxii, lxvii, lxix, 14, 44, 61, 63, 73n, 76–78, 97, 99, 102, 107
housing xvi, xxix, xxxviii, lxviii–lxix, 4, 5, 8–9, 21, 23, 25, 29, 32–33, 37, 60, 62–63, 75, 87, 96–97, 99

illegitimacy xvii–xviii, xxxvi–xl, xlii–xliii, liii, 14, 15, 20, 22, 29n, 52–53, 56–58, 72, 85, 87, 89–91, 112, 115–116
incest xlii, 14

knitting xxiii, xxviii–xxix, liv, lxi, 4, 6n, 10, 11–12, 15–16, 20, 23, 24n, 37, 78, 80

labouring work 4, 18, 19n, 72n
labour, recruitment of xv, xxix–xxx, liv, 6, 8, 21, 25–26
leisure and spare time xxi, xxiii, xxxiv, xlvi, lxvii, 4, 20, 21–22, 24–25, 30, 37, 43, 51, 73, 80, 86, 92, 95
literacy xvi, xix–xxi, xxii–xxiv, lx–lxi, 4, 5n, 9, 15, 22, 28, 37, 63, 73, 74n, 79n, 80, 89n, 92, 99, 105n

machine-making business (mechanics' trade) xv–xvi, xxxiv, liv–lviii, lx, 4, 6–7, 16, 23–24, 26, 28n, 30n, 33, 37–38, 41n, 42–45, 47, 53–54, 55–56, 59–60, 62, 64, 66, 88, 90, 93, 96–97, 110, 113n
mangling lxii, 79
markets lxi, lxvii, 11
marriage xvi–xvii, xix–xx, xxi, xxxvii–xxxviii, xli–xliv, xlv–xlvii, 5, 15, 18–19, 30–31, 32, 41, 56, 61, 76–78, 86, 96–97, 100, 105, 107
    breakdown of xxxviii, 105, 107
    companionship within xlvi, lxv–lxvi, 104, 108n
    disagreements within xvii, xix–xx, xlii, xlv–xlvii, lxxiii, 34, 44, 61, 64, 76–77, 97, 107
    faithfulness before/during xlii, xlvi, 18, 19, 28–29, 31, 78
    freedom of the unmarried 16
    unhappiness within 3, 19–20
    violence within xliii, 19, 86
medical treatment xvi–xvii, xl, lv, lxiii–lxiv, lxvi, 28, 35, 48–50, 65, 82, 91–92, 96, 108, 115–116
mental disturbance 2, 81n, 82
middle-class aspirations xlvi, lxx, 44
migration xv–xvi, xxvii–xxxi, xxxii–xxxiii, lxvii, 3, 5, 7, 10, 13–14, 16–17, 21, 25–26, 28–29, 32–33, 36, 72–75, 78, 80–81, 85–87, 97, 105, 109, 112
militia and armed forces xliii, 8, 16, 18, 29, 36, 71, 79, 84–85, 86, 109
mills and factories xv–xvi, xviii, xx, xxiv–xxv, xxvii, xxix–xxx, xxxviii, lii, liv–lv, lvi–lx, lxii, lxiii, lxvii–lxix, 6–8, 12, 14, 24–26, 28, 29n, 32–33, 36–37, 38n,